PREACHING as ART

Biblical Storytelling for a Media Generation

DARIUS L. SALTER

BEACON HILL PRESS
OF KANSAS CITY

Copyright 2008
By Darius L. Salter and Beacon Hill Press of Kansas City

ISBN 978-0-8341-2359-5

Printed in the United States of America
Cover Design: J.R. Caines
Interior Design: Sharon Page

Library of Congress Cataloging-in-Publication Data

Salter, Darius, 1947-
    Preaching as art : biblical storytelling for a media generation / Darius L. Salter.
        p. cm.
    Includes bibliographical references.
    ISBN 978-0-8341-2359-5 (pbk.)
    1. Preaching. 2. Mass media—Religious aspects—Christianity. I. Title.

    BV4211.3.S25 2007
    251—dc22

                                                                    2007046443

10 9 8 7 6 5 4 3 2 1

contents

INTRODUCTION
preaching in a media world

the illusion of virtual reality

Imagine the resurrection of Christ taking place in the 21st century. Mary Magdalene would have scanned a camera phone across the empty tomb. She would have immediately dialed Peter and John for a "check this out." No need for the breathless sprint to the burial site. The evidence would have been sealed with a face-to-face encounter. All the disciples with a video cell phone would have been in on the first greetings from the resurrected Lord. No mistaking Him for the gardener. That first word uttered by Christ, "Mary," would have been more than a word; it would have been a full-facial body exposure, simultaneously witnessed by the disciples and forever preserved on film! A simulcast of the risen Lord! The first visit by Jesus to the disciples meeting "behind locked doors" would have been recorded by security cameras. Instead of Thomas saying, "Unless I see the nail marks in his hands and put my fingers where the nails were, and put my hand into his side, I will not believe it" (John 20:25), the disciples would have said, "Look at this."

But how would Thomas have known that "looking at this" is "looking at this"? Nothing is more illusionary than a "screen." Forrest Gump talks with Richard Nixon and appears with George Wallace at the University of Alabama; John Wayne appears in beer ads, and SUVs run up the side of glaciers; Spider Man spins a web across Manhattan, and Bruce Almighty walks on water. Reality and illusion have been fused together, and it has become almost impossible to distinguish the real from the fabricated. Virtual reality is no reality. It attempts to experience reality in an artificial setting, removed from the reality that the technology attempts to reproduce. Nicholas Mirzoeff notes in *An Introduction to Visual Culture* that "at New York's Empire State Building, the queues are longer for the virtual reality New York ride than for the lifts to the observation platform. . . . . Virtual reality has long been favored by the military as a training arena, put into practice in the Gulf War at great cost of human life. This is visual culture. It is not just a part of your everyday life, it is your everyday life" (Mirzoeff 1999, 3).

Cinematography creates an illusion. The people watching it, unless they are doing technical or critical evaluation, are oblivious that they are viewing still frames. Movie cameras capture their objects sequentially by depicting different motion positions. Thus, unless one is filming a still object, each frame (actually three frames) will be slightly different from the one before and after it. Unlike the great artists of the Renaissance, or contemporary photographers such as Richard Avadon, cinematographers close the gap between picture and voyeur because life is motion; anything that moves must be real. Edward Branigan explains the process:

> Recall that literally only *still* frames—24 per second, each flashed 3 times—are projected onto the screen. Each individual frame on a strip of film is moving through the projector only while the shutter of the projector is blacking out the screen (which is about 40 percent of the time). In fact, literally nothing is moving on the screen in front of us—not images, characters, objects, or a camera; if it were otherwise, there would be only a moving vertical blur on the screen as the film strip raced past the projector lamp (Branigan 2006, 11).

screenland

All of us are constantly assaulted by visual images, images that either outright dupe us or reduce life to a question mark: "Will I really look like that?" "Will I really be the center of attention if I drive that vehicle?" "Will my hair really grow back if I dab it with 'automatic full head of hair in 30 seconds'?" Virtual reality possibilities and alternative lifestyles are bombarding us via screens—screens of PalmPilots, video phones, computers, iPods, TVs, DVDs, and marketing marquees that change images every 10 seconds, almost all for the purpose of seducing us. Seduction has gone high tech. Neil Postman has labeled the constant assault of media a "peek-a-boo world":

> From millions of sources all over the globe, through every possible channel and medium—light waves, airwaves, ticker tapes, computer banks, telephone wires, television cables, satellites, printing presses—information pours in. Behind it, in every imaginable form of storage—on paper, on video and audio tape, on discs, film, and silicon chips—is an ever greater volume of information waiting to be retrieved. Like the Sorcerer's Apprentice, we are awash in information. And all the sorcerer has left us is a broom. Information has become a form of garbage, not only incapable of answering the most fundamental human questions but barely useful in providing coherent direction to the solution of even mundane problems (Postman 1992, 69).

Screenland is here to stay. It enables us to be omnipresent. We can attend an NBA basketball game, Princess Di's funeral, and the inauguration of a president. Time-space dimensions have been collapsed into a sheet of plasma or, if you will, expanded to a six-story IMAX. Whichever, we all become participants, performers in our favorite sport, music event, celebrity celebration, or game show. Even as I write this, I'm informed that 65 million people voted for their "American Idol"—more than for any American president. And 35 million people tuned in last night for his crowning, just slightly behind the 39 million who watched this year's Academy Awards.

There are several plausible explanations for our incessant movie attending and TV watching: a search for an alter ego, a yearning for transcendence over the tedium of everyday existence, a fascination with celebrities in the absence of real-life heroes, a longing for altered states of consciousness, and the pursuit of adventure without risk. Marshall McLuhan argued that the business of film is to "transfer the viewer/reader from one world, his own, to another, the world created by typography and film." This "self-fulfillment without delay" meant that "the World eagerly lined up to buy canned dreams" (McLuhan 1994, 291).

The reasons for movie watching are almost endless. One of the most fascinating explanations is that on a screen, the real becomes more real than real. Peter Lorrie's eyes bulge out more than eyes can protrude, and Robert Redford's hair glistens more than hair can glow. That which we would pay little attention to in real life takes on a gargantuan life of its own. A vivid cinematography moment takes place in my favorite western, *Once upon a Time in the West*, when the camera zooms in on a fly flitting on the face of Jack Elam. On camera the fly becomes an immense biological creation worthy of voyeurism, but in your kitchen, your only thought would be to kill it. Colin McGinn writes,

> What we are looking at, by looking into the apparatus before us, is the world as it might be seen by another type of being, with more acute vision than ours. This is a kind of magical effect, as if conferring a God-like power on our perception of reality. Not only does the screen let us look through it to a world not our own; it presents that world, in startling magnified dimensions and detail, adopting the position of a microscope (McGinn 2005, 24).

None of the above is meant to discredit the technology of visual communication. Even when I refer to computers, movies, and television as vicarious and voyeuristic, I'm aware that vicarious experience can be transformative, whether it's being drawn into the dilemma of *Sophie's Choice*, hearing Oscar Schindler helplessly agonize "If I could have saved just one more," or to be present at the crucifixion of our Lord in the *Passion of the Christ*. Film is a critical medium for spiritual, political, and social transformation, negatively or positively. Films change worldviews, carve out vocations, model virtues, funnel resources, and expand information undreamed of by our ancestors. Everybody has a "God's eye view" of everything. We continue to decipher, code, explore, research, and penetrate both the universe and DNA molecules. All of this is collected, frozen, and magnified on film. I know! A camera just traveled down my esophagus. If it isn't on camera, it isn't real. It didn't happen.

the technologically driven church

At least that is the conviction of our age and now the Church. Sanctuaries have become screenlands, video images magnify performances, film clips illustrate sermons, and telecasts allow preachers to communicate with multiple congregations at the same time. Incarnation is being traded for images that are sharper and larger than the sacramental fare that has been our diet for the last 2,000 years. Compared to Joel Olsteen preaching to 35,000 persons and to millions more via cable TV, most preachers simply aren't cutting it. We have determined that what will fix our plight is visual and auditory magnification, and if that doesn't satisfy us, we can do a satellite hookup to the preacher of our choice. Thus, the ante for preaching has been upped. Never has the communication market been more cutthroat, the voices for spiritual options more competitive, and the possibilities for parishioners to find the homiletical medium of choice more numerous.

My prediction is that the American church will become less theologically driven, less worship style driven, and even less economically driven. It will increasingly be media driven. Visual magnification, electronic accessibility, audio amplification—all feeding a cult of celebrity religion—will vie for our spiritual attention. Nobody really cares that John the Baptist said "He must become greater; I must become less" (John 3:30) when they magnify the preacher with 20-foot-wide screens on each side of the sanctuary. Techno-access preempts theological conviction. Visual images backed by rhythmic beat fill large sanctuaries just like the media blitz that assaults us 24-7. Church has decided that it needs to be on a technological continuum with the world's Oprahs. Thomas De Zengotita has labeled this "more real than real," this "unlimited source of unlimited media titillation," as the "Blob":

The moreness of everything ascends inevitably to a threshold in psychic life. A change of state takes place. The discrete display of options melts into a pudding—what I call the Blob, usually a metaphorical entity, shimmers into visibility at this moment, the moment when you stand amazed before the vast display at the MegaStore (Zengotita 2005, 23). And should we say megachurch?

The technical 21st-century term for the Blob is "media," the sights, sounds, symbols, sound bites, and pictures mediated to society. These messages, overt and covert, are for the most part aimed at product consumption, a marketing niche that is sophisticated and subtle. Rarely are commercials communicated via rational argument, logic, and comparative analysis. Instead they plant an idea, an ideology via image, metaphor, relationship, and analogy. For instance, Michelin tires offers no statistical analysis as to why one should buy their tire over, say, Goodyear. They simply show a child swinging on a Michelin tire. The clever suggestion? One would be an irresponsible parent to place their child in a vehicle with anything other than Michelin tires.

This graphic revolution has resulted in "Hundreds of corporate icons that no longer require any phonetic descriptor for them to be recognizable. Icons such as McDonald's golden arches, the Target bull's-eye, Apple's apple with a bite . . . no longer need words for people to identify their meaning" (Hipps 2005, 72). Eternal Image, Inc., a burial container company, advertised that anyone could have the logo of their Major League Baseball team engraved on their urn or casket, as "a way to make team loyalty a final statement."

Advertising icons create desire and modify behavior. They maintain the myth that a person's worth is predicated on not what a person produces but on what he or she consumes. As an American society, we are convinced that loneliness, alienation, and a sense of insignificance can be mollified by the "arts of impression management," a status "founded purely on one's ability to purchase, construct, and present a viable social self" (Ewen 1988, 68). Personal worth throughout the 20th-century industrialized world became defined and valued by patterns of consumption. Labels denoting distinction and prestige increasingly indicated, according to Stuart Ewen, "an epic crisis of identity that lurks within the inner lives of many Americans" (Ewen 1988, 58). Ewen argues and documents that

by the middle of the 19th century, the expanding market in appearance was helping to feed a nation of class defined primarily in consumptive rather than productive terms, highlighting individual above common identity. The idea of an American "middle class" constructed out of images, attitudes, acquisitions, and style was emerging" (Ewen 1988, 62).

But not all of the media avalanche is for the purpose of mercantilism. We market ideas, ideologies for the purpose of transformation, salvation from addiction, the wiping out of disease, the adoption of political perspectives, and persuasion to the justice of a social cause. Within the last 24 hours I stared at a poster that depicted a casket with flowers on it. The caption: "He beat her 250 times. She only got flowers once." The message was clear: spousal abuse is a serious issue.

the scriptures as media art

The above asks the simple question: Is the preacher with Bible open before 100, 200, 300 listeners about to become extinct? Yes, if he or she thinks that parishioners will continue to listen to a person who monotones and monologues pedantic erudition and theological esoterica to persons who listen because of some type of denominational obligation, institutional habit, or attendance at church, because that's what normal people do, at least, if they live in Indiana or Ohio.

What I am suggesting in this book is that the Scriptures were the media form for the Hebrew people and subsequent Christian Church. The Bible abounds in repetition, alliteration, symbols, images, puns, allegories, analogies, metaphors, and parallels—it is an exquisite art form of literary devices, often lost in translation. But they are more often lost by and on the church because we fail to let Scripture be Scripture. Allowing the Bible to be the Bible means to treat it as an exquisite piece of art as sophisticated and powerful as any multimedia, multimillion dollar ad campaign. The words of Scripture are *imagologies,* sensuous audiovisuals meant to be both heard and seen and in turn to transform. Scripture employs a range of literary devices to sensually entice us or, at the other end of the spectrum, to bludgeon us into what Eduard Riegert refers to as "imaginative shock." God majors in communication. He means to get our attention. God creatively and imaginatively dispatches words to perform His intention to destroy and deliver, tear down and build up, through visual, sensory discourse. The words of Scripture were to be read, both in public and private meetings, so that they created Kingdom boundaries for God's gracious activities. Imaginative language addressed both mind and heart, body and soul, the cognitive and affective.

the scriptures as iconic communication

Monotheism and subsequent Christianity have from their inception been iconic. (The English word *icon* comes from the Greek word *eikon,* meaning image.) Judaism began before written language, and Christianity was born into an age that was still largely illiterate. Christianity exhibited the genius of mastering the iconic creativity of the ancient Hebrews and at the same time mastering abstract thinking that would take root in the worlds of Greek and Roman thought. Christianity was disseminated through both engraved symbols on catacomb walls and by a hybrid Roman Jew who had been trained by Gamaliel, a "teacher of the law, who was honored by all the people" (Acts 5:34). Paul, who wrote a third of the New Testament, could pile logic upon logic to both the defiance and delight of the brightest philosophers. Yet, Paul excelled at verbal image making. For example, note the graphic metaphors that Paul created in his second letter to the Corinthian Church for the purpose of conveying truth: "fragrance" (2:14); "peddle the word" (2:17); "you are a letter from Christ" (3:3); "beholding as in a mirror" (3:18, NKJV); "treasure in jars of clay" (4:7); "earthly tent we live in" (5:1); "Christ's ambassadors" (5:20); "supply and increase your store of seed and will enlarge the harvest of your righteousness" (9:10); "weapons of our warfare" (10:4, KJV); and "a thorn in my flesh" (12:7).

Throughout the centuries abstract reasoning and iconic communication have vied for position in Christianity's worship, preaching, and evangelism. Theological integrity seeks to combine the best of both worlds. Pictures without reason often result in either spectacle or relativity, and reason without metaphor and image will tend toward irrelevance and boredom. Right and left brain thinking will incorporate a gospel of both the spoken and visible word. Preaching that connects will maintain theological depth with both rational paradigms and word pictures from everyday life; it will use images that clearly convey the explanation. Thus, the preacher who desires that his or her homiletical efforts not be deemed as obsolete as an inkpot, and who would not reduce preaching to a relic of the past, will take seriously Patricia Wilson-Kastner's argument that the Hebrew world of communication was very similar to our present-day media mix. This mix understands that an additional survey of knowledge is hardly ever sufficient to change us:

A preacher who wants to preach to the whole person will find such a world congenial because its language is imaginative, grasping people at the place in their hearts and minds where the intellect and emotions meet, where we at once think and feel and act. But the preacher needs to be prepared to engage in a complex encounter, because the dynamic that imagery sets up is a different form of discourse from the more familiar forms of the logician or scientist (Wilson-Kastner 1989, 36).

sermonic entrance into a media world

If the spoken word is to gain accessibility to a postmodern mentality deluged by visual expressions, several things will have to happen. First, there will have to be a new confidence in the Bible as an unsurpassed art form. Jesus and the prophets before Him spoke in language meant to be both heard and seen. As Amos Wilder states concerning the communication of Christ, "This utterance is dynamic, actual, immediate, reckless of posterity; not coded for catechists or repeaters" (Wilder 1964, 211).

Jesus had no intention of leaving behind another law code to memorize but a revelation of himself and His incarnation of the Kingdom. The Sermon on the Mount is not an argument but an overthrow of the prevailing moral order of the universe. Jesus' words are not a prescription for success, but the song of a new creation culminating in the Book of the Revelation, the most profound vision ever had by humankind. Wilder calls it "a masterpiece of surrealism. For the interpretation of its cumulative dramatic levels we may well call in depth psychologists and the anthropologists as well as the modern literary critic" (Wilder 1964, 128).

Second, the 21st-century preacher will have to fight the temptation to completely succumb to technology. Concession can be stymied only by a new birth of Spirit-anointed creativity. In a day of visual stimulation, sermons will have to be word pictures. This is not to say there is no place for film clips, object lessons, and scenic images on screen, accompanying both song and sermon. Creativity is hard work and heart work, and the temptation to fill sermonic space with imported artistry is often banal and far less profound than the "word" that it needs to convey. Elizabeth Achtemeier accurately defines creative preaching as "the fashioning of a sermon into such an artistic and reflective whole that the word of God spoken through the text is allowed to create that reality of which it speaks within the individual and corporate lives of the gathered congregation" (Achtemeier 1981, 11).

Creative exegesis is not simply about parsing verb tenses and identifying the correct case of nouns, but allowing the creative God to shine forth in His transforming power. Only the gift of creative speaking will allow a creative God to continue to create and recreate in us the Living Word.

Third, imagination worthy of worship need not be secondhand but can be God's gift "for such a time as this" (see Esther 4:14). Spirit-anointed words as gifted by God and mediated through a person called to a particular context are priceless, nonnegotiable, and irreplaceable. The right word at the right time transcends and supersedes graphics and images purchased from the world's media supermarket. Performative certitude enables the preacher to stand by his or her calling in a degree and dimension that goes above and beyond communicative technique, no matter how slick and sophisticated the technology. God's promise to Isaiah is more relevant for the 21st-century Christian Church than the latest project from DreamWorks: "So is my word that goes out from my mouth: It will not return to me empty, but will accomplish what I desire and achieve the purpose for which I sent it" (Isa. 55:11).

Is it possible that the importations of visual accessibility from the experts of efficiency and entertainment undermine the authority of theological categories? Postman writes,

> In *Technopoly*, all experts are invested with the charisma of priestliness. Some of our priestly experts are called psychiatrists, some psychologists, some sociologists, some statisticians. The God they serve does not speak of righteousness, or goodness or mercy or grace. Their God speaks of efficiency, precision, and objectivity (Postman 1993, 90).

theological limitations of media technology

The inability to weave the concrete and abstract within a meaningful pattern is often the failure of video clips separated from theological reflection. A recent church I visited showed a trailer from *Facing the Giants*, a movie curiously produced by a church in Georgia and released by Samuel Goldwyn. Never have the church and Hollywood been on more friendly terms. The movie climaxes with a small Christian school facing a dominant football powerhouse for the state championship. Because the plot is so formulaic, I'm not really giving away the ending when I tell you David beats Goliath. The 50-plus-yard field goal by a kid who before the season had never kicked a ball through the uprights (in the script, had never played football) was probably more improbable than David's marksmanship with a slingshot. The movie has many redeeming factors, among them, the exhibition of faith, courage, and determination. After the triumph the coach has each player respond to the question "What's impossible with God?" Only subsequent theological dialogue would sharpen the dichotomy between the grace of humility and the glory of winning a football game. Technologies imported for the purpose of preaching and worship aids are often foiled by advantaging us rather than glorifying God.

McLuhan argued that all modern media produces four effects: it enhances, it reverses, it retrieves, and it obsolesces (see explanation in Hipps 2005, 41-43). Gutenberg's printing press enhanced literacy, reversed community, retrieved the message of justification by faith, and obsolesced the sign acts of Christian worship. Thus, the priesthood of believers, a critical concept for the Reformation, has for Protestant Evangelicalism often demeaned the communal and consensual parts of the gospel. In other words, many of us have inherited a highly individualistic form of piety.

McLuhan's grid would be helpful in evaluating technological innovation in the church, for instance, the projection of a biblical text on a screen as it is read in a worship service. It enhances the ability to see (I'm not sure about this), reverts to graphics written on a cave or prison wall, retrieves a common text from a single version, obsolesces the carrying of one's own Bible. I have even noted a hint of hypocrisy as upfront persons feigned memorization while reading from the back wall. My own assessment of projecting the text on a screen, unless it is read in unison, leaves me with more minuses than pluses.

McLuhan defined media as extensions of ourselves: the photograph is an extension of the eye, the telephone is an extension of the ear, clothes are an extension of the skin, money is an increased mobility of grasp, and the car as an extension of man "turns the rider into a superman. It is a hot explosive medium of social communication" (McLuhan 1994, 221). Thus, McLuhan warned that we serve these objects instead of being served, as gods or minor religions (McLuhan 1994, 46). Or stated another way, "we become what we behold" and "we shape our tools, and thereafter our tools shape us" (McLuhan 1994, xi).

The question deserves to be asked: Does the use of media in the church extend us in ways that glorify the created rather than the Creator? One may ask this question about the preacher projected on large screens on either side of the auditorium. The extension of the ego becomes even more pronounced when the preacher is present at one location while his image is projected to multiple worship sites. Shane Hipps's indictment is worth contemplating:

> The message of a video-venue sermon is that the authority to preach is derived from talent and celebrity, not character or communical affirmation. A televised event doesn't communicate anything about a person's character, it can only affirm or deny talent attractiveness. We don't watch movies or TV shows because we respect or want to know the personal

character of the actors. We watch because we are enamored by their beauty, talent, or celebrity (Hipps 2005, 151).

None of this is meant to discourage learning from the world of media art. Keep in mind that the superstitions of the Church have often been preempted by scientific discovery. When Copernicus humbly advanced his heliocentric hypothesis, Martin Luther called him "a fool who went against holy writ." Thus, all technological questions need to begin with the question, "Is God being displaced or is the Church being challenged?" Does my implementation of this tool tweak the bureaucracy or glorify God? For C. S. Lewis bureaucratic technology incarnated Satan:

> I live in the Managerial Age, in a world of "Admin." The greatest evil is not now done in those sordid "dens of crime" that Dickens loved to paint. It is not done even in concentration camps and labour camps. In those we see its final result. But it is conceived and ordered (moved, seconded, carried, and minuted) in clean, carpeted, warmed, and well-lighted offices, by quiet men with white collars and cut fingernails and smooth-shaven cheeks who do not need to raise their voices. Hence, naturally enough, my symbol for Hell is something like the bureaucracy of a police state or the office of a thoroughly nasty business concern (Lewis 1961, iv-v).

God does not intend to marginalize the church to the hinterland of technological irrelevancy. Neither does He intend for the uniqueness of preaching to be preempted by the latest technological advance so that the next 500 years of the church will be an endless experiment with secular techniques for capturing the world's attention. God's Word is timeless! It will continue to redeem and transform, to create worlds of hope and freedom, to surpass the best creativity of "screenland." The imagination of God, infused into the imagination of the preacher, will continue to capture the minds and hearts of all who have ears to hear and eyes to see. Nothing else but preaching will do. Screenland may enhance but never replace. Colin McGinn explains:

> The visual image can only take in what is happening now to the outside of a person; it cannot go straight inside to the mind and range back and forth through time. To achieve these effects, it must resort to indirect methods, such as flash backs and flash-forwards. The directness and economy of language are not available to the visual image. Nor can it easily abstract away from irrelevant features of a scene to give us an isolated detail. The visual image always offers up a totality of details (McGinn 2005, 120).

If McLuhan was correct that the essential nature of media is the extension of the self in its efficiency, amplification, and success, only a carefully thought through theology of technology will save us from the pitfalls of a consumer market that searches for a church that will mirror rather than challenge the prevailing worldview. God's audiovisual was Christ. Upon His ascension, Christ transferred His audiovisual representation to the Church. Christ's Body conveying truth, love, and grace has been for the last 2,000 years and will continue to be God's primary media on earth. The media-driven spectacle that defines much of Christian worship often subtracts from the possibilities of an incarnational encounter with one another. People often attend worship services as they do rock concerts and movie theaters, never realizing that they are to be a sacrament to and within the togetherness of Christ's Body. Again Hipps offers a prophetic word: "However, left unchecked, spectacle actually works against the creation of authentic, missional community. Spectacle creates publics not communities. Publics are made up of people who share the same affinities but are otherwise leading disparate lives" (Hipps 2005, 149).

And when you think about it, the images of screenland can never stand alone. They need emotionally charged music, manipulative cinematic technique, and illusions that only the most skilled director and editors can create. Often the very technologies we propose for enhancing worship activities such as singing and preaching are counterproductive. Sut Jhally suggests that video CDs, music accompanied by video, marginalize if not eliminate the imagination of the ear. Interpretation becomes frozen and loses the relationship of dynamic creativity that exists between music and listener: "The realm of listening becomes subordinated to the realm of seeing, to the influence of commercial images" (Jhally 1995, 83). We who fulfill the roles of prophet-priest are called upon to discern when technological innovation is reducing active engagement to numbing passivity. While arguing that Christian education needs to adjust to an audiovisual culture, Pierre Babin exclaims, "What a terrible power audiovisual language has! It is able to drive one to love vibration just for the sake of vibration itself to the point where it is separated from the human need to understand" (Babin 1991, 62).

In contrast, I am proposing that we give new attention to the reality of Scripture to rediscover its creative voice, that is, to step into its world and find it to be amazingly and frighteningly similar to our own. After all, the task of the most contemporary preacher is the same as the most ancient writer, to bring God's heart to bear on the human heart. This book dedicates itself to the practicality of that process. I have one goal in the following pages: to help the Christian preacher proclaim the Word in such a way that people will listen and, in turn, become more Christian than they already are.

one

PREACHING as ART

god's idea

The preacher is a craftsperson. If when we create something we are most truly ourselves, I suspect the sermon is still the most creative act that the pastor accomplishes. Nothing is more composite of the pastor's identity than the preaching moment; it aggregates—or at least exposes—the preacher's personality, experiences, gifts, quirks, willingness to work, self-security, ego strengths, compassion for people, and above all his or her relationship with God in a way that no other pastoral act does. Thus the preacher, by the power of the Holy Spirit, sustained inquiry, and a God-given gift of creative art, will strive to offer a preaching sacrifice pleasing to God and fitting for the people to whom he or she is called to minister. God has created persons or mediums through which His Word is to be spoken.

God has encased salvation in a narrative powerful enough to transform us. Preachers are called to carry on the tradition. Surprising to most preachers and to far more churchgoers is that God's story is entertaining, enjoyable, intriguing, fascinating, and captivating, as well as paradoxical, dialectical, mystifying, and at times downright bewildering. What we have in Scripture are stories, songs, poems, metaphors, images, letters, and almost innumerable figures of speech that were the polished art of accomplished communicators. God is anything but dull, and His story is anything but dull. God has not simply told us a story; He has told it with the imagination, creativity, and art that characterize His mind.

God was the first preacher. He spoke worlds into existence. Preaching takes part in God's creative work through the power of the Holy Spirit. Even as the Word became flesh, the ultimate purpose of preaching was to incarnate the Living Word in the life of every believer. Unless the creative power of God is active throughout the total process of preparation, presentation and penetration, the spoken word will not participate in God's creative transformation. Ezekiel described the creative intent of every sermon: "I will give you a new heart and put a new spirit in you; I will remove from you your heart stone and give you a heart of flesh" (36:26).

scripture as art

Biblical writers expressed truth through verbal art. Some were far more intentional about this than others. David was far more aware of literary craft when he wrote a psalm than was Paul when he dictated a letter. But whenever Paul struggled for a word or a more acceptable way to say something, even his letters became an art form. Note the number of artful metaphors that Paul used, say, in the Pastoral Epistles: "the good fight of faith" (1 Tim. 6:12), "suffered shipwreck" (2 Cor. 11:25, KJV; 1 Tim. 1:19, KJV and NASB), "seared with a branding iron" (see 1 Tim. 4:2, NASB), "spread like gangrene" (2 Tim. 2:17), and "itching ears" (2 Tim. 4:3). Did these analogies simply drop on his head from heaven, or did he give time and thought to their appropriateness? None of the biblical writers pursued the exhibition of craft as their ultimate goal or purpose, but they were well aware that form must be congruent with substance. And if we believe the Old Testament scholar Gerhard Von Rad, biblical writers were not unaware of the artistic nature of their labor. "Many of these narratives are, in addition, products of a determined intent at art and were in those days certainly evaluated as works of art" (Von Rad, 1980, 12).

All good art conveys a message and is not an end in itself. If we allow Scripture to creatively deliver God's message to a longing, hopeful congregation, then it will be congruent with the worship that precedes it. Worship consists of verbal, visual acts. If sermons are only logical, conceptual, pedantic, and propositional, they interrupt; they are incongruent with what has gone on before and what will go on after we preach. In Calvin Miller's words, "We have done far too little to let the Bible stand and be celebrated as art in our services. It is time to wake ourselves to the literary glory of that which we handle in such mundane fashion" (Miller 1996, 106).

C. S. Lewis said that "to interest is the first duty of art." Note that he said first duty and not ultimate duty. But if preaching fails to do its first duty as art, why would anyone listen? There is just too much competition in the marketplace for people to listen to dull preaching. Those who preach only out of duty produce listeners who listen only out of duty, a miserable exchange of boredom.

Contrary to many sermons, the Bible is an interesting book. No one book has ever contained more murder plots, love stories, betrayals, adulterous affairs, heroic feats, tragedies, and triumphs than does the Bible. To fail to carry on God's tradition of composing and creating is to engage in homiletical reductionism. Rather than diminishing God's story, the call for preachers is to imaginative speech that issues in daring, provocative, colorful, and—yes—entertaining proclamation.

Many of us are wary of the word *entertainment*. Entertainment often carries the connotation of the bizarre, the shallow, or—to use a David Wells

phrase—the "slick and the slack." Worship and preaching as primarily entertainment often accommodates to the fad and fashion of the moment, the
applause of performance, and the consumer-driven marketing of the gospel.
But "entertainment" has a more basic meaning than amusement. It is derived
from two French words, *entre* meaning "between," and *tenir*, "to hold." "To
entertain" means "to hold between": your speech and their reception, the
biblical world and their world, the material and spiritual, and so on. Entertainment overcomes, transcends, and preempts the disconnect between the
Word of God and persons who often liken a sermon to a root canal: "The
only thing good about this is that it will soon be over."

the aesthetic quality of preaching

How disappointing it would be to visit the Louvre in Paris or the Getty in
Los Angeles and discover that its most esteemed piece of art had a drape or a
veil over it. Instead, you would like to find it in a setting and light that most
enhances its magnificence. Obscuring the Scriptures with trivial commentary,
poor form, dull speech, and impotent moralisms insults the task to which
God has called us. Preaching is an exercise in aesthetics. When it is not, it is
reduced to moral platitudes and utilitarian pragmatism. A person who reduces everything to the practical—to borrow some Craddock language—
would "fry rose petals in the fat of swine rather than smell the flowers"
(Craddock 1981, 87).

Preaching needs to at least sometimes leave persons with the fragrance of
inspiration rather than the urgency to chloroform the earth or even the
neighborhood. Henry Thoreau stated at least a half truth when he said, "I
came into the world not chiefly to make this a good place to live but to live in
it be it good or bad" (Thoreau 2004, 11). Living in the world, for Thoreau,
was not to ignore the good, but to embody that good in an art form, one of
the half dozen greatest pieces of American literature. Appreciating God's art
transforms us into artists. Craddock writes,

> Man in his struggle for survival has never been so reduced that his pri-
> vations snuff out his aesthetic life. Put man in the simplest cabin and he
> will plant petunias about the door; drive him into a cave and he will play
> the artist on the wall; leave him nothing but sticks and he will devise a
> flute; bind him in chains and he will drag them to some remembered ca-
> dence; imprison him and he will sing hymns at midnight. The song leader
> of America has been the Negro; what right has he to sing? Our country

has been led in laughter by Jews who cannot remember when Israel did not have crepe on the door (Craddock 1981, 89).

The art form in which we proclaim the gospel is no less important than the right frame for a painting. The right frame would be carefully chosen for texture, color, and dimension. Imagine placing my daughter's wedding portrait in a poster frame purchased at Wal-Mart. Many of the forms and frames of reference in which we package God's revelation diminish the truth. Blowing up the headquarters of the antichrist with a laser missile (a reference to the Left Behind series) is a long way from casting the "beast" into the "lake of fire." The Book of the Revelation deserves much better framing.

great art

What makes art great? It seems to me art that is considered great in a small geographical area by a small group of people over a short period of time but considered mediocre or trivial outside these limits of space and time would be something less than great. I would like to suggest that part of the Bible's universal appeal beyond space and time, its cultural transcendence, is due to its archetypical art forms such as narrative, image, and poetry. Tolstoy identified congruency of emotion between the artist and the one experiencing the art as an essential criterion for greatness. The intensity of emotional congruency varies with sincerity, clarity, and infectiousness. If these qualities abound, the recipient or observer is brought to the realization, "That is what I would say or make if I had the ability." Thus, great art accomplishes a union of souls. Art is assessed not only by its "contagion" but by the values that it seeks to make contagious. Art for Tolstoy was great only to the extent that it increased love for God and humankind.

Preaching is great only to the extent that it causes a congregation to long for the presence of God and increase in love for both God and humankind. Preaching for art's sake, so that observers will be awed by its eloquence and entertainment value, destroys the ultimate purpose for preaching. Art conceals itself for the purpose of inclusion, drawing the listener into the plot without him or her knowing; or to use another analogy, the sermon becomes a Trojan horse, not for the purpose of betrayal or trickery, but because persons do not respond best if they are hit on the head with a platitudinal plank. As Max Lucado argues, if truth arrives a bit "incognito," people are more prone to receive it (Lucado 2006, 8).

postmodern indirection

Søren Kierkegaard used the art of parable to communicate to the Danish church. He delivered his art as a "dialectical knot" of jest and earnest that the listener must untie. He saw this as far more effective than lecturing, direct communication that would offend and therefore be immediately rejected. The art of indirect communication, Kierkegaard argued, is grounded in the Incarnation, the God who came to earth incognito. The indirect communication of art employs a greater faith than does direct communication. Of indirectness Kierkegaard wrote, "It does not, like direct communication, employ enticement and warning and threatening—and then gradually and quite unobserved the transition is brought about little by little, to the point of accepting it, as regarding oneself as convinced by it, of being of the opinion, etc." (Kierkegaard 1967, 140).

If postmodernity is a triumph of mystery over logic, impression over rationale, aesthetic creation over empirical demonstration, and transformative symbolism over print-based discourse, preaching in the 21st century should have a heyday, what Ronald Allen refers to as a "homiletical promised land" (Allen 1997, 164). The Scriptures, laden with symbol and image, solve the communication problem of postmodernism's deep distrust of the Enlightenment emphasis on rationality. Michael Glodo argues that "if our view of Scripture be right the Bible should be able to 'out-image' any contemporary imaging because of the divine character of Scripture and because of God, the end of Scripture" (Glodo 2001, 111).

Functional utility is not the stuff of art, neither is it the primary purpose of the sermon. Sermons that make me a more positive thinker, more generous husband, more perceptive parent, and more astute financial manager and yet bypass the transformative power of Jesus Christ have failed. In fact they may be moral lectures, fireside chats with a Cub Scout troop, or instructional how-tos, but not Christian sermons, much less biblical sermons.

Postmodernism is a disillusionment created by the failure of modernism to make the world an increasingly better place to live. Technological utopias never happened. A world filled with war, violence, and poverty continues to assault our sensibilities, mocking our hopes for a better tomorrow. Emancipation is yet to come. Competition increases to tell the best, most attractive, and most compelling master narrative. As Gerard Loughlin correctly asserts, "Most of us want to be mastered or written into a narrative that is larger, longer, and stronger than our own" (Loughlin 1996, 8).

Postmodernism longs for a metanarrative of emancipation—freedom from our fears, estrangements, sins, and guilt. This kind of emancipation marches toward wholeness as sure as the Israelites left Egypt and headed toward Canaan. The march to wholeness advances on reality—the truth about God, myself, and the surrounding world. Art is not reality but, by not being reality, points us to reality. It leaves those in its presence confessing, "I am like that." Thus, art serves as a trap for meditation. Good preaching, like good art, arrests us the way the eyes of a master portrait do when they follow us as long as we are in the room. Rowan Williams writes, "As the perspective 'bears down' upon the beholder's eye, the eye of the iconic figure acts, searches, engages. The skill of looking at icons, the discipline of 'reading' them, is indeed the strange skill of letting yourself be seen, be read" (Williams 2000, 184). If the preacher consistently allows the sermon to read him or her, the possibility that others will let the sermon do the same in their lives is much greater.

iconic participation

Biblical preaching does not enumerate suggestions for suburban living in the 21st century. Instead it evokes images that are so primal and universal that the communal and individual verdict is, "I've been found out. I've been discovered by the blinding light of God's Word. After my eyes adjusted to the light, I saw myself and everyone and everything else much more clearly." Preaching as art does not simply explore the components of life as work, worship, and play but arranges them with depth and perspective. Perspective is the all-consuming passion of the preacher as artist. Perspective provided by Spirit-anointed words places life at God's disposal. The hearer leaves convinced that the disposal does not result in God's thrashing us, but in God returning life to us immeasurably richer and fuller than we ever dreamed it could be. Good preaching paints God's dreams for us, leaving worshipers confessing, "Why in the world wouldn't I want that?"

Art allows the listeners to participate. In other words, the listeners cease to be just listeners; they are also performers. Preachers or professors of preaching who concentrate on technically correct ways to preach often miss the point, for there are very few if any technically right and wrong ways in preaching. Absorbing a congregation is hardly a technique but an ethos, an emotion, a drama that causes listeners to become participants who transcend time-space barriers between themselves and the biblical narrative. Good preaching invites persons to become players in the live drama, to become performers in the action of the triune God, to make all of life sacred.

Don Cupitt argues that the "Holy Scriptures still provide the strongest of all forms of the idea of a master-narrative. Not a story we made up but the story that makes us up, conscripting us into its plot; writing God into every step of our lives and every step of our lives into the plan of God" (Cupitt 1991, 87).

The pulpit will elicit and evoke powerful enough images to displace the gods of this world, tell the story that comprehends life in its complexities, and make a declaration that dwarfs the limp and feeble claims of the prevailing culture. None of this can be done outside of hard work and reliance on the Holy Spirit to convert that work into a "sharp two-edged sword" (see Heb. 4:12) that reads the innermost consciousness of human beings and supplants guilt and fear with grace and hope. The ultimate aim of preaching is the realization by both preacher and hearer that I and the world in which I live cannot only be different but will be different by the grace and power of God. The sermon is iconic in that it enables both preacher and hearer to participate in the nature and image of God.

art as subtle awareness

A word of caution about preaching as art. It may not get the quick results that have been our habit and goal. In fact the better the art form, the more forceful the art, the less the immediate pragmatism. Good art is absorbed, soaked in, pondered, and may leave the observer/listener crying "I am undone" or "what must I do," rather than turning to a quick fix, because the quick fix may not be what is really needed; in fact, a quick fix is often impossible. This in no way limits the grace of God. Those who followed Christ in the New Testament were called to a lifetime of discipleship and thus a lifetime of transformation.

The sermon as art is not so much precept or proposition (though these may be implicit or explicit) as it is quickened and heightened awareness. The more subtle the awareness the better; the mature observer and listener will be willing to say at least once in a while, "I've been had." This is what Roger Hazelton refers to as the "shock of recognition" or "effective surprise" (Hazelton 1967, 33). This is exactly what happened or should have happened when Jesus told the story of the "good Samaritan" or the "prodigal son," unless the Pharisees were too dense to see themselves deftly painted by Jesus into the word picture. Imagine the following story told by an Army chaplain to fresh recruits, or a Sunday School teacher to a class of single adults. The story demonstrates that the rhetoric of narrative is different from the rhetoric of critical-rational discourse.

It appears that a truck driver was driving through the Mojave Desert, where he picked up a hitchhiker—a young woman who was very beautiful. More to the point, she was available and willing. They stopped at a motel, where they had an afternoon tryst. Afterwards, the truck driver fell asleep. When he woke up, the hitchhiker was gone, and on the pillow there was a note that read, "You're number sixty-three. Welcome to the world of AIDS" (Camery-Hoggatt 2006, 468).

Good art begs a response, which is what separates it from a fence post. It encounters us beyond emergency or utilitarian measures. It reveals ultimate things, of which no work of art is more indicative than the Book of the Revelation. Thus the question is raised, "Does art obscure or make clear?" The answer is yes. Ominous mysteriousness, shrouded in symbolism, enhances clarity. Not a clarity about neat formulas, easy answers, and simple predictions; ultimate clarity about ultimate things and the ultimate Person. *The appearance of the One who leaves no doubt to whom I owe allegiance.* It's amazing how the message is lost when people treat the Bible as an almanac rather than a work of art. The message delivered through the art of Scripture is clear. There's one thing needful and that is to fall down and worship the King of Kings and Lord of Lords.

art as restrained radicalism

A religion that demands total abandonment of self demands language of equal extravagance. Art is the medium of language that can entice us to radicalism, without at the same time scorching us. It acts as both a buffer and a detonator. Instructions on a can opener are for the purpose of disseminating practical information for quick, strain-free consumption of both the contents of the directions and the can to be opened. Very little of Scripture, if any, is in the form of technical advice. The art forms of narrative, prophecy, poetry, and epistle are congruent with the mysteries and paradoxes that complicate trust in God in the midst of life's complexities. Preaching is a form of counseling. Counseling at its best knows that truth cannot always be swallowed whole. Though the attitudes and values of the counselee may best be killed, an AK-47 would execute both the patient and the problem. Donald Capps writes in *The Poet's Gift:*

Again and again, pastors confess that they have been unable to communicate a theological "answer" to a parishioner in distress, not because the pastor did not know what such an answer would be, but because this answer would violate the experience that the parishioner and the pastor felt was warranted at the time. In such situations, pastors have much in common with poets (Capps 1993, 3).

Art serves as a demilitarized zone, time and space granted for exploration, a search for symbolical artifacts and signs by which we discern life's critical indexes. Art connotes a "come ye apart" invitation quite unlike reading a traffic sign, which demands a reflexive response. Artists do not demand, trap, and corner; rather they evoke, entice, provoke, and enable. In this vein, Elizabeth Achtemeier writes, "The restraint of the artist respects the integrity and privacy of the listener and gives the personality of the hearer space in which to feel and think and respond and thus to move into a new reality" (Achtemeier 1981, 35).

Thomas Troeger emphasizes the necessity of revitalizing "religious imagination so that it gives the sense of open space in front of people" or, in Parker Palmer's famous dictum, "creates sufficient space for obedience to truth." And as Troeger points out, sermons that are technically accomplished, that is, biblically sound and lucidly organized, may fail to deliver in spite of being well spoken. He forms the question that should frame all of our homiletical endeavors: "How, then, do preachers find a poetic and communal idiom that will speak with authority to a society whose verbal medium is technical and individualistic?" (Troeger 1988, 215). Troeger answers his own question by stating the preacher will seek to integrate the ancient wisdom with contemporary knowledge so that "the religious imagination may be reengaged in the cause of personal and social transformation" (Troeger 1988, 229).

Precept is often for immediate consumption, such as slogans, pithy statements, and aphorisms. While Scripture is not completely devoid of these, such as the Book of Proverbs, it deals mostly in "percepts" that need to be seen, microscopically examined, and telescopically viewed from as many angles as possible. As Bernard Meland points out, because we live more deeply than we think, concepts often fail to represent life, and let me add worship (Meland, 1976, 28-29). The Book of the Revelation does not give us an argument for worship, but a verbal picture of the 24 elders falling prostrate before the Lamb. The ultimate end of all preaching is the worship of the triune God!

scripture and preaching as literature

For those who are uncomfortable with treating the Bible as literature, what Robert Alter refers to as the "multi-faceted artistry of the Biblical narratives" (Alter 1981, 179), allow me to say that we are not arguing that the Bible is only literature. I am firmly convinced that the Holy Spirit enabled the authors in the creative use of linguistic devices, such as repetition, reversals, juxtapositions, creative montages, and folding events within future events, to accomplish God's purposes. For instance, the differences between the Gospel accounts are often accredited to the limited perspectives and biases of the authors. Rather than liken the biblical writers to the proverbial blind men that examined the elephant, why not approach the writings of the four evangelists as men who wrote with theological imagination and conviction? For instance, Luke rearranges the temptations of Christ because he envisions the ascending order of the temptations differently than does Matthew. I'm confident that some exegetes would read Luke's creativity much differently than I would. That is a risk I must be willing to take.

For those who would agonize that treating the Scripture as an art form results in a reduction of the "inspired Word of God," they may want to consider that God's inspiration encompasses both form and content. The first reference of persons being filled with the "Spirit" in Scripture concerns the artists of the tabernacle, Oholiab and Bezalel. The enablement of craftsmen for a house of worship is hardly more critical than the enablement of the words that would fill the house. When David Daiches declares the Psalms "the greatest lyrics of world literature" (Daiches 1984, 211), and Samuel Sandmel argues that the literary prophets "represent the artistic pinnacle of the Bible" (Sandmel 1972, 237), they are not imposing on the Scriptures literary criticism that was foreign to the purposes of God. God envisioned and enabled language sufficient and efficient for the message He wished to convey, knowing, as Meland argues, that language is always inadequate, particularly in God talk.

adequate language for preaching

The constant battle of all communication is the discovery of adequate language. As Abraham Lincoln rode the train to Gettysburg, he made repeated copies of his address, each time hoping he would come closer to representing the enormous sacrifice of the battle that, more than any other, saved the Union and freed African-Americans. Lincoln's speech not only reflected what had happened at Gettysburg but also created what was to arise from it, "a new birth of freedom." Lincoln creatively drew upon obstetrics, referring to conception and birth no less than three times. Lincoln accepted the daunting task of making sure that the thousands that died at Gettysburg did not die "in vain." Lincoln's artful use of metaphor, juxtaposition, alliteration, imagery, repetition, contrast, and parallel structure ensured that the life of "increased devotion" rose above the graves of those who had given the "last full measure of devotion." The preacher tries to create for every generation what arises from the birth, death, and resurrection of Jesus Christ.

Lincoln relied on metaphors of spiritual imagination rather than advice, statistics, and strategy, all of which would have cheapened the occasion. A nation faced with the carnage of thousands of its best lost in battle demanded what Philip Wheelwright referred to as "tensive language." Stenic language is closed, propositional, and informational, while tensive speech is multivalent, dialectical, and paradoxical (Wheelwright 1962, 45-69). The tension and divisions within the nation called for Lincoln to grope for words that represented that tension, to "capture a vision which would bare the traces of the tensions and problematic character of the experience that gave it birth" (Wheelwright 1962, 46). Lincoln used an archetypical symbol, birth, artfully placing it in a new context to offer hope in the midst of America's apocalypse. He would have agreed with Wheelwright: "Tensive symbols may perhaps offer hints about the nature of things which straight-forward techniques must either ignore or distort. If reality is largely fluid and half-paradoxical, steel nets are not the best instruments for taking samples of it" (Wheelwright 1962, 128).

"Steel nets" remind us of Søren Kierkegaard's observations that truth is not nimble on its feet or, in Craddock's words, truth is often "heavy-footed" and "pedestrian" (Craddock 1978, 16). The preacher grasps for forms that transcend the heavy footedness of boredom and commonness by realizing that the vehicle that delivers the truth is as important as the truth, because when the vehicle breaks down, so does its rider. The pragmatic engineering of the vehicle is insufficient in itself to deliver truth. All cars have a steering wheel, four wheels, seats, and an engine. To just get there will not do for Americans, either in their choice of cars or sermons. In contrast to sheer utilitarianism Craddock writes, "We are of course talking about artistry. Art implicates and involves the reader, listener, or observer in ways more complex than agreeing or disagreeing, . . . a bit of artistry can lay hold of heart or mind and not let go until thoughts and feelings long dormant are stirred" (Craddock 1978, 98).

Allow me to say that this book is not about the preacher being clever or fascinating. The desire to be a "great preacher" subverts the necessity to allow God's Word in its redeeming solvency to be heard by the person who could care less for preaching as linguistic giftedness. This book is about giving the biblical text the exploration it deserves so that all people will receive the message they deserve "for such a time and place as this." The preacher aims at resonance and attempts to open eyes and unstop ears by using language palatable to hearers while not reducing the truth the language means to convey.

I tell seminary students that I would like to give them a gift after they graduate. I would hand them, if possible, a language transformer (all of us have electrical transformers outside of our houses that regulate and transform electricity into a usable amount. If not, the full current coming from the outside wires would fry the electrical sockets and blow the electrical panels off the wall). My gift would be used to translate all technical jargon, "seminariese," into usable, palatable, and artful language. The art transformer (risking a mixed metaphor) would enable the following seven transformations.

ONE
UNSEEN INTO THE SEEN

Artists render that which can be seen. Art by its very nature is a hands-on enterprise that imagines and produces that which can be physically experienced. Museums post the injunction "Do not touch!" for the very reason that art can be touched. In fact, the artist would have failed if the temptation to touch never occurred in the minds of the art's admirers.

Art grants physical access to worlds that are beyond the domain of most of us in the same way that preaching enables access to another world. God asked Jeremiah, "What do you see?" Jeremiah responded, "I see a boiling pot, tilting away from the north." God then said, "From the north disaster will be poured out on all who live in the land" (Jer. 1:13-14). The primary reason that the Old Testament prophets are visual communicators is that God communicated to them in pictures and objects that were as tangible and true to life as the events that would happen to Israel. God enabled the prophets of Israel to see so that the people of Israel would be able to see. God enabled His messengers to excel in object lessons. Ezekiel 21:9-10 is a case in point: "A sword, a sword, sharpened and polished—sharpened for the slaughter, polished to flash like lightning!" Ezekiel told Israel that since God could not get their attention with a rod, He would now try a sword. A sword flashing like lightning would, if not startle, at least wake up most congregations.

Before Zerubbabel rebuilt the Temple in Jerusalem, God spoke through

the prophet Haggai: "'I will take you, my servant Zerubbabel son of
Shealtiel,' declares the LORD, 'and I will make you like my signet ring, for I
have chosen you'" (Hag. 2:23). A signet ring was a work of art; no other ring
in the world was like it. The imprint of the ring on a document left no doubt
as to the officialness of the communication. The signet ring carried the authority of the king and his kingdom. God tangibly and artistically communicated to Zerubbabel, "My seal is on you. You cannot fail because you are my
chosen vessel." The signet ring was the sign of God's enablement stated by
Zechariah to Zerubbabel: "Not by might nor by power, but by my Spirit"
(Zech. 4:6).

All the parables of Jesus could be prefixed by "Imagine this," or "Picture
this." When Jesus told the story of a man going down from Jerusalem to Jericho, most of His hearers immediately perceived a rocky, winding, dusty road,
the perfect haven and workplace for thieves. Imagine the ludicrous incongruity Jesus created when He told the Pharisees and lawyers, who "picked the
places of honor at the table," about the poor, ragged, and diseased beggars
who were sitting around a sumptuous banquet table laden with silver plat-
ters, filled with culinary masterpieces to be washed down with the finest wine
(see Luke 14:7-13).

Sermons work best as artistic visions that are a curious combination of
improvisation and painstaking work. Before Tolkien wrote his Lord of the
Rings trilogy, he meticulously outlined every scene and what it contained (as
is displayed in the main library at Marquette University). The Renaissance
painters Rubens, Leonardo da Vinci, and Michelangelo crafted designs that
would guide them in giving form to the vision that would require painstaking
labor. Pliny the Elder in the first century told the story of a painter attempting to depict the froth coming from a dog's mouth. After several attempts at
painting the froth and being disappointed at the results, he flung the
"sponge ful of colours that he had wiped out, full against that unhappy place
of the table which had put him to all this trouble: but see what came of it!
the sponge left the colors behind, in better order than he could have lied
them, and in truth, as well as his heart could wish" (Gayford 1998, 455).
Artistic expression that gives visibility to that which is difficult to make visible
will seldom happen in a fit of exasperation but will more often appear as a
result of long-suffering patience. The story is told of James Joyce, author of
Ulysses, slumped over his writing table in a posture of despair. A friend asked
him how many words he had been able to write today.

"Seven," came the exasperated answer.

"Seven, well that's pretty good isn't it—at least for you."

"I suppose it is, but I can't find what order they go in," replied Joyce (King 2000, 146).

No profession should be more aware of the symbiotic relationship between word and picture than Christian preaching, Christianity has produced more visible manifestations than any other cultural or sociological movement in the world. God was made visible in Jesus Christ. The events of Christ's life could be captured by both two- and three-dimensional art objects, which served as instruments of remembrance. Art as a means of grace was given formal affirmation, after much controversy, by the ecumenical council of A.D. 786. Concerning the events of Scripture the synod stated, "For the more frequently they are seen by means of pictorial representation, the more those who behold them are aroused to remember and desire the prototypes and to give them greeting and the worship of honor" (Nichols 1980, 81). One hundred years later Nicephorus, patriarch of Constantinople, was even more pointed: "The humanity of Christ if bereft of one of its properties is a defective nature, and Christ not a perfect man, or rather not Christ at all. He is lost altogether if he cannot be circumscribed and represented in art" (Nichols 1980, 86).

Only preaching that can be seen will lead to parishioners confessing, "I see." From the Greek word *Ideÿ*, "I see," we get the word *idea*. Neither Jesus nor the Hebrew prophets would have attempted to communicate a concept without material objects. Jesus used 20 different visible metaphors in His sermon on the mount. John Milbank writes, "When we seek to isolate a material content for a word, we must use other words, with their preestablished associations of ideal value. As with language, so we thought, we must write and think through the opaque natural world, which we reactivate through metaphor" (Milbank 1997, 75). The essence of postmodernity is "sight," the visual that grasps an idea. In Nicholas Mirzoeff's words, postmodern culture is "most postmodern when it is visual" (Mirzoeff 1999, 4).

When Ann Sullivan enabled Helen Keller to utter a sound symbol for water, she rewound Helen's life to the first word that was ever spoken. Language forms from object to object and the words that connect those objects. Thus, we think much more in *percepts* than we do in *precepts*. This was certainly true for the Hebrew prophets. Speaking in percepts came far more naturally for cultures who communicated orally rather than in written language, especially in language that uses the words of theology and philosophy. In his book *Visual Thinking*, Rudolf Arnheim states, "What is needed, it seems to me, is a systematic training of visu-

al sensuality as an indispensable part of any educator's preparation for his profession" (Arnheim 1969, 315). As a teacher, Frank McCourt hit "pedagogical
paydirt" by dissecting a ballpoint pen. "The spring makes the pen work." The
"spring" is the noun of the sentence and "makes" is the verb. "So you can see a
ballpoint pen is like a sentence. It needs something to make it work. It needs action, a verb. Can you see that?" (McCourt 2005, 124).

TWO
ORDINARY INTO THE EXTRAORDINARY

The Basilica of St. Josaphat towers over a Polish neighborhood in Mil-
waukee. This community in the early 20th century produced one of the most
remarkable churches in America. The copper dome, modeled after St. Peter's
in Rome, rises 20 stories above the ground. The copper work, hand-carved
marble, stained glass, ornate wood carvings, and paintings that grace the
walls rival anything in Europe. The vividness of the colors reminds one of St.
Paul's in London. The grandeur and exactness of the cathedral's proportions
project a simple beauty that both defies and exalts the simple houses surrounding it. The descriptive brochure states, "The twin towers, cross-shaped
floor plan, hand-carved marble pulpit, columns, and baldachina represent
the same passion and triumphant spirit of European cathedrals."

But what defies imagination is not so much the exquisite artwork that covers the interior of the majestic dome but the discovery that the cathedral was
built from the ruins of a Chicago post office dismantled in 1901. What kind
of ingenuity would it take to convert a post office into a cathedral? Is there a
better example of the ordinary becoming the extraordinary, the common becoming uncommon? The commonness is accented by the fact that the entire
project was funded with pennies given by poor people who worked long hours
in the machine shops and breweries of the city. The Basilica of St. Josaphat
stands as a testimony to the fact that every job and task can take on a meaning beyond the simple carrying out of trivialities and minute details.

Most of us are not involved in building a cathedral; in fact, most of us are
not involved in building anything. We simply take our places on the assembly
line of so-called progress, hardly ever able to say, "I had a major hand in producing that." Sitting in a six-by-six-foot cubicle staring at a computer screen
seems far removed from a Swiss woodworker crafting a meticulously carved
clock in a previous century. In a day that almost totally dismisses the possibilities of taking pride in a finished project, most lives become abstractions,
minuscule points in an endless line of routine with no particular direction.

A critical objective for preaching is to enable people to get the big picture, to envision that life is more than getting up and going to work. Sermons place life within the overall scheme of God's providence. Sermons work when they consecrate the most menial responsibility to God's eternal and universal scheme and they reduce the CEO of a megacorporation to obscurity, unless he or she is engulfed by God's superintendency over human affairs. Americans are increasingly depressed people, gulping down megadoses of antidepressants, largely because they are lost in a world that controls them rather than able to lay claim to their rightful domain. Paul asked the Corinthians when they were embroiled in lawsuits, a depressing activity for anybody, "Do you not know that the saints will judge the world?" (1 Cor. 6:2). Sermons ask the simple question, "Why would anyone want to grovel in the give-and-take that ensnares and enslaves most of us when we can be a major player in God's scheme to redeem the world?" Enticing our parishioners to trade the trivialities of mundane existence for Kingdom citizenship shouldn't take a whole lot of persuasion, but it will demand our best imagination.

THREE
PROFANE INTO THE SACRED

Homiletical imagination expands the borders of spirituality. Transforming the secularity of our existence into a sacred ordering with holy dimensions demands a refocusing of much of the church's business. Sunday business is about moving God out of Sunday and into the totality of existence. Enabling parishioners to get out of bed, not to go to work, but to embark on a daily mission of the Holy Spirit would infuse the church with a renewal of energy for bringing God's kingdom to earth. Preaching explores creative ways in which parishioners may write God's signature on all of existence. A teacher prays over the desk of every student, and a shopworker conducts a Bible study during lunchtime. The job of preaching is to enable life to become more than economic consumption, technological progress, and creature comfort. True biblical preaching continually drops clues to the God-dimensions of life. Church business is to translate nonchurch business into sacred business.

In *Silas Marner*, the novel by Mary Anne Evans (better know by her pen name, George Eliot), Silas visits the home of Dolly Winthrop. She offers Silas some lard cakes, less distinguished by their taste than by the inscription of the letters "IHS" on each of them. Dolly cannot even read the letters much less interpret them. She only knows that they must be good because they are also sketched on the cloth that hangs over the pulpit in the church. Dolly says to Silas, "I prick 'em on all the loaves and all the cakes; though sometimes they won't hold, because o' the rising for, as I said, if there is any good to be got we've need of it in' this world—that we have; and I hope they bring good to you" (Eliot 1999, 82). George Eliot was not only trying to fuse the profane and sacred, but in the words of her biographer, Frederick Karl, to resolve the "major faultlines in Victorian religion and social thought" (Eliot 1999, 15). It is not an accident that she, like Silas Marner, was ostracized from the church and thus forced to discover the holy in unconventional ways.

Sermons that go beyond the four walls of the church find the sacred in the profane, the holy in the unholy, and transform all of life into a theological enterprise. Thinking theologically is not primarily the gift of formal education, but in daily activity finds, in Elizabeth Browning's words, that "Earth's crammed with heaven and every common bush ablaze with God, but only he who sees takes off his shoes, the rest sit around it and pluck blackberries."

But what Elizabeth Browning missed, at least from my perception, is that holy ground provides excellent fertility for blackberries. The presence of God knows no boundaries, as the psalmist noted: "If I make my bed in hell you are there" (139:8). The problem is seeing and perceiving God in the hell of life, when the fumes and smoke obscure even His silhouette. Artists make God known in the sweat-drenched vocation and dreary toil of life even as Jean François Millet depicted the two peasants in a field bowing their heads for prayer as they stood between the rows with hoe in hand. Such is the message of the cross created from over 4,000 pieces of wheat placed at the front of the Cathedral of the Plains in Victoria, Kansas, the symbol of God's redemption. The cross sprouting from the navel of America's wheat harvest is a fitting reminder that all of business—even the provision of the world's most common staple—is God's business. I suspect that's what Zechariah was trying to say when he wrote,

> On that day HOLY TO THE LORD will be inscribed on the bells of the horses, and the cooking pots in the LORD's house will be like the sacred bowls in front of the altar. Every pot in Jerusalem and Judah will be holy to the LORD Almighty, and all who come to sacrifice will take some of the pots and cook in them. And on that day there will no longer be a Canaanite in the house of the LORD Almighty *(Zech. 14:20-21)*.

FOUR
REDEMPTION OUT OF TRAGEDY

Preaching is an act of pastoral care. It attempts to find good in evil, to explain the existence of evil, and to transform tragedy into triumph. The difficulty

lies in there being some events that are so overwhelmingly tragic that any explanation or theological rationale often sounds trite and empty. Evil has never
been sufficiently explained, and all rational constructs end in contradictions.
That God is all powerful and yet He allows evil in the world is a paradox that
defies the most systematic and comprehensive theology. Thus, art accomplishes that which logic cannot defend or support, giving expression to the sorrow
and contradictions that accompany all tragedy whether it be personal or national. Eugene Peterson claimed that "Job made poetry out of what in many of
us is only a tangle of confused whimpers" (Peterson 2002, 39).

Art lends objectivity to tragedy. It places or positions a tragedy within a
painting, a sculpture, or a poem so that it can be handled and explored. Creativity projects grief and guilt on a carving or painting, thus serving as a
catharsis for emotions that, if left to smolder within the unconscious, would
eventually destroy or debilitate life's normal functions. Art gives expression to
our deepest hurts and innermost pinings for redemption. Where language
fails, art succeeds in turning the destructive forces of life into building blocks
of hope and resolution. Feelings are so powerful and unruly that they can only be managed through artful expression. Emotions that otherwise might be
expressed in violence to self or others are channeled into meaningful expressions of creativity. Ellen Dissanayake writes in *What Is Art For?* "The numerous
ends that violent behavior seems to serve—release, communication, play, self-
affirmation, self-defense, self-discovery, self-destruction, flight from reality,
assertion of truest sanity in a particular situation—are very like the motivations that are often proposed to underlie art" (Dissanayake 1990, 139). Pastors who stood before parishioners on the Sunday after the destruction of
the World Trade Center defused and dispelled the rage that filled the collective heart of America. They are much like the New York City policeman who
inscribed the following words on a security barrier around the rubble that
was once the Twin Towers:

The Road to Heaven*

While traveling along
It's never too late.
Take the road that leads to love
Not the one to hate.
Hate is what took these buildings down,

---

*I am indebted to one of my students, David Tate, for finding this at the former loca-
tion of the World Trade Center in New York City. Author unknown.

With love is how we'll remember those,
No longer around.
Take the right road and you will see,
How much sweeter life will be.
The road may be uphill and strewn with stones
So get rid of the weight
And lighten the load
At the summit there is a beautiful view
All of God's peace
Open to you.
A Police Officer
NYPD

The story of the sinking of the *Medusa* off the coast of Africa in 1816 is a study in incompetence and survival in the cruelest circumstances. Some 80 of the ship's sailors boarded a makeshift raft 65 by 23 feet. What was supposed to be a quick four-mile trip to shore became a 12-day nightmare of fighting, starving, cannibalism, and dying either of thirst or from drinking salt water. On July 17 a sister ship, the *Argus,* rescued 17 survivors, 10 of whom would live to tell of the disaster.

For 18 months, between February 1818 and July 1819, Theodore Gericault painted the rescue of the 17 survivors, choosing not to depict the *Argus* alongside of the raft, but as a small tip of a sail barely visible on the distant horizon. To achieve exactitude and reality, Gericault had torsos and body parts hauled in for the purpose of anatomical study. Live models afforded him the reality of figures in all sorts of agonizing postures. One sailor aided by fellow survivors who braced him up, frantically waves a scarlet and white cloth signaling their need for rescue. Out of all that Gericault could have symbolized in his painting—the shipwreck, mutiny, cannibalism—he chose redemption. Julian Barnes, in his *The History of the World in Ten and a Half Chapters,* wrote, "We are all lost at sea, washed between hope and despair, hailing something that may never come to rescue us. Catastrophe has become art but this is no reducing process. It is freeing, enlarging, explaining. Catastrophe has become art: that is, after all what it is for" (Gayford 2000, 232).

Every Sunday pastors stand before parishioners stemming the tide of tragedy, death, divorce, and even national calamity. Tragedy defies neat answers and comprehensive formulas. Only art in the form of song, prayer, and sermon, of which the Psalms are all three, will do. The preacher becomes the medium for his or her people expressing the deepest hurt, frustration, and anger of their existence. Emotions of the congregations flow through the pastor even as they did the psalmist as he stood before Temple worshipers and sang:

> The eyes of the LORD are on the righteous and his ears are attentive to their cry; the face of the LORD is against those who do evil, to cut off the memory of them from the earth. The righteous cry out, and the LORD hears them; he delivers them from all their troubles. The LORD is close to the brokenhearted and saves those who are crushed in spirit. A righteous man may have many troubles, but the LORD delivers him from them all *(Ps. 34:15-19)*.

FIVE
ORDER OUT OF CHAOS

Much of God's creativity in Gen. 1 is focused on giving order to what has already come into existence. The desire for order is more than a compulsion for neatness. Order in the divine image has more to do with purpose, direction, and meaning. Rick Warren's *The Purpose-Driven Life* struck a responsive chord with the most affluent society that has ever inhabited the earth. An innate hunger to know that my life counts for something more than acquisition resides within every human heart. God wants every individual to know that he or she can be caught up in something bigger than themselves. Thus, one of the purposes of art is to enable persons to literally "get the big picture."

We need to know that we are going somewhere. God whispers in every Christian's ear, "You are special and you can be caught up in My plan." Obviously several, if not many, of our parishioners, at any one time will be overwhelmed with confusion. Life doesn't make sense and there is no goal to be achieved and no destiny at which to arrive. Sermons are for the purpose of confirming for all persons that they are God's vocational elect, individuals of destiny.

Simon Winchester tells the sad and fascinating account of William Minor, who murdered a man in London on February 17, 1872. Because Minor was found to be insane (today he would be diagnosed as paranoid schizophrenic), he was sentenced to life at the Broadmoor Criminal Lunatic Asylum. This institution had replaced the Hospital of St. Mary at Bethlehem, which in the 15th century became a hospital prison for "lunatics." The word *bedlam* is a corruption of the word *Bethlehem* and came to be understood as a place for mentally deranged persons. Webster's dictionary describes "bedlam" as "any scene of uproar and confusion." We can only speculate why Minor's mind was increasingly haunted by imaginary thieves and attackers, which he believed to come up through the floor at night. The best conjecture is that because he, as an army doctor in the Civil War, was forced to brand a Union soldier in the face for desertion, he feared the deed would be returned upon him.

The Professor and the Madman details how Minor's confused life found meaning from his prison cell by becoming a prolific contributor to the *Oxford English Dictionary,* the most orderly creation ever produced by humankind. Through a "chance" appeal that fell out of a book he had ordered, Minor became a longtime friend of the *Oxford English Dictionary* editor, a polymath genius named James Murray. Concerning the *Oxford English Dictionary,* a lexicographical monument finally finished in 1927, Winchester writes, "The lonely drudgery of lexicography, the terrible undertow of words against which men like Murray and Minor had so ably struggled and stood, now had at last its great reward. Twelve mighty volumes, 414,825 words defined; 1,827,306 illustrated quotations used, to which William Minor had contributed scores of thousands" (Winchester 2005, 219-20).

Winchester has produced a work of art that inspires, gives hope, and discovers meaning in the most pitiful of circumstances. That is exactly what the hundreds of narratives in the Scriptures become in the hands of verbal artists who realize that the ancient biblical writers left for us an art form that needs to be recrafted and re-created for each new generation. Sermons that restore order to both the universe and individual lives, lives that are often out-of-whack, will never go out of business. Dissanayake argues that it "is inherent to the human condition to seek order for its own sake, to find delight and satisfaction wherever it is recognized and to actively seek or long to impose it on ourselves." She then states, "Giving shape and form to the amorphous or erratic which occurs invariably in the arts can be seen as an intensification or the intentional exercising of this general structuring proclivity" (Dissanayake 1990, 114).

SIX

DISSONANCE TO RELEVANCE

Preaching is supposed to be boring. Cartoons spoof benign and sedate preachers putting parishioners to sleep. Dullness is the sine qua non of the preacher who is out of touch with reality, having little influence on what goes on in the *real* world. Parishioners that face the *real* world of managing unruly kids in a classroom, trying to please an overdemanding boss, putting in an eight-hour day at Wal-Mart, and changing bed pans at Medical Research

Hospital are convinced that pastors are not in touch with the real world. The list stretches on as far as the line of the people who do the daily tasks of maintaining society, whether it be staring at a computer screen or folding shirts at a dry cleaner.

Do preachers assume that parishioners leave all of the above behind when they go to church to learn about Moses crossing the Red Sea and Paul escaping his persecutors by being lowered in a basket over a wall? But most people don't have Pharaoh's army bearing down on them, and they aren't ducking rocks thrown by people who don't like their theology, which is precisely the point. Nobody cares enough about theology to hiss or spit, much less throw a stone. Other than the practice of yoga and the mental benefits of contemplation, theology is relegated to seminary classrooms, the peculiar prerogative of those of us who don't have a real job. Sermons often leave parishioners murmuring, "If he only knew the stress I face. If only he knew how tight our finances are he wouldn't talk about tithing so much."

The word *relevant* comes from the Latin, meaning to "lift up again" or "to relieve." The critical relief for sermon tedium is the growing or sudden awareness that the preacher is talking about "what concerns me." Obviously this cannot be in the confrontational mode of a bolder and more uncivil day when preachers such as Charles Finney called parishioners out by name in the congregation. Relevance will only happen as a preacher connects the biblical narrative to what is foremost in parishioners' minds. The only way for a preacher to hold attention is to know where *their* attention lies. Relevance is the result of theological imagination, the artistic ability to focus the light of God's interests on the interests that preoccupy the most nonchalant and routine church attender. As a person at the health club told me, "I go to church Saturday night and get that over with." This attitude to church attendance is alive and well because the church often is an out-of-date institution that just might offer some fire insurance to keep us out of the place where there are no air-conditioners. And if that possibility even remotely exists, why not give it an hour a week? But if that is the most relevance that the church can engender, sermons will continue to be relegated to the half hour when people balance their checkbooks.

For a year, Barbara Ehrenreich, who holds a Ph.D. in biology, immersed herself into America's workforce doing minimum wage labor as a kitchen aide in a residence home for the debilitated, a maid at a hotel, a cleaning lady for a maid service, and a stock checker at Wal-Mart. Ehrenreich's solidarity with those who enable most of us to live in ease and comfort was motivated by the fact that 30 percent of the American workforce labors for $8.00 an hour or less. The poorest 10 percent earn 10 percent less than they did 30 years ago, and housing devours 37 percent of the average paycheck. Sixty percent of America earns less than $14.00 per hour. All of this sounds like remote facts to which I respond, "Oh, my!" or "I'm glad that data doesn't describe me." It isn't the facts that grab our attention but the sights, sounds, and smells that engulf those who "nickel-and-dime it." Ehrenreich described her experience as a waitress:

> The kitchen is a cavern, a stomach leading to the lower intestine that is the garbage and dishwashing area, from which issue bizarre smells combining the edible and offal: creamy carrion, pizza barf, and that unique and enigmatic Jerry's scent, citrus fart. The floor is slick with spills, forcing us to walk through the kitchen with tiny steps, like Susan McDougal in leg irons. Sinks everywhere are clogged with scraps of lettuce, decomposing lemon wedges, water-logged toast crusts. Put your hand down on any counter and you risk being stuck to it by the film of ancient syrup spills, and this is unfortunate because hands are utensils here, used for scooping up lettuce onto the salad plates, lifting out pie slices, and even moving hashbrowns from one plate to another (Ehrenreich 2001, 29-30).

Relevance focuses on the grubby details of life. Biblical revelation comes in sights, sounds, smells, images, and often the texture of life that does not merit a G rating. The Bible does nothing to blunt life's ragged and raw edges. Stark realism is the motif of Scripture rather than romanticism. Von Rad argues that the prophets did not adhere to the code of "devout language," but rather, "they often spoke in down right scandalous language about God, and it is quite clear that they wanted thereby as iconoclasts to destroy conventional ideas about God" (Von Rad 1974, 16). We are quick to gloss over God's actions as if we need to protect God. Rather than needing our defense, God invites us to explore Him, to know Him in all His mystical, paradoxical, and politically incorrect actions. Why, Jesus didn't even thank that poor Pharisee who had invited him home for dinner but immediately lit in to him with an invective: "Inside you are full of greed and wickedness" (Luke 11:39).

SEVEN
ABSTRACT TO CONCRETE

The academy has often enslaved theology with manacles cast from polysyllabic words, circumlocution, and long complex sentences. The guild (a conspiracy against the laity according to Bernard Shaw) has obscured God with abstraction tinged with Greek Platonism and German idealism. To abstract an idea is to think it apart from any particular instances or material objects. Sermon preparation constantly asks, "What does this thought, for instance, God's providence, look like? What is the concrete form for this quality, virtue, or attribute that I'm trying to express? Sermons become plausible only as we give concrete evidence that ideas can become reality. Faith is quickened only to the extent that sermons provide "evidence of things not seen" and "the substance of things hoped for." The burden of truth lies with the preacher; thus, John wrote, "We declare to you what was from the beginning, what we have heard, what we have seen with our eyes, what we have looked at and touched with our hands, concerning the words of life" (1 John 1:1, NRSV).

Mark Galli and Craig Larson argue that for preaching to connect it will have to pay close attention to how newspaper writers use true stories, short sentences, and graphic details rather than vague references. Journalism excels in trading the vagueness of generic language for particulars. "Being specific means saying Luger, rather than weapon; '89 Taurus, rather than vehicle; adultery, rather than sin; the nails through Christ's palms, rather than Christ's suffering; Bob, the 45-year-old, overweight Chicago detective with the scar on the back of his hand, rather than the officer. The gunpowder is in specifics, the more precise the better" (Galli and Larson 1994, 72).

Thomas Troeger compares two wedding sermons, one in pedantic, abstract language "the sacred words of promising covenant" and a "visual sermon for the mass media generation." In the latter sample a photographer takes the couple's picture in wedding clothes each anniversary for the next 50 years. The pictures include stacks of bills, doctor's appointments, the countenances of acid words, tired visages, and eventually musty and yellow wedding garments, no longer capable of being zipped and buttoned over inflated, fleshy carcasses. The words "In sickness, and in health" had flowed nonchalantly out of their mouths 47 years ago. But now as a husband who has had two heart attacks holds his wife's hand, knuckles swollen and knobby, they pose for the flash of the camera. "In looking into each other's eyes, they see something more beautiful than the prize pictures in their anniversary album; the grace and the glory of a promise kept" (Troeger 1990, 47).

First, translating the abstract into the concrete takes place in frames of reference that identify everyday life. Concrete preaching laces language with rhetorical devices that empirically represent the everyday world. Calvin Miller calls for substantive thinking and preaching, strong nouns and verbs rather than modifiers. "His mood froze his face in furrows of grudge" communicates more effectively than "his face was hard and cold" (Miller 2006, 158). But modifiers sparsely used enhance vividness as William Faulkner's description of "Emily" demonstrates: "Her eyes, lost in the fatty ridges of her face looked like two small pieces of coal pressed into a lump of dough as they moved from one face to another while the visitors stated their errand" (Faulkner 1965, 170).

The following rhetorical devices demonstrate visual speech:

Contrast

He built a house but failed to build a home.

"The Bobos are trying to build a house of obligation on a foundation of choice." —David Brooks (Brooks 2000, 228)

Simile

Grace is like water, you can receive it but you can't hold onto it.

"I began to conceive that my mind itself was like one of those out-moded small-town telephone exchanges being gradually inundated by flood waters." —William Styron (Styron 1992, 47-48)

Hyperbole

"He's so tight that if he opened his wallet in January a Junebug would fly out of it."

"Writing fiction, especially a long work of fiction, can be a difficult lonely job; it's like crossing the Atlantic ocean in a bathtub, there's plenty of opportunity for self doubt." —Stephen King (King 2000, 210)

"The sluggard buries his hand in the dish; he will not even bring it back to his mouth!" (Prov. 19:24).

Comparison

"They may like you, they may love you, but they are young and the business of the young is to push the old off the planet." —Frank McCourt (McCourt 2005, 255)

"Too many of the things we do in our lives, large and small, have come to resemble channel surfing, marked by a numbing and seemingly endless progression from one option to the next, all without the benefit of a chart, logistical or moral, because there are simply too many choices and no one to help sort them out." —Alan Ehrenhalt (Brooks 2000, 245-46)

Second, narrative illustrations are an essential delivery system for theological visuality. The right illustration capsulates, summarizes, highlights, and clarifies truth conveyed to people, who at times, including me, think no more deeply than a gnat looking for its next full head of hair. Illustrations are the horse sitting on the table, the 5,000-pound squid lying in my bed, and the giraffe who doesn't have enough head room in my car. Illustrations are as numerous as the leaves that fall from a New Hampshire maple, as free as the sand that sticks to my feet when I step out of the surf on the Outer Banks of North Carolina and as sparkling as the stars on a dark clear night in West Texas. Only a 24-7 dialogue with the universe, whether I am reading a book, taking a hike through the Colorado Rockies, or standing on a Chicago street corner will secure adequate illustrations. History, contemporary news, everyday events, literature, art, conversations, and—above all—interactions with my family are the stock and trade of the preacher. All of these need to be told with graphic detail without demeaning, trivializing, or simply piling on words to attract attention to myself rather than illuminate the idea.

To be illustrious as opposed to illustrative is to attract attention to oneself, even as a decorator lamp desires to be noticed but fails to illuminate its surroundings. Well-placed illustrations do not attract attention to themselves but shine light on truth, making it attractive and appealing. Even more importantly, illustrations retrieve and download concepts for portable transportation. Parishioners often carry away only the illustration. Thus, I emphasize to students that the closing illustration needs to incorporate not simply the final point but as much of the sermon as possible. One of my closing illustrations narrates an anecdote from one of my favorite people, Francis Asbury. This story concludes my sermon on Jesus' words in Luke 22:29, "Just as My Father has granted Me a Kingdom, I grant you" (NASB). I preface the anecdote by saying, "I'm not aware of anyone who claimed more of the Kingdom than did Asbury. Between 1771 and 1816 he rode 250,000 miles on horseback, preached 15,000 times, crossed the Allegheny Mountains 60 times, and ordained 4,000 men. Asbury was referred to as "infinite toughness."

At Georgetown, South Carolina, he reaped a seed sown some 20 years before. He had spent 10 minutes sharing the gospel with a slave; crossing a small bridge, Asbury bid the slave "good day," and continued to ride. Some distance away, the Holy Spirit nudged the bishop: "You need to speak to that man about his soul." Asbury turned his horse around and rode up to the large and poorly clad black man. Dismounting, Asbury asked the slave his name, to which he responded, "Sir, I don't rightly know what my name is. They call me Punch because I am always getting into fights." Asbury asked Punch if he ever prayed, to which the slave responded, "No, sir." Sitting down on a rock, Asbury read some Scripture, sang a hymn, and had prayer with Punch, then departed.

Twenty years later there stood Punch, having located the bishop at his

Georgetown stop. "Sir, you know that day you stopped and prayed with me; I went back to my cabin and got down on my knees, and my cabin was all filled with light. Since that day I haven't wanted to fight anymore, curse anymore, play cards anymore. I haven't even wanted to fish anymore. There are now three hundred of us, and they want me to be their preacher." Asbury thought to himself, "Better to witness to one slave than to rule on the highest throne on the face of the earth" (Salter 2003, 323-24).

As a preacher I have to be careful not to constantly illustrate through preachers and, in my case, to laden my sermons with history, of which I am far fonder than most. Everydayness is the best stuff for morphing abstractions. Persons incarnate sermonic truth. As an example of suffering and perseverance, John Ortberg introduces us to Mable, as told to him by Thomas Schmidt. I reintroduce her to congregations as a living, breathing example of one who knows the "fellowship of Christ's suffering."

As I neared the end of this hallway, I saw an old woman strapped up in a wheelchair. Her face was an absolute horror. The empty stare and white pupils of her eyes told me that she was blind. The large hearing aid over one ear told me that she was almost deaf. One side of her face was being eaten by cancer. There was a discolored and running sore covering part of one cheek, and it had pushed her nose to one side, dropped one eye, and distorted her jaw so that what should have been the corner of her mouth was the bottom of her mouth. As a consequence, she drooled constantly. I was told later that when new nurses arrived, the supervisors would send them to feed this woman, thinking that if they could stand this sight they could stand anything in the building. I also learned later that this woman was eighty-nine years old and that she had been here, bedridden, blind, nearly deaf, and alone for twenty-five years. This was Mabel (Ortberg 1997, 25).

Gifted and diligent are preachers who can depict persons living out Christianity in the nitty-gritty of everyday experience. Minute particulars, diaper rash and diminishing cash, create the friction of life. Too often, our illustrations exalt spiritual giants who know little about (and if they did they never told us) applying spirituality to nagging children, unfolded clothes in overfilled baskets, clogged toilets, and bagworms in my shrubs. Such is not the case for E. T. Eberhart who told parables for "20th-century Christians," this one about "the mother who had some difficulty with her lot":

Her mornings began twenty-four hours late. She arose with yesterday's leftovers still in place. This was due to the heck-with-it attitude that snagged her when sleep finally floored the boys for the full count. The dinner dishes would keep 'til morning, and no company coming tonight, so let the scattered clothes be, ditto for the toys, dusting and vacuuming having already received a rescheduling.

Now she did crack a whip, but it could not be heard, the happy sounds being too loud. So one afternoon she did a learn-by-example touted by leading authorities. They cozy couched with her holding her favorite magazine, the boys nestled close. She showed them selected pictures, giving the moral about picking up their debris. This she said would give them a magazine-pictured home and wasn't that what they wanted. Before she took her third breath the youngest wanted cookies and milk, big brother kicked the five-year-old in the shins making him cry, and the dog crawled under the couch chewing an old beef bone (Eberhart 1977, 81-82).

This book will argue for myriad art forms, forms as varied as the text they communicate and the situations in which they are communicated. No art should be created in a vacuum but with a certain audience in mind. Persons who read novels and attend plays need a different kind of preaching than those who do neither. This is not to say that preaching needs to be less artful for the less educated or elderly. But no single art form will appeal to everyone. For example, my taking of scenic side trips during the sermon often leaves some of my meat-and-potato listeners wishing I would not sacrifice straight-to-the-point communication for aesthetic packaging. Many seminary students who have been taught to preach impressionistic, suggestive, artful sermons will have to adjust to the parishioner who says, "Preacher, tell me what you're going to say, tell me, tell me what you said." No preacher should stand back from his best sermon and say, "What a masterful work of art!" while his parishioners remain in darkness.

Bear in mind that there are great preachers that know little about what this book professes to teach. They have determined "to know nothing but Christ crucified" (see 1 Cor. 2:2), and they have come before their congregations "not with wise and persuasive words, but with a demonstration of the Spirit's power" (v. 4). They live in the Bible, absorbing Scripture, spending much time in prayer, and faithfully preparing a message appropriate for both time and place. They communicate certainty in their convictions, passion in their voice, and love for their people, with a high agreement between what they preach and what they live. When Matthew Arnold, the 19th-century historian and poet, took a friend to hear Charles Spurgeon preach, the friend remarked to Arnold upon leaving the Metropolitan Tabernacle, "I don't believe what he was saying." Arnold responded, "That doesn't make any difference, he does." I remind students, "If you can't show as much enthusiasm for announcing that Christ is risen as a weatherman does in prophesying climatic changes, you are in the wrong business." This book is offered to those who go about the business of carving out of Scripture something to say week after week, to those who wander in a dry and thirsty land, with the hope that preaching will once again become the "power of God unto salvation" (Rom. 1:16, KJV).

two

PREACHING as BIBLICAL narrative

the bible as story

Story is so basic and constant to human communication that it is difficult to define. We know a story as opposed to a laundry list, a set of instructions, a code of rules, and so on, when we hear one. A story is a chronological sequencing of events—events connected by time, space, logic, consequence, or cause and effect that make sense to the listener, or will make sense once the story is completed. If some facet of the story is unintelligible, the teller may be asked to provide some connective detail or clue so that the events cohere in a more understandable form. The preacher tells God's story, the story that defines all other stories, and places his or her hearers within that story. So my students have heard it a hundred times. When someone asks me what I do for a living, I say, "I'm a storyteller, I tell the story surrounded by a whole lot of little stories. You have heard the story, haven't you? God became man and died for you."

The Bible is a story or, if you please, two stories that are connected. It is not a completed story; the end is yet to be written. In that sense, no sermon is ever complete. The jury is always out, at least part of them. They keep returning, demanding more evidence, wanting to hear the story one more time. "Tell that part again." The Bible tells a story of redemption, the rescue of humanity by God with what Joel Green calls a "single, coordinating and unifying plot" (Green 2003, 28).

In the Old Testament, God rescues the Israelites from Egypt, and in the New Testament God rescues whosoever will believe from the power of sin and Satan. Both of these historical events proliferate hundreds of biblical stories, domino events that unfold throughout the biblical narrative and are still being played out in the histories of nations and individuals. Scriptural narrative begets narrative. Stories spawn stories. Events foretell future events and one tale often portends another tale.

Some of the stories told in Scripture did not actually happen. Others so actually happened that their historical verification is critical to faith in the Bible's theological framework. For the Christian, the core story in Scripture is not optional. It is a story that if proven to be historically false invalidates faith. Paul wrote, "If there is no resurrection of the dead, then not even Christ has been raised. And if Christ has not been raised, our preaching is useless and so is your faith" (1 Cor. 15:13-14). Not all biblical stories imply an external reference to historical fact or event, but if the Bible was mainly a tale written in a vacuum with no validating observation recorded in any historical record other than itself, faith would consist of an illusion. George Stroup has written, "The assumption that meaning and truth do not necessarily cohere, that the world of the text is not the real world of historical event, that the truth of the narrative is a matter of the correspondence between its claim and its historical reference, make it virtually impossible to read a text 'realistically'" (Stroup 1981, 140). To read the text realistically is to read it with the firm conviction that the characters and settings described by the author happened within time and place. If they didn't happen, they certainly could have, surely in the parables of Christ.

story as meaning

Each time a local Christian congregation comes together, it enacts several memories: the Christological drama, the story of the Christian Church throughout 20 centuries, the history of its denomination (if it participates within an affiliation of churches), the narrative of the particular community of the gospel that meets at Fifth and Grand. All these memories interweave with national and political histories that provide identity. The memory that is not optional for the local congregation to enact and reenact in creed, song, prayer, sermon, and sacrament is the biblical narrative. Unless the church is scripted by Scripture in word and deed, it ceases to be a Christian church. It could be argued that the sermon has done more to provide the church its narrative identity than any other single act. Thus, the preacher is in the serious business of not only maintaining ecclesial identity but also transforming identity, because transformation, the creation of new worlds, always results for those who sincerely hear the biblical story. Walter Brueggemann writes, "Preaching as interpretation is always a daring, dangerous act in which the interpreter, together with the receivers of the interpretation, is consuming a text and producing a world" (Brueggemann 1988, 131-32).

My life finds meaning only in a story that extends both backward and forward beyond my finite existence. The biblical narrative is uniquely eschatological, not in a horoscopic or crystal ball sense, but in God's intention for the ultimate good to forever triumph. God's story, which embraces and encompasses my story, lets me know that my life did not begin at conception and will not end in death. It began long before and will continue long after.

the essential elements of good storytelling

What makes narrative good? The basic ingredients are plots, characters, scenes, and conversations that are full of eccentricities, intrigue, emotions, and many other interesting traits. The Bible story depicts a constant life-death struggle. Humankind from the very beginning is on the brink of ruin, beset with murder, deceit, treachery, betrayal. Humanity almost completely destroys itself. God often intervenes at the last moment when all seems hopeless. But all of this isn't without its light moments. In fact much of the time the reader doesn't know whether to laugh or cry. Scripture allows us to do both. Preaching that takes Scripture seriously will cause listeners to be drawn into the text, to sense the emotions of the text, to participate vicariously in the struggle of the text.

Good plot always includes conflict, and no literature excels more with incorporating conflict than Scripture. Good conflicts with evil; book after book, chapter after chapter, depict protagonists and antagonists in life-and-death struggles. Though Scripture is interspersed with song, proverbs, and apocalyptic literature, it is mainly a story about people with problems. Biblical characters provide the preacher with a constant supply of fascinating subject matter. In the development of a main character, J. Kent Edwards writes, "You will begin to see your protagonist as more than just a disembodied attribute or a walking theological lesson. Your goal is to get to know the protagonist as well as his mother, spouse, and best friend knew him" (Edwards 2005, 83).

narrative profluence

No family has ever been more conflicted than those folks from whom God attempted to form a nation. A very elderly couple has a son. They named him Isaac, meaning "laughter," or "Is this a joke?" He and Rebecca become the proud and partial parents of two sons. One of them is captain of the football team and the other is the only boy in home ec class. Guess which parent sides with which child? The family squabbles, resulting in the home ec kid having to flee for his life.

When Jacob arrives at the home of his mother's brother, Laban, the first person he encounters is the girl of his dreams, Rachel. What a knockout! She tells him that the stone over the mouth of the well is so large that they will have to wait until evening when the other shepherds arrive to draw water. No problem. Mama's kitchen helper pronto leaps to the well and flips off the stone like it was the lid on a tube of Pringles potato chips. It is amazing what can happen when all the hormones are aligned in a single direction. Where are we going with the above anecdote? What meaning does it have to the story? Actually, more dysfunctionalism, which further complicates the plot. The side plots are drawn together in what Philip Gerard calls "narrative profluence" (Gerard 1996, 133).

"Narrative profluence" asks a simple question: is the sermon going somewhere? Sermons always move in one or more of the following directions: dilemma to resolution, loss to gain, defeat to victory, question to answer, problem to solution, conflict to reconciliation, negative to positive, and evil to good. God's story always moves toward solution, though there are individual lives and events that end in disaster. However, unlike Greek tragedy, the underlying premise for every disaster is "things could have been different" (though I admit that the premise is severely challenged in the stories of both Pharaoh and Judas, but in both of these persons, God uses their rebellion and greed for good). God's narrative means to convince us that His predetermined plan to redeem His Bride can never be overruled. Exquisite pieces of narrative tapestry in the lives of Jacob and his 12 sons abound; comparison, continuities, parallels, ironies, and the scrapes of life cause the reader to ask, "How is he going to get out of this fix?"

Robert Alter highlights Judah's sexual impetuosity (see Gen. 38) with Joseph's abstinence; the kid required by Tamar and the kid that was sacrificed to provide the blood that deceived Jacob; the inability to immediately recognize Tamar with the inability to immediately recognize Joseph; and the reversal of first-born status for the twins born to the illicit liaison, a theme found throughout Scripture. The artful intentionalities preserve the literary unity of the text and are provided by a "brilliant literary artist" who knew how to carefully "splice" his sources. Judah is trumped by the triumph and revelation of both Tamar and Joseph. And it seems to me that any good Jew would have camouflaged that it is Tamar who falls within the lineage of the kings of Judah and not Joseph (and for us who carry the story into the new covenant, the lineage of Christ). But the artist does not allow his nationalistic bias or theological presuppositions to undermine the "indeterminate" schemes of God. Hardly anything goes according to a neat theodicy. At first glance, Tamar seems despicable, tricking her father-in-law into a sexual escapade, a sin that the Mosaic Law would later condemn under penalty of death. Judah's self-righteous condemnation of Tamar to be burned to death is completely exposed. The biblical writer highlights the contrast present in

the actions of Judah, whose "sexual appetite would not tolerate postpone-
ment though he has been content to let Tamar languish as a childless widow
indefinitely" (Alter 1981, 8).

preaching as literary analysis

Giving close attention to the literary skills of the narrator yields invaluable
material, making the story come alive to the modern reader and hearer. Alter
defines literary analysis as giving "minutely discriminating attention to the artful use of language, to the shifting play of ideas, conventions, tone, sound, imagery, syntax, narrative viewpoint, compositional units and much else" (Alter
1981, 12). In other words, the Bible is great literature, unsurpassed narrative to
which we should give at least as much attention as we would give any other
great piece of literature such as that of Dante, Tolstoy, Fitzgerald, or Steinbeck.

As we read through these stories, especially in the Old Testament, we are
repeatedly astonished at the perverseness and evil that often end in good. No
literature exercises better denouement—surprise ending—than does Scripture.
Genesis sets the pace. The ebb and flow of disgrace and redemption spirals at
a lung-sucking pace. Joseph, the son of promise, languishes in a prison hopelessly forgotten by anyone connected to anyone who could be of help. Even
the wine master, who had every vintage from the last 100 years memorized,
ungratefully blocked out the one person who gave him hope as a prisoner. The
scene of Joseph sitting alone in the dark of a cell trying to figure out what
went wrong or what he did wrong is the perfect literary device, what the
British writer Joyce Carey refers to as the "sketch of a central episode working
back to a beginning and outworking an ending" (Buttrick 1987, 15).

The ending reveals that God was behind much of the treachery, not causing it, but seeing that it ultimately turned out for good. Joseph's betrayal by
his brothers translates into their own salvation. The greedy Ishmaelite traders
marched Joseph smack dab into the center of world events. The oblique analogy, not so oblique, is to the betrayal of Christ at Passover, the most central
Jewish festival, something that the Jewish leaders swore not to do lest the
deed attract far more attention than they desired. In the biblical narratives,
God is constantly correcting marginalization, snatching us from the oblivion
of insignificance or annihilation.

Hope creates the narrative line for Scripture, a hope that is always embodied in persons inflamed by passion, a hope almost snuffed out by greed
and stupidity. But if we communicate with the text long enough, the mysteri-

ous God may reveal His motives. God does not allow Abraham to kill Isaac, the incarnation of hope. He does order Abraham to sacrifice misplaced hope; the thing or person that we think we cannot do without must be traded for the God that we really cannot do without. David Buttrick reads the story as liberation. Abraham is "wrapped up" in Isaac "holding on for dear life," rather than living in the constant everyday grace that "God will provide" (Buttrick 1987, 357-68).

arrangement of the story

Arranging narrative is more intuitive than conventional, what Buttrick refers to as a "logic of consciousness," which we know when we see it. We possess even more certitude when we don't see narrative progression. Daniel Defoe's *Robinson Crusoe* stated, "Being the third son of the family and not bred to any trade, my head began to be filled very early with rambling thoughts" (Defoe 2003, 5). Most of us would desire preachers to possess such self-awareness. Sermons cannot afford to have rambling thoughts. They do not offer the same opportunity for meandering as do novels. They more resemble short stories. Although the reader does not immediately perceive the reason for an anecdote, a side trip into another time and place, inclusion needs to be readily apparent in retrospect. The reason an element is in a sermon may not be readily apparent to the listener, but somewhere there should be an "Aha, I see why she included that."

Narrative sequencing discovers its direction through causal, substantive, or chronological connectedness. Often an event or a scene employs all three. For instance, the sentence "We desperately searched for the lost engagement ring, wondering if the waves would deliver it to us or wash it beyond our frantic efforts" doesn't make sense unless there is a prior discovery that the ring has been lost. Narrative profluence exercises patience, attempting to avoid what Lajos Egri calls jumping, the impetuosity that negates a steady rate. "No honest man will become a thief overnight; no thief will become honest in the same period of time" (Egri 2004, 153-69). Even for those of us who believe in miraculous transformation by the grace of God, the events of prevenient grace precede momentous changes. As the sermon progresses, the importance of what is shared becomes more strategic.

The experienced preacher bewares of starting a sermon with his or her best stuff, most dynamic story, because it diminishes everything else by comparison. Sermon fatigue is worth fighting. Not that the sermon must end in a grand revelation, a surprise ending, a knock-your-socks-off, mind-bending revelation. Rebecca McClanahan reminds us, "Mystery extends beyond revelation of uncertain outcomes. It also involves *how* a story is told—how description is created and controlled, how characters are developed, and how the plot unfolds" (McClanahan 1999, 194).

Eugene Lowry offers help to those of us uneasy with the simple assumption that storytelling carries its own inner logic. Classical narrative sequence for Lowry means that the sermon consists of opening conflict, escalation, reversal, and proleptic closure (an ending that has been anticipated by an earlier clue). No text better fits the pattern than the story of the prodigal son (see John 15:11-32). The youngest son's situation steadily grows worse. Reversal takes place when he decides to throw himself on his father's mercy. The key to the ending is that his father saw him "a long way off" (v. 20). However, the narrative of the elder son thwarts convenient adaption to the model. The story ends with a stalemate. The narrative does not tell us that the older brother came into the house and joined the party, but the text does not tell us that the father came in either. The father's invitation to the elder son is still good.

Lowry illustrates four ways that the preacher can unfold the story. "Running the story" follows the sequencing of events in the same order as the text. "Delaying the story" opens with a parallel story, the door of analogy, a contemporary prologue that provides entrance into the text. For the text Mark 6:30-34, which recounts Jesus' command to His disciples to feed the thousands, Leander Keck opens with a contemporary analogue before reading the text. "I am concerned now with that gnawing, demoralizing sense of inadequacy which often seeps into the seminary community . . . indeed, the curriculum appears to be designed to rob a student of confidence . . . all the critical analysis has gotten to us—a pretty good sign that the faculty is doing its job" (Lowry 1989, 80-81). Keck's analogy places seminary students in the disciples' predicament; both of them inadequate.

For the third model "suspending the story," Lowry chooses one of the most bewildering narratives in Scripture, the vineyard owner who paid all of his laborers the same, no matter how long they had worked (see Matt. 20). After working through the injustices of the text, Lowry zooms ahead 2,000 years to a school board that pays women and blacks less than they pay white males. "This story is the same kind of issue, just in different form. I say this is a good cause for the National Labor Relations Board, don't you think? In fact, I am shocked." Lowry then returns to the text to find the answer to this injustice.

Fred Craddock models the last narrative strategy, "alternating the story," with a sermon titled "Praying Through Clenched Teeth." "Alternating" features the recurring movement of the sermon from inside to outside the story. Woven in and out of the text, a text that conveys reasons why Paul was originally bitter toward Christianity, are contemporary scenarios that suggest bitterness. The sermon closes with a family adopting a stray cat, a cat inclined to hiss and scratch but is transformed by the family's loving care. "Not too long ago God reached out his hand to bless me and my family. When He did, I looked at His hand, it was covered with scratches. Such is the hand of love, extended to those who are bitter" (Lowry 1989, 148).

development of dialogue

Ninety percent of a script in a play or movie is given to dialogue. Biblical narratives differ in the amount of dialogue they record; some are sparse, others are replete. Lengthy dialogues take place between God and Abraham concerning the future of Sodom (Gen. 18:16-33); Jacob and Laban (30:25-34); Joseph and his brothers (25:1-14). Other times we can only imagine the conversation that took place, say between Rebecca and Isaac as they positioned their sons for success, all the while professing to openly and honestly love one another. Was it something like "You always take his side," or "I notice you spend a lot more time with Esau than Jacob," or "Why are you always protecting him?" or "It won't hurt that boy to do a good day's work." There must have been a lot of conversation in the home to promote competition, even jealousy, all of those domestic crosscurrents that wire us for success or failure, psychological security or neurosis. The taunts that are meant to be funny, said in jest, actually detonate as hand grenades. Did Isaac say, when the twins were 10 years old, "I'm getting Esau a new bow for his birthday. What are you getting Jacob, some cake pans?"

The preacher makes decisions as to whether he or she is going to bring the conversation into the 21st century or leave it in its historical context. One can imagine Tamar saying to her father-in-law when Jacob asked him how much he owed her for her sexual favors, "Well I'm not set up for MasterCard, why don't you pay me with a goat?" Judah said, "Well, I don't happen to have a goat in my wallet, allow me to leave the family seal for collateral until I return." If one is trying to cover his or her tracks, one probably would not want to leave a family album or birth certificate. Sort of like the guy who robbed a church; since the priest didn't have any money, he took a check. In his book *Preaching: The Art of Narrative Exposition,* Calvin Miller chooses for a model text the request by Balak for Balaam to curse Israel (see Num. 22–24). The following provides an excellent example of imaginative reading between biblical lines:

> Balaam smiled. He was good at divining things. He could split a frog gigged from the Red Sea at midnight, and from the splay of entrails tell who would rule Egypt for the next one hundred years. He could predict things too. He foretold the collapse of a tower in the Delta of the Nile, and predicted the droughts that plagued the Negev, merely by burning the feathers of a raven which died in the Wadi of Death. He was the wizard of wizards, and the king would pay him major shekels to whomp up a curse and spew it out over the advancing hordes of Moses (Miller 2006, 156).

The above "fictional overtones" may leave some of my readers feeling uneasy. History, like all other writing, demands rhetorical style. Gratefully, even historians such as David McCullogh, Steven Ambrose, and Doris Kearns Goodwin have demonstrated how plausible reconstruction makes history come alive for those of us who find facts, figures, and events becoming a monotonous blur. Interesting recalling of events demands interpretation, and interpretation demands imagination. Reading between the lines suggests what could have taken place, allowing the story to be heard anew. Thomas Troeger states, "By imagining that there is more to a biblical story, we practice an ancient way of interpreting the gospel to people living in different times and places" (Troeger 1996, 22). Then he goes on to imagine what the married couple in Cana did with almost 150 gallons of wine left over from their wedding.

Narrative with characters demands emotions and attitudes between the characters. Doubt, fear, blame, and the whole range of relational attitudes are best revealed not through declarative attribution but through imaginative conversation. In his sermon "Malchus's Ear," Dennis Kinlaw accents the importance of Peter cutting off the ear of the high priest's servant in the passion narrative. The subsequent healing of the ear by Christ and Malchus's return to his boss's home must have resulted in the following dialogue:

Caiphas: Malchus, how did it go?

Malchus: Well, it went very interesting, sir.

Caiphas: Well, did you have any problem?

Malchus: Well, not too much, a little.

Caiphas: What kind of problem did you have? Did you get him?

Malchus: Oh, yeah, we got him all right.

Caiphas: What kind of problem did you have?

Malchus: You see this ear.

Caiphas: Of course I see your ear, I see it every day. What about your ear?

Malchus: You know that guy that we arrested. He had a servant that had a sword. As we started to lay hands on him (Jesus) that servant pulled his sword, and swung and clipped it right off.

Caiphas: What do you mean he clipped it right off? Looks like it's hooked on all right now, you're standing there pulling on it.

Malchus: That's right, it is hooked on all right now. But you see that's the thing that concerns me. When he clipped it, it fell right down there on the ground. And the guy we arrested, reached down, picked it up and put it back and it's perfectly all right. And my buddy says it looks all right.

Caiphas: Are you kidding me?

Malchus: On your honor, sir. You can ask the other fellows. (After a pause.) Do you really think we got the right guy?

Kinlaw goes on to interpret the interchange as Christ's last love note to Caiphas. "I'll send him one last note to let him know who I am and who it is he is rejecting." Every time that the boss and the servant intersected, which must have been several times a day, all Caiphas could see was that ear. In every individual there is a Malchus's ear, a reminder of what God is trying to say. When we share the gospel with someone, a witness of grace, a token of God's love is often already present (From a tape, "Malchus's Ear," used by permission).

development of character emotions

Filling in the blanks can be creatively done by asking the questions: What emotions could have been felt? What could have happened? What could have been said? What bodily positions could have been assumed? What was he or she really thinking? What were his or her motives? No characterization can take place without attempting to get into the skin of the persons who are interacting with one another. A key way to get on the inside of a story is for me to read my own emotions or try to imagine what my emotions would have been like in that situation. What did it feel like when the chair fell out from under me in a crowded auditorium? What levels of anxiety do I experience when I am waiting for a biopsy report. Ann Hood writes in her helpful book *Creating Character Emotions,* "A hefty part of writing is being able to explore our own inner lives, to tap into our own emotions and histories, to revisit things that perhaps are unpleasant, like my days as the ninth-grade weirdo" (Hood 1998, 10).

Characterization succeeds to the extent that the artist/preacher infects the viewer/listener with the feelings of the character. Preaching constantly attempts to limit the emotional distance between the characters portrayed and the audience. It is for this reason that *All Quiet on the Western Front* succeeds on an affective level and why most Hollywood war movies fail. *All Quiet on the Western Front* focuses on one German student who joins the German army in World War I. The scene that best depicts the ambiguities, horrors, contradictions, and bewilderment of war isn't of two faceless armies slaughtering each other in some momentous battle, but of our protagonist suddenly finding himself in the same foxhole as a French infantryman. The German soldier immediately stabs the intruder, but that does not end the relationship between the two men. For 10 minutes the camera zooms in on the German as he watches a fellow human being die. The man whom he has just killed has far more in common with him than what separates them. The most poignant moment is when the German empties the contents of the French soldier's wallet to find a picture of his family. This nameless soldier takes on a history of love, care, hard work, and decency—all reasons for extending a life rather than snuffing it out.

The above scenes of distraughtness and psychological agony repeat themselves throughout Scripture: David grieving over Absalom, God's instruction for Hosea to marry a prostitute, Jesus' command to "the rich young ruler" to go and sell all that he owned. Or the rich farmer whose life was snuffed out simply because he built extra barns. All of these people had a history. For the farmer who expanded his business, I would paint him as a faithful husband, good dad, coach of a Little League baseball team, hard-working Rotarian, and his golf game wasn't bad either. If I picture him any other way, that is, begin with showing what was wrong with him, I will set him up in a we/him dichotomy between my listeners and the text. Instead, I intend to raise the question, "Well, what's wrong with this man? Sounds as if he has some good old American upper middle-class values. It seems so unjust for God to strike him with a heart attack on the day after the local feed co-op honored him for being a model farmer and serving as its president for the last 20 years. The man had only one slight problem: "I" was at the center of his life rather than God. He used the personal pronouns "I" and "my" 10 times within the space of three verses (Luke 12:17-19).

What were the memories that came flooding into David's mind when he heard of Absalom's death? The best-looking son he had. The most athletic kid in the high school. Full ride football scholarship to Notre Dame. All the times they had spent together. Did he get out the scrapbook and look at the newspaper clippings? Absalom knew that he was special; David treated him as special. It was difficult not to brag at the barber shop when you have a kid that good. "Did I mention Absalom?" "A can't miss first-round draft choice," they said. "In all Israel was no one as handsome as Absalom, so highly praised; from the sole of his foot to the crown of his head, there was no defect in him" (2 Sam. 14:25, NASB).

psychic time

The above frame of reference in a movie or play was what Arthur Miller called psychic time. Miller scholar Christopher Bigsby writes that for Willy Loman, the central character in *Death of a Salesman,* there were "Memories which crash into his present, creating ironies, sounding echoes, tormenting him with a past, which can offer him nothing but reproach" (Miller 1998, xi). The Bible majors in these archetypical moments, when a person's life or a nation's history has collapsed into a single act, recognition, or choice. These parenthetical observations abound throughout Scripture, such as the psalmist's summation of the Israelites badgering of God in the wilderness: "So he gave them what they asked for, but sent a wasting disease upon them" (Ps. 106:15).

How often does the preacher superficially dismiss the message of Pilate's wife to her husband: "Don't have anything to do with that innocent man, for I have suffered a great deal today in a dream because of him" (Matt. 27:19)? What was in her dream? What would the guilt and shame of executing the most righteous man that ever lived look like in a dream? Would it be the horror that Truman Capote captures in a blatant killing, the senseless spilling of innocent blood? Would it be something worse than the terror created in a Stephen King novel? Dreams do not consist of the world of logic, cool rational constructs of cause and effect. They rather shock, traumatize, dismantle, unnerve, and make immediate both our past and present in choking dosages. Mrs. Pilate may have felt as if she had been sucked into a black hole of hopeless doom with all the demons of hell grabbing at her ankles. She held on to the bed post while pleading with her husband. Like most husbands, he should have listened more carefully.

the mystique of contradiction

No interesting narrative is void of interesting characters. Intriguing characters incarnate contradictions, idiosyncrasies, inconsistencies, and besetting
sins in which we are far more interested than we ought to be. Arthur Miller
referred to Willy Loman as a "bleeding mass of contradictions." Willy's
speech constantly betrays him: "Oh, I'll knock 'em dead next week. I'll go to
Hartfield. I'm very well liked in Hartfield. You know, the trouble is, Linda,
people don't seem to take to me" (Miller 1998, 23).

Massive contradictions plague biblical characters. Not long after Noah so
faithfully captained the ship, we discover him as a drunken sailor, wasted out
of his mind. Abraham, who could defeat four kings at once with an army
made up of his immediate family, protected his own skin by betraying his
wife. When confronted by King Abimelech, who had confiscated Sara, Abraham responded, "There is surely no fear of God in this place, and they will
kill me because of my wife" (Gen. 20:11).

All great people bear within the depth of their souls what Carl Jung called
"antinomies of opposites." Often these antinomies are blind spots camouflaged by defense mechanisms, or outright pathologies. Paul Johnson capital-
ized on the glaring inconsistencies of famous people in his book *Intellectuals*.
Bertrand Russell destroyed his family or families because of selfish and my-
opic choices, while preaching love and goodwill and participating in benevo-
lent causes. Jean-Paul Sartre declared, "Man will be judged not by his words
but by his deeds," but did nothing to aid the Jewish resistance in his native
France. His existentialism, which he claimed could not be explained but only
lived, must not have afforded him much security. One biographer estimated
that his daily intake of stimulants included "two packets of cigarettes, several
pipes of black tobacco, a quart of alcohol (chiefly wine, vodka, whiskey and
beer), 200 milligrams of amphetamines, fifteen grams of aspirin, several
grams of barbiturates, plus coffee and tea" (Johnson 1990, 240). Tolstoy attempted to love humankind, especially the peasants, while at the same time
neglecting his family. Johnson indicted Tolstoy's "disastrous case of self de-
ception" by saying, "It is remarkable that Tolstoy who thought about himself
as much as any man who ever lived—including even Rousseau—who wrote
about himself copiously, and much of whose fiction revolves around himself
in one way or another, should have been so conspicuously lacking in self-
knowledge" (Johnson 1990, 114).

These self-deceptions are displayed in an abundant variety by biblical characters. They accent the need for God's grace, grace that reveals and heals if we acknowledge and confess the contradictions that plague all of us. David, the man after God's own heart, scoffed at his need for Saul's armor, which included a sword, a sword so large that David couldn't even walk with it. Remember that Saul was tall. When David belted on the sword, the sheath must have drug the ground. The confidence of this unarmed, scrawny kid echoed throughout the valley of Elam. "I will give the carcasses of the Philistine army to the birds of the air and the beasts of the earth, and the whole world will know that there is a God in Israel" (1 Sam. 17:46).

After David killed Goliath, Scripture simply notes there was no "sword in his hand" (v. 50). But if one follows David's life carefully and honestly, we discover that David becomes addicted to the sword. David's confidence inexorably drifted into snow banks of insecurities, exemplified by his need to shore himself up by men who could wield a sword. David ordered his military commander Joab to conduct a census with one purpose, discovering how many men in his kingdom owned a sword. This distrust in God's ability to protect his people translated into dire consequences. God slew 70,000 people.

These inconsistencies within God's servants are not limited to the Old Testament. Peter is the New Testament exemplar of character flaw. No one better combines boasting with failing, climaxed by his blasphemous denial that he ever knew Christ. And not all of these hypocrisies are solved by post-Resurrection and Pentecost experiences. Paul exposed Peter's pretensions to inclusiveness (after all, he was the first missionary to the Gentiles) by censoring him for his aloofness to the Gentiles while in the presence of Judaizers. But what about Paul himself who wrote so eloquently that love "is not provoked, does not take into account a wrong suffered" (1 Cor. 13:5), and yet he was so unforgiving of John Mark? To Paul's credit, he later reversed his opinion (see Col. 4:10 and 2 Tim. 4:11).

An argument for the authenticity of Scripture is that it does not, for the most part, gloss over tarnished heroes. Complications and inconsistencies riddle authentic characters, unless they're going to manifest what Nancy Kress calls the "depth of wallpaper" (Kress 1998, 2). Few people are one-dimensional; everyone is interesting if we get to know them. But even more importantly, if we camouflage the flaws of biblical characters, we will, first of all, make them different from the rest of us, who are plagued by inconsistencies, and second, we will minimize the necessity of God's grace that seeks to reconcile the conflicting antagonisms that reside deep within the human consciousness. Paul confessed, "For the good that I want, I do not do, but I

practice the very evil that I do not want" (Rom. 7:19, NASB), but later testified, "There is now no condemnation for those who are in Christ Jesus. . . .
who do not walk according to the flesh but according to the Spirit" (8:1, 4,
NASB). One of the goals of preaching is to unmask "Christian Pollyanna" and
to translate her into a boldface oxymoron. Though biblical grace is opti-
mistic, it does not hide behind the pretensions of a blind naïveté.

character description

Enabling congregations to know our sermon characters demands detailed
and graphic description. We learn by noting how others go about characterization—both fiction and nonfiction. C. S. Lewis described his friend Charles
Williams: "He was nervous (not shy) to judge by the trembling of his fingers.
One of the most characteristic things about him was his walk. There was
something of recklessness, something even *panache* in his gait" (Lewis 1966,
iv). Perhaps Truman Capote's real gift was not in his detailed characterization of the killers Perry Smith and Richard Hickock but in bringing to life the
Clutter family, boring farmers living in a boring small community in the boring wheat fields of Kansas. Capote described Herbert Clutter: "Though he
wore rimless glasses, and was of but average height, standing just under
5'10", Mr. Clutter cut a man's-man figure. His shoulders were broad; his hair
had held its dark color, his square jawed, confident face retained a healthy-
hued youthfulness, and his teeth, unstained and strong enough to shatter
walnuts, were still intact" (Capote 1994, 6).

All fiction writers thrive on the idiosyncrasies, the strangeness of their
characters. Only as the individuality of others is highlighted, do we come to
discover that we are not alone in our own strangeness. No psychiatrist has
ever more keenly analyzed a patient than did F. Scott Fitzgerald when he described Jay Gatsby: "An instinct towards his future glory had led him some
months before to the small Lutheran College of St. Olaf in southern Min-
nesota. He stayed there two weeks dismayed at its ferocious indifference to
the drums of his destiny, to destiny itself, and despising the janitor's work,
with which he was to pay his way through" (Fitzgerald 2004, 105). Which
one of us has not thought we were too good for an assignment, an assigned
job that was "surely beneath our talents"?

Rob Staples in his sermon "Holy Ground Once More"* argued that

---

*Message delivered at the Nazarene Theological Seminary, Kansas City, September
11, 1992.

Moses became a man the day he righted an injustice by slaying the Egyptian slave driver. Before this event Moses "had it made, driving his own souped up four-horse chariot with a sign on the back 'Egypt, Love it, or Leave it.'" He exchanged lounging by the pool sipping lemonade for tending sheep that belonged to his father-in-law on the backside of an arid, hot desert. He could have been elsewhere had he exploited his Egyptian connections and played his cards right. "But on a common ordinary day, in a common ordinary place, with a common ordinary bush, God broke the back of mighty Egypt with a shepherd's staff and a stammerer's tongue."

narrative as desperation

Acclaimed writers of fiction tap into the emotions and attitudes that universalize our collective unconscious. Narrative preaching with trenchant appeal necessitates getting on the inside of people. Riveting fiction does multiple radial imaging of the psychological quirks and motives that either spur us to action or paralyze us. In *The Treasure of the Sierra Madre*, B. Traven transmutes the greed of the antagonist Daubs into a fear of neurotic proportions:

> As he stood quietly for a moment, he thought he felt somebody behind him. So close he felt the sensation of breath on his neck. He imagined he felt the point of a knife on his back. He sprang forward, drew his gun, and turning, aimed at nothing. No one was threatening him. He saw nothing, but the dark shadows of the burros, grazing peacefully near the camp. Daubs looked at them and thought for a second, "How happy animals are because they cannot think as human beings can" (Traven 1963, 261).

Daubs is a metaphor for greed and disillusionment, his own worst enemy. Daub's self-consumption is contrasted to Howard, who turned his back on the treasure of the Sierra Madre to be a respected medicine man in a small Indian village. The loss of the gold was for Daubs a curse, but for Howard, redemption. The Traven tale is parabolic, even as were the stories of Jesus. When Howard discovered that the gold dust, which he, Daubs, and Curtin had labored for 10 months to collect, had been mistakenly poured out by the Indians, he let out "such a roar of Homeric laughter that his companion thought him crazy" (Traven 1963, 305). As any good novelist, Traven has his character grasp for theology: "Anyway, I think it's a very good joke—a good one played on us and on the bandits by the Lord or by fate, or by nature, whichever you prefer" (Traven 1963, 305). Thus, Traven has accomplished what both the novelist and preacher attempt according to Sallie McFague, "participation, empathy, identification." If the listener or reader learns what the parable has to teach him or her, "it is more like a shock to the nervous system than it is like a piece of information to be stored in the head" (McFague 2005, 122).

What Daubs and Gatsby both have in common is desperation. As Lajos Egri states, "A good pivotal character must have something very vital at stake" (Egri 2004, 111). An all-consuming passion pulls a reader or listener into the death struggle, alarms the senses, strains the muscles, and stomps on mundane trivialities. We experience whatever emotions that the character is processing. Good preaching evokes an experience rather than creates a philosophical argument. John Gardner writes that "the great novelists such as Tolstoy and Dostoevsky have a gift for rendering the precise observations and feelings of a wide variety of characters, even entering the minds (in Tolstoy's case) of animals" (Gardner 1999, 30).

The Gospel writer Mark creates the desperation of a woman who had uncontrollably bled for 12 years with a precise diagnostic history: "She had suffered a great deal under the care of many doctors and had spent all she had, yet instead of getting better she grew worse" (Mark 5:26). Not only was this woman diseased, but also she was shamed by her disease. It's one thing to have an illness; it's another to have an unmentionable illness, at least unmentionable in polite society. Her illness was not beyond the firing range of gossip and stares. She could feel piercing eyes as she walked by the chariot garage, and the whispers at Sarah's Super Salon were never muffled enough for her not to hear.

How emaciated was this lady? What was her hemoglobin count? How difficult was it for her to get out of bed. What would she do? Perhaps just lie in bed and allow herself to go into a coma. That would be a good way to end her miserable life, or would it? She had no family or friends, at least that we know of. She concocted a plan. She would steal a miracle. If she couldn't buy one from a physician, she would steal one. Her insurance having been cancelled, her bank account empty, her credit at "Abraham's Pretty Good Grocery" (to borrow a Garrison Keiller institution) having been denied, she had one last resort, to steal a miracle.

An entourage of disciples surrounded Jesus. The crowd that followed showed little respect for life, knocking the less stalwart out of the way. A reputation for raising people from the dead almost always gets up a crowd. How was this 78-pound embodiment of emaciation going to push and shove her way through the hundreds of others just as desperate as she was? How many times did she almost touch him? How many times was she knocked out of the way or thrown to the ground? No thief has ever been more reckless and daring as this skeleton of a woman, who repeatedly lunged at a man at whom she had never gotten a clear look, much less ever met.

And then to make matters worse, Jesus embarrassed her. "Who touched me?" Didn't Jesus know that civil propriety would allow this woman to save face? But no, Jesus isn't going to take one step further until the lady fesses up. Should she shrink into the crowd or cry out "It was me. I did it?" What a moment of agony. Maybe Jesus would reverse the healing if she made herself known. Maybe He would take back what she had stolen.

What a disgrace to be stealing from God himself. When she thought she couldn't sink any lower in the eyes of her neighbors, now she would sink even lower than that. She could see the headlines in the *Capernaum Gazette,* "Untouchable Steals from God." The apartheid newspaper would tell how this nobody got in the way of Jesus who was on His way to heal the daughter of a somebody. And what about Jairus, the synagogue official, certainly a type A personality, who is doing his best to see that Jesus keeps moving in the right direction? Jairus, the somebody, and this unnamed lady, a nobody, separated by social taboo, were on a collision course that day, a meeting brought about by one universal trait—desperation.

The impropriety of Jesus finds its resolution in His addressing this woman as "daughter," the only recorded incident in the New Testament of Christ's calling anyone "daughter." The key to the text is that the healing in all three Synoptic Gospels always takes place on the way to Jairus's house for the purpose of healing Jairus's daughter. On that day Jesus made a loud and clear statement: "Nobody is a nobody in the Kingdom of God." This daughter of God was just as important as a daughter of an important official. Jesus could have just spoken a word and Jairus's daughter would have been healed without taking the across-town trip. The main purpose for marching down Main Street was to intersect the woman who had far too little strength to touch God, had God not been longing to touch her. And of course, no one can ever steal a miracle, because miracles are absolutely free.

visual circumstances

Attention-getting narrative does not deal with people as abstractions but as persons in concrete circumstances with distinguishing characteristics: flabby arms, scoured faces, ample waist lines and hips so large they could hold up a tractor tire. Words such as "depressed," "happy," "disappointed," and "encouraged" beg for content and lose the battle of recognition if they are not incarnated in individuals. Stephen King writes, "If on the other hand, I can show you a silent, dirty haired woman who compulsively gobbles cake and candy, then have you draw the conclusion that Annie is in the depressive part of a manic depressive cycle, I win" (King 2000, 190). Dorothy Sayers described one of her characters as a "very much made-up lady with a face set in lines of habitual peevishness" (Sayers 2002, 383).

The preacher boldly imagines gossip, speculation, innuendo, and the flaws that represent the uniqueness of a person. If the preacher is uneasy about describing details that may or not be true, the statement can always carry the caveat of "imagine" or "perhaps" or "maybe." "Perhaps" David was sitting in his hearth room, the embers dying in the fireplace, the sword that killed Goliath in a trophy case over the mantle, shadows flickering on the 14-foot-high gray stone walls. His eyes, which at one time had drawn a bead on the forehead of Goliath, could barely distinguish the shadows on the walls from the servants that came and went at his beckoning.

The ebbing heat of the hearth reminded David of his own life, which was about to be extinguished. Had he secured his legacy? "Maybe" the armies of the Philistines were at that very moment gathering outside the palace, ready to storm it, seize him, and mock him by putting his eyes out. David longed for the day when he was virile, when he slew his 10,000, when his exploits were the talk of every barber shop and blacksmith's forge. Instead of the courage that once ran through a troop and leaped over a wall, David's bravado retreated before the serpent of fear. It caused him to doubt the very existence of God. "Maybe" even before he ordered Joab to conduct a census, he commanded a servant girl to check the lock on the front door.

Concrete details rather than vague abstractions deliver characters to listeners. Words such as "beautiful," "special," "great," and "wonderful" make benign impressions, thus, should be excised from speech. The question must be asked, what will make this person memorable, whether she be an actual person, or a fictional construct. Robert Heilbroner described Adam Smith, author of the *Wealth of Nations,* and the father of capitalism as a man with a

> protruding lower lip thrust up to meet a large aquiline nose, heavy bulging eyes looking out from heavy lids. All his life Smith was troubled with a nervous affliction, his head shook and he had an odd and stumbling manner of speech. He was attired in a light colored coat, knee britches, white silk stockings, buckle shoes, flat broad-brimmed beaver

hat, and cane, walking down the cobbled streets with his eyes fixed on infinity and his lips moving in silent discourse. Every pace or two he would hesitate as if to change his direction or even reverse it. His gait was described by a friend as "vermicular" (Heilbroner 1999, 45).

No one exceeded Thomas Wolfe in finding the exact word to describe a person's idiosyncrasies. Most of the characters created in *Look Homeward, Angel* are thinly disguised persons that he actually knew in Asheville, North Carolina. It is unlikely that any of us can detail biblical characters without watching people with fascination. Fascination with people creates fascinating persons. Wolfe described the brother of Eugene, the main character in *Look Homeward, Angel,* as "cheaply and flashily dressed with peg-top yellow shoes, flaring striped trousers, and a broad brimmed straw hat with a colored band, he would walk down the avenue with a preposterous lurch and a smile of strained assurance on his face, saluting with servile cordiality, all who would notice him" (Wolfe 2004, 37).

Rarely, if ever, do we find the above kind of graphic caricature in the Scriptures. However, the writer or storyteller often gives details that are too quickly passed over by the preacher. In the story of the rich man and Lazarus, Luke 16, one finds two characters for whom Jesus supplies much detail, almost to the point of exaggeration, or extreme type. "Now there was a rich man, and he habitually dressed in purple and fine linen, joyously living in splendor everyday" (v. 19, NASB). The purple and fine linen allude to the outer and inner garments of the priests in the Old Testament. One has to be particularly vain to wear not only expensive, designer clothes, but high priced underwear as well. The King James Version translates "the joyously living in splendor" as "faring sumptuously" and *The Message* as "wasting his days in conspicuous consumption." Since the man never exercised and ate a smorgasbord several times a day, I wonder how big he got. I'm confident that he spoke with an aristocratic accent, aspiring to emulate a Roman senator, though that position was as unlikely as me playing in the NBA. The greater the pipe dream the greater the pretension. And thus, he strutted rather than walked, with his chin tilted at a 45-degree angle, never making eye contact with those he felt to be inferior to him, which was just about everybody.

In describing Lazarus, Jesus means to repulse us. Lazarus is nothing less than grotesque, covered with sores, dressed in rags, smelling like the dogs that licked his sores. Homeless people have a real problem with hygiene. Did he stake out squatters rights, much as the Joads in John Steinbeck's *Grapes of Wrath,* going from camp to camp? Or was he delivered to the rich man's gate by a friend for eight-hour shifts seven days a week? Whichever, from my perception, Lazarus wasn't very bright. Though he was perpetually hungry, this pale, skinny vagrant, who begged garbage, as far as we know, never received a crumb. Did the thought ever occur to him that he should be panhandling for at least a few days, perhaps down at 5th and Main?

The rich man and Lazarus are exaggerated archetypes created for the purpose of contrast, lest anyone would miss the point. In this life the rich man had everything and Lazarus had nothing. Thus we are at liberty to treat them as composites, imaginative types with which we can play like a child with Legos. Authors such as Wolfe, Steinbeck, and Fitzgerald majored in these kinds of archetypes lest their point be lost. Robert DeMott, a Steinbeck scholar, writes, "Steinbeck summoned all the concrete details of human form, language, and landscape that ensure artistic verisimilitude, as well as the subtler imaginative nuances of dialect, idiosyncratic ticks, habits, and gestures that animate fictional characterization" (Steinbeck 1992, xxxii). To do this, Steinbeck was a keen observer of life, spending time in the migrant camps and canneries where his stories take place. Preaching that does not capture the details which occupy the ordinary person will fail to connect. For this reason Fred Craddock suggests that imaginative preaching begins not with expression but impression, "a sensitivity to the sights, sounds, and flavors of life about him, that is not easily maintained by the minister, or by anyone else" (Craddock 1981, 80).

action as keys to character

The Scripture narrators are far more interested in action than they are the details, which would enable us to imagine what a person looked like. When the Bible does give us a clue to appearances, it's almost always critical to the unfolding of the story: the height of Saul, the ruddy good looks of David, the long hair of Samson, and the hairy body of Esau. Remember, Rebecca had to be highly creative in deceiving her husband. The Scriptures waste no words in describing physical appearances. If a biblical writer reported that a person sat on a park bench feeding squirrels, the observation would be essential to the story, not simply reported for scenic effect.

Robert Alter refers to the above action essentials as "bound motifs," characteristics critical to the unfolding of the story, as opposed to free-floating motifs, which are rarely ever found in the Bible. Details are dropped as clues, which the preacher will allow the listener to discover and in turn develop a plot, just as Agatha Christie or Sir Conan Doyle turned their readers into sleuths. We are often forced to draw our own conclusions. Alter writes, "We are compelled to get at character and motive, as in impressionist writers Conrad and Ford Madox Ford, through a process of inference from fragmentary data, often with crucial pieces of narrative exposition strategically withheld, and this leads to multiple or sometimes even waivering perspectives on the characters" (Alter 1981, 126).

Thus, the preacher will give high priority to discovering how action information provides the moral and spiritual direction for the story. King Asa's sending silver and gold to the King of Aram as treaty collateral portends Asa spending the last days of his life as a cripple. If Asa needed the crutch of a treaty with another nation, God would take such dependency to its ultimate and personal conclusion (see 1 Kings 15-16). In contrast to the above clues to disaster, biblical writers often report actions of positive contribution, such as Hannah's yearly trips to the Temple and Ruth's accompanying Naomi to her home country and her subsequent gleaning in the fields. The novelist Henry James asked, "What is incident but the illustration of character?" The translators for the King James Version certainly understood this observation when they recorded that Jesus "must needs go through Samaria" (John 4:4), a grammatical construct in the original language no different than the other "musts" in Jesus life. Since this is the only time we find "must needs," the translators of the Authorized Version believed this highly intentional action of Jesus to be terribly critical to the story. Hardly anything just happens in Scripture, in particular, the actions of Christ.

In Scripture, speech is often a clue to later action. Careful analysis of what is actually said renders essentials for sermon development. If one quickly scans what is said rather than giving minute examination, it will be all too easy to assume generic interpretations, what one has always heard about the text. When Adam defended his disobedience by saying, "The woman you put here with me—she gave me some fruit from the tree, and I ate it" (Gen. 3:12), he was not ultimately blaming the woman, but rather, he was blaming God. When David was accused by his wife of making a fool of himself, by cavorting or exposing himself among the young maidens (he was wearing a linen ephod), he responded by saying, "It was before the LORD, who chose me rather than your father or anyone from his house when he appointed me ruler over the LORD's people Israel" (2 Sam. 6:21). David's pompous statement of exclusion ends with the following historical data, about which we can only speculate. "And Michal daughter of Saul had no children to the day of her death" (v. 23).

the perspective of the reporter

Most often, a narrator will choose an omniscient perspective. An omniscient perspective knows all the details of the story, because the reporter is outside of the story. Variety in preaching can be provided by assuming a character either identified already in the biblical narrative or created by the preacher. The reasons for incarnating oneself in the story are sometimes more intuitive than rooted in an objective literary advantage. In the story of Jesus casting the demons from the demoniac in the country of the Gerasenes (see Luke 8:26-39), I choose to place myself within the story as someone not identified by the text. Because this story takes place in a coastal village and I was raised in a commercial fishing village, there is a comfortable fit for me as opposed to the story taking place on a sheep farm. I enjoy being present on the sunbathed placid morning when Jesus and the 12 disciples oar the boat into a small inlet allowing the bow to nudge the rocky beach.

I choose to interpret the story of the prodigal son by becoming the offended brother. Because he has such a good case and we often facilely dismiss his protest, I choose to place myself in his shoes. Since most of us do not have a *National Enquirer* story to tell, one for which we can sell television rights (as does the prodigal), we find ourselves identifying with the elder brother, if he is adequately re-created by the preacher. What kind of father, "God," is this who would allow his son to work 12 hours a day in a hot field, arms aching, shoulders stooped, drenched with sweat, hands callused, up and down, up and down, and up and down the field behind a plow, and never once taking him to McDonald's or expressing appreciation? Wouldn't it be nice if God would once in a while announce a Darius Salter day, complete with party favors and testimonials? It seems unconscionable that the elder brother discovered a party as he came in at sunset after a long day's work, rather than a servant fetching him from the field.

J. Kent Edwards recommends that preachers use a first-person perspective in a half dozen sermons per year. "Choose a character who has much to gain or lose and is emotionally involved, possesses character flaws, and whose life is headed for a dramatic climax or unexpected twist." Edwards suggests that first-person character stories be told through "the mono-mythic" method that uses the seasons of the year: summer—state of bliss; fall—destabilization and dissent into tension and discontent; winter—life has bottomed out; spring—the turn of grace toward renewal and life. Edwards chooses for his sample sermon the story of Samson, definitively drawing us, by way of first-person narrative, into the tragedy of a man who could not be captured by an army but could be defeated by the whims of a woman. In spite of his triumph at the end of his life, the strongest man whoever lived was left with a chilling confession: "What bothers me, however is that when people like you remember me, they think of me only as a strong man. Not a great man. And I could have been great. I should have been great." Obviously the Samson story provides plenty of opportunity for graphic details, psychological motivation, and haunting memories:

> I met the woman. Hah . . . she had black hair. She had olive skin. She had eyes that would just melt you. Boy, could she fill a dress. She captured your imagination. She enthralled you. Her beauty, her wit, her charm . . . everything about her was ideal . . . If you dreamt of the perfect woman, you would be dreaming of my Delilah. This was the perfect woman; she had everything a man could ever want. You couldn't imagine anything else. Except for one little thing . . . she was perfect except . . . she was a nag. She was easy on the eyes, but she was a nag (Edwards 2005, 152).

historical versus a contemporary setting

Encouraging genuine empathy with characters is a far more effective way to get listeners to apply the truth of the text to themselves than is employing side comments to make relevancy clear. Good application is never made; it is discovered by both speaker and hearer, with the confession, "Oh goodness, that's me." At times this relevancy can be intensified by bringing the story forward into a contemporary setting. One of my former preaching students, Chad Wilkes, in telling the story of the prodigal, transformed himself into a cook at the Father's business, "Frank's Truck Stop and Burger Barn," complete with chef's hat and apron. Such creative parody intensifies personal crisis, while at the same time providing comedic relief.

Insights into the above kind of parody can be gained by reading Neil Simon's *God's Favorite*. The laughs of the early part of the play slowly descend into the angst of confessing that most if not all of us practice a utilitarian relationship with God. After Sydney Lipton reads the list of Joe's coming attractions (ills): "A hernia, gastritis, a double impacted wisdom tooth, a root canal job, the heartbreak of psoriasis, constipation, diarrhea, piles, dysentery, chills, fever, athlete's foot, lumbago, a touch of gonorrhea and a general feeling of loginess. . . . All this, mind you, is on the left side of your body," Joe confesses, "I am an infinitesimal speck on the eyelash of the universe . . . but God sees me" (Simon 1971, 537-38).

In the '60s, Clarence Jordan chose to translate whole books of the New Testament into the idiom of the racist south. His translation caused the Scriptures to assume a prophetic immediacy: "And I'm telling you straight there were a lot of white widows in Georgia during the time of Elijah. And the skies were locked up for three years and six months. And there was a great drought everywhere, but Elijah didn't stay with any of them, instead he stayed with a Negro woman over in Terrell County. And there were a lot of sick white people during the time of the great preacher Elijah, but he didn't heal any of them, only Naaman the African" (Jordan 1969, 25). Throughout the *Cotton Patch Gospels* biblical towns are transported to a segregated south. The Pharisees become white corrupt politicians and fig trees become peach trees, all scripted with southern vernacular.

Some homileticians are squeamish about lacing ancient settings and narrations with contemporary idioms. It is my perception that both preacher and listener will be well served by indexing the narrative with what the biblical setting or character would look like in 2007, say, in Cleveland, Ohio. Thus, placing Matthew Levi in a cubicle behind a computer at the RIRS office (Roman Internal Revenue Service) or clothing Joseph with Tommy Hilfiger, if nothing else, will raise a smile. In all likelihood, contemporizing will shed light on the bewilderment of meandering in strange lands with alien customs. The golden arches of McDonald's that blot the freeways of Kansas City serve as reminders of sterile modernity, but may be a welcome reference point for seven-year-olds weary of riding camels in an arid country.

Preachers are translators for persons who have little ability to read between the lines or understand what a statement would sound like if uttered by a modern person rather than an ancient Middle Easterner. When Jesus' hearers, muttering their surprise that He could voice such profundity, said, "Isn't this Joseph's son?" I think they meant "Isn't this the kid who carried his dad's tool box?" or "Isn't this the kid who struck out with the bases loaded in the ninth inning of the state championship baseball game?" No wonder Jesus said, "No prophet is accepted in his hometown" (Luke 4:24).

managed segments of the sermon

Earlier, we discussed sequencing. Now the preacher makes critical decisions about the amount of the story that will be told and how the story will be broken up into manageable parts for both speaker and listener. David Buttrick refers to these manageable parts as "moves," three or four sentences that elaborate on a single idea. The move has lost its unity if it cannot be summarized in one clear sentence. Narrative moves for Thomas Boomershine become episodes: "An episode is a story unit of two to four sentences. The sentences and episodes are the foundational components of a biblical story's structure" (Boomershine 1988, 24). In the Lukan birth narrative, the episodes are keyed to (1) the explanation of the historical purpose of the trip to Bethlehem, (2) the birth of Christ, (3) the appearance of the angels to the shepherds and their response, (4) the message of the angels to the shepherds, (5) the trip by the shepherds to the manger, (6) the aftermath or response of both Mary and the shepherds to what had happened. Boomershine suggests that names be given to each of the episodes and they be memorized as themes or images. "My names for these episodes are the enrollment, the birth, the shepherds, the announcement, the confirmation, and the responses" (Boomershine 1988, 27).

The complexity of the task intensifies with longer portions of Scripture, where narrative takes side trips and themes have many meanings. The narrator disciplines himself or herself to choose a plot line that includes those elements critical to the story, those episodes that illuminate the idea being developed by the narrator. I suggest that the story be reframed in the teller's own words, using language and references suitable for a 21st-century congregation. A word or phrase represents an episode so that the preacher can stay on course with a quick glance at his or her notes.

My sermon preparation has changed over the years. Immediately after seminary, I wrote out a full manuscript and, as a final step the night before preaching, made a list of notes. In recent years, I have ceased to write a full manuscript. Instead, I begin early in the process audibly articulating the message, listening for rhythm, graphic imagery, vehicles that will carry the message, better or best words, and sentences concisely constructed. If I write out a manuscript early in the process, I freeze the message rather than allow it to accrete or evolve over several days. Hopefully, I allow the sermon to be a living, dynamic organism throughout the complete process of both preparation and delivery. As organic evolution, the sermon is a life-form maintaining a growing, creative edge until the last amen. Also, if I write a manuscript, I am left with the task of transforming it from written prose to spoken vernacular. I prefer to apply the dynamic of oral communication throughout the process, leaving the message open-ended as long as possible. Knowing 99 percent of what I am going to say when I stand in the pulpit, I will sometimes add a word, renuance a thought, and/or reframe a sentence that will transform what I planned to say, so that it will be more adequate for the present moment.

One never memorizes a 25- to 30-minute message. The preacher commits to memory 10 to 12 moves or episodes of 2- to 3-minute duration each. Though some of the exact phrasing may be mentally locked in, I prefer to not think of committing to memory as rote memorization. Rather, I have audibly rehearsed it, each time increasing the comfort level in telling it. The message absorbs me, because I am increasingly gripped by its necessity for me and the congregation, whom I had in mind throughout the process of preparation. As the text increasingly grips me, I am aware that it has something to say to others, who live at the same address as I do, on the avenue called Humanity. Not until I have placed myself under the text for both its judgment and hope am I ready to deliver the message to the community of the gospel.

To illustrate this process, I choose the life of Elisha. One cannot talk about Elisha without including his mentor, Elijah. This tale of the two prophets is filled with weirdness, irony, paradox, miraculous power, humorous juxtapositions, psychological complexities, political intrigue, and conflicts between good and evil. The wild ride finds its destiny in the grace of God, grace that is operative in a scrawny, bald-headed farm kid who aspired to be twice as great as the most powerful prophet in the history of Israel. I choose as my text 2 Kings 13:14-21, the story of Elisha's last encounter with Joash, King of Israel, and the casting of a corpse on the grave of Elisha that subsequently "came to life and stood up on his feet."

Episode One—1 Kings 17

The relationship of Elisha and Elijah in a historical setting and the historical setting in which they lived. Key sentences: Elijah was not the kind of person who would have been invited to the mayor's ball. He would not have been invited to be grand marshal in the Rose Bowl Parade or any other kind of parade. Reigning on the throne of Israel were the two most wicked people to reign on a throne anywhere, Ahab and Jezebel.

Episode Two—1 Kings 18

The showdown with the prophets of Baal, the superbowl of calling down fire. Key sentences: Elijah was not beyond making fun of the prophets of Baal: "Your God must be on a vacation, he must be taking an afternoon nap" (see 1 Kings 18:27). Once when I was in Kyoto, Japan, I was shown a 30-foot-tall Buddha that had a rope running from its head to the floor. Attached to the rope in front of its face was a bell. I was told that if a person wanted to pray, he or she could shake the rope that rang the bell and wake the Buddha from his nap. But on Mount Carmel, where Elijah built his altar, there was a God present who neither slumbers nor sleeps. Elijah prayed a humble prayer, and fire came down from heaven and consumed the sacrifice and the stones of the altar and licked up the water that was in the ditch around the altar.

Episode Three—1 Kings 19

Elisha's radical and irrevocable decision to follow Elijah. Key sentences: Elisha killed the oxen, made a fire out of the plow, placed the pieces of the oxen on the fire (in Kansas City we call that a barbecue), and called all of his neighbors in for a going away celebration. He wasn't coming back to farming any time soon. For the next five years, Elisha followed Elijah, carrying his attaché, his gofer, go for this and go for that (see 1 Kings 19:21).

Episode Four—2 Kings 1

The falling of Ahaziah, king of Israel, from upstairs to the first floor of his house and the subsequent prognosis of Elijah. Key sentences: "You go back and tell your king he ain't goin' to get better; he is going to die." Ahaziah did not like that prognosis and wanted a second opinion from the same person he had gotten the first opinion. He sent three groups of 50 soldiers to confront Elijah to see if he could change the prognosis.

Episode Five—2 Kings 1

The calling down fire from heaven and consuming the first two groups of 50 soldiers that confronted Elijah. The third captain fell down on his face and begged for mercy and Elijah spared him. Key sentences: Have you ever thought that calling down fire from heaven is a very secure kind of gift? A sure way to take care of all of your problems. The perfect road rage when someone cuts in front of you. I would like to call down a little fire from heaven at about two in the afternoon, just to get my students' attention. Elisha must have been watching all of this and thinking, "I don't have the gift of calling down fire from heaven, and when my master is gone, they are going to hang me up from the highest tree. I wonder what's going to happen to me when he is gone? I wonder what is in my future?"

At this point, I use Elisha's question to digress to Elijah's question, which I speculatively place within his thinking. "I wonder who is going to take my place? I wonder to whom I am going to pass the baton?" This enables me to seize a metaphor, an image that serves as a vehicle to carry the sermon to its conclusion. It doesn't make any difference how fast you run the race, if you don't make a good handoff with the baton. One bad handoff with the baton and everyone on the relay team becomes disqualified. To cement this idea into the minds of my listeners, I make my first illustrative digression by telling the story of the Taylor family, best known of which was James Hudson Taylor, who passed the baton from generation to generation. Some would have heard of the famed missionary to China, but few would have known that his great-grandchildren were imprisoned by the Japanese along with Eric Lydell, God's flying Scotsman, popularized in the movie, *Chariots of Fire*. Eight generations of Taylors passed the baton to one another, having been obedient to the call of Christ.

Episode Six—2 Kings 2

Elijah's hunt for his successor at the prophetical schools and his question to Elisha, "What is it that you want?" Key sentences: "I want to be twice the man that you have been, I want a double portion of your spirit." What an audacious answer! Remember that Elijah had raised the dead. I figure that when you have raised the dead, you have arrived spiritually. When a student accomplishes that at Nazarene Theological Seminary, we go ahead and give that student a diploma and exit him or her out. We don't have anything more to offer such a person.

Episode Seven

A quick rehearsal of the life of Elisha to demonstrate how audacious Elisha's request was. Key sentences: Elijah lived in a cave. He was fed by birds. He was depressed. He dressed funny. A tailor in the desert made his clothes. Elisha said, "I want to be twice as weird as you have been," which is the real snag, the obstacle to doing God's will and passing the baton to others. I don't want to be weird. I want to be a normal American with everyone liking me. Would I be willing to risk being different for a double portion of God's spirit?

Episode Eight—A Revisit of 2 Kings 2:9

Key sentences: It wasn't that Elisha thought he could be twice the man Elijah had been. He thought, "It will take twice what he has got, for me to be half of the person he has been." Francis of Assisi was asked, "Why are people always hanging around you, following you, listening to you?" Francis answered, "God couldn't find anyone more worthless and sinful than I am.

God has chosen me to confound the nobility, learning, and beauty of this world."

Episode Nine

The chariot of fire comes, and as Elijah breaks gravity, he passes his mantle (baton) to Elisha. Key sentences: Elisha purifies the water in the well at Jericho, and fills a widow's pot with oil so that she can pay her debts. He gives a childless couple a son, and when the son dies of a heat stroke, Elisha raises him to life. He heals the feared Syrian, Naaman, of leprosy. He restores a man his livelihood by causing his axhead to surface. Wherever Elisha goes, he brings healing.

Episode Ten—2 Kings 13:14-21

To protect a corpse from a maurading band of thieves, some Moabites hide it in the sepulchre of Elisha. When it touches the bones of Elisha, it comes to life. Key sentences: After I am dead and gone, and worms have destroyed this body, and whatever is biodegradable about me has returned to dust, could I continue to pass the baton, cast a shadow, have an influence on the next generation and the next generation, until Christ returns? Could it be that life is more than technological progress, economic consumption, and creature comforts? Can life be lived in the dimension of a double portion of God's spirit so that it becomes more than going to work, more than earning a living, more than breathing and eating? It can be lived by God's power in a redemptive dimension that brings healing to everyone within my sphere of influence, even after I'm dead.

Episode Eleven

Joash, king of Israel, visits Elisha because he is about to go to battle. Key sentences: Elisha tells Joash, "Strike the ground with those arrows." Joash struck the ground three times and stopped. Elisha was angry with him: "Why didn't you strike the ground twice as many times?" (See 2 Kings 13:18-19.) The refrain of his question? "Why didn't you ask for a double portion of the Holy Spirit?" Why don't I ask for a double portion of the Holy Spirit? Why don't I ask now?

Second Kings 13:14-21 provides a double garage in which to park two homiletical vehicles, two propositions, both of them vital to one another: passing of the baton and the double portion of the Holy Spirit.

three

PREACHING
as ICONIC
creativity

the land of metaphor

Martin Luther King Jr. hurled images on the one million persons who gathered in front of the Lincoln Memorial, August 28, 1963. Preaching at its best is a dream, a dream filled with images. We will never forget the images: "I have a dream that one day my four little children will live in a nation where they will not be judged by the color of their skin but by the content of their character . . . that one day right there in Alabama little black boys and black girls will be able to join hands with little white boys and white girls as sisters and brothers." The oratory reached such heights of imaginative arousal that we forget that King began the speech with the simple metaphor of a check: "In a sense, we have come to our nation's capital to cash a check. When the architects of our republic wrote the magnificent words of the Constitution and the Declaration of Independence, they were signing a promise that all men, yes, black men as well as white men, would be guaranteed the inalienable rights of life, liberty, and the pursuit of happiness. It is obvious today that America has defaulted on the promissory note so far as their citizens of color are concerned" (Washington 1986, 217-20).

King was convinced that the essence of a sermon is an appeal to the imagination. King scholar Richard Lischer assessed that King "dwelled in the land of metaphor all of his days," which he had inherited from the vivid colorfulness and concrete imagery of slave preachers. A slave preacher, long before King, had described the river of life in the Book of the Revelation as a "ribbon danglin' from the bosom of old mother earth." A former slave referred to her conversion as a "fiddle in my belly." King was a master of metaphor as metonymy, a trading of one name for another, the likeness of which is immediately apparent: "the iron feet of oppression, the dark chamber of pessimism, and the tranquilizing drug of gradualism" (Lischer 1995, 122-23).

Martin Luther King Jr. stood as the inheritor of those who have modeled preaching at its best, preaching that can be both heard and seen. Good speech abounds with images, images that represent values, desires, fears, ambitions, and all other human emotions. The world's images clamor for our attention, attempting to sell us secularity, ruggedness, individualism, manhood, womanhood, and exquisite delights for the palate. Never mind that I will never ski the Alps; by drinking the right beverage I can join the persons who do. Never mind that I will never grace the cover of Cosmopolitan magazine; I can wear the same perfume as the woman who does. In a world that markets icons, the economy of fantasy displaces the marketing of facts. The advertisers normally do not offer disclaimers that their products will probably not increase my sexual attraction, driving expertise, or prowess in the world of sports. In other words, the images of the world, if they don't outright lie, they almost always tell a half-truth. Thus, we might define preaching as enabling persons through God's power to exchange old images for new. Elizabeth Achtemeier claims that "if we want to change someone's life from non-Christian to Christian; from dying to living; from despairing to hoping; from anxious to certain; from corrupted to whole, we must change the images—the imaginations of the heart—in short, the words by which the person lives" (Achtemeier 1981, 24).

kingdom iconography as antidote to the world's images

Biblical preaching scripts life with Kingdom iconography, displacing the world's gods with Kingdom images. Kingdom iconography unmasks, dismantles, and brings to light icons of deceit that subvert truth. A subtle lie is wrapped around every commodity; even though Coca-Cola is drunk from a bottle in the shape of a curvaceous woman, it will not increase my testosterone, and the scantily-clad woman doesn't come with the tires, even though I buy four of them. Preaching as iconic pedagogy would alert consumers to intentional built-in obsolescence, obsoletism and discontent that quickly discards items purchased. Christian iconography, borrowing language from Leslie Newbegin, saves us from the apparent goods of life for the real goods of life. Jesus' images of salt, light, cornerstones, and foundations on a rock offer clear options for laying up "treasures in heaven where moth and rust do not corrupt, and thieves do not break through and steal."

Preaching serves as an iconic sieve, a critical index for sifting through the world's messages. Hidden persuaders beckon for time, money, and energy, exacting a price in relationships, physical health, and peaceful living in God's creation. "Image management," the pretense of style, is contrary to the authenticity and transparency that is found in Jesus Christ. Christian preaching is constantly about the business of drawing boundaries between Kingdom territory and the conspicuous consumption communicated by images that define the "American Dream."

If the task of preaching is to displace the world's definition of blessedness with God's definition of blessedness, some knowledge of the enemy's arsenal is a must. Commercial icons emphasize style over substance, evanescence over permanence, and false options overrule real possibilities. Ubiquitous

symbols, subliminal and sensuous, picture a life without limitations and contradictions. Jean Kilbourne in "Beauty and the Beast of Advertising" claims
that women are in a "double bind: somehow we are supposed to be both
sexy and virginal, experienced and naïve, seductive and chaste" (Kilbourne
1995, 124). Kilbourne charges that the women in advertisements are more
like mannequins, without wrinkles, pores, scars, blemishes, and—above all—
no signs of advancing age. Stuart Ewen charges that we are able to establish
little critical distance between us and the allurement of iconic hype.

Thus, preaching may need to become, in the words of Douglas Kellner, "a
development of competencies of reading images critically," a postmodern
pedagogy "in order to survive the onslaught of medias, images, messages, and
spectacles which are inundating our culture" (Kellner 1995, 126). In a day
when logos, tattoos, and labels define life's allegiances, every Christian deserves to know that he or she can be sealed with the Holy Spirit, the Hound of
Heaven, given to sniffling out the hidden persuaders that lurk throughout our
society. Preaching will border on naïveté, if not outright obscurantism, if it
does not give high priority to iconic stewardship. The seductive music of the
world's images, erotically inviting us to the table of conspicuous consumption, may be the single greatest issue the American church faces.

images despite the enlightenment

The guillotine of the enlightenment has received far more credit for cutting off the head of imagination than it deserves. Every effective (and affective) communicator before and after Voltaire has employed images, often exaggerated images. No one ever outdid John Donne, the early 17th-century
Anglican preacher: "Thou passeth out of the world as thine hand passeth out
of a basin of water, which may be somewhat fowler for the washing of it, but
retains no other impression of Thy having been there." (It is said that Donne
slept with a casket in his bedroom to remind him of his mortality.) The poet
Walter Scott referred to the Anglican Church of Scotland, which had been almost totally eclipsed by the Presbyterians, as a "shadow of a shade." The
Scottish Presbyterian preacher James Stewart, who spanned most of the
20th-century, referred to the New Testament characters who thought they
were so high and powerful—Tiberius, Pilate, Herod, Lysanias—and all their
pomp and might as "mere foam on the face of time's hurrying stream" (Wilson 1992, 166).

All of the image makers did not reside on the British Isles. In his most famous sermon, "Sinners in the Hands of an Angry God," Jonathan Edwards described God as one who "holds you over the pit of Hell, much as one holds a spider, or some loathsome insect over the fire, abhors you, and is dreadfully provoked: his wrath burns toward you like fire." As a precocious child, Jonathan had demonstrated keen observational powers in "natural science." Early essays on rainbows, insects, and, in particular, spiders foreshadowed stark images that he drew from everyday life for preaching material. Richard Bushman writes that "aside from purely scientific curiosity, something held Edwards's attention to spiders hour after hour. During his observations, he continually drew parallels to people, and at the end, he discussed the ways of God with small creatures in a universal moral order" (Bushman 1977, 232).

However, I would not argue that all well-known preachers have majored in metaphor. Reading the sermons of 19th- and 20th-century greats, such as Theodore Parker, Phillips Brooks, Horace Bushnell, and Harry Emerson Fosdick, yields the conclusion that much American preaching, with the exception of the African-American Church, has been in the form of carefully reasoned logic. In possibly the best-known homiletical text used in seminaries in the first half of the 20th century, James Broadus stated that "preaching and all public speaking ought to be largely composed of argument (Broadus 1943, xii). Such logical, tightly-woven discourses are beyond the listening powers of most 21st-century Americans, accustomed to receiving most of their information through sound bytes and visual stimuli. The attention span of most Americans is shorter than a Christmas list of our favorite IRS auditors. Unfortunately, the postmodern world, as Mark Taylor charges, can only speak, think, and hear in fragments. It is this that the world of advertising media completely accepts and capitalizes on. "Media philosophy is an attack on the institution of rational, systematic, analytic, supposedly value free unmediated, objective thought. It sets itself against every form of critical thought that remains prisoner to the abstract" (Taylor 1994, 5).

the recovery of metaphors for preaching

Effective preaching displaces the world's images with God's images. Metaphors of blessedness construct an alternative worldview. A metaphor captures the meaning of a word, sentence, paradigm, or complete ideology. The word *metaphor* is derived from the two Greek words *meta,* meaning "over," and *pherein,* meaning "to bear"; thus metaphor means "to bear over." A metaphor carries and presents an idea in graphic form. Proverbs, aphorisms, and axioms are made memorable through metaphoric images; for example, "Those who live in glass houses do not throw stones." Glass houses represent those of us who are vulnerable, flawed, and fragile. The stones that we throw at others may be readily returned on us.

Walter Brueggemann suggests that we will need to "re-imagine" preaching because our former models are increasingly regarded as "patriarchal, hierarchic authoritarian, and monologic" (Brueggemann 1995, 313). While Brueggemann's judgments on didactic and doctrinal preaching, in my view, are more negative than they need to be, his point for would-be communicators to postmoderns needs to be taken seriously. "The work of preaching is an art of imagination, an offer of an image through which perception, experience, and finally faith can be recognized in alternative ways" (Brueggemann 1995, 323). Brueggemann argues that communication as narrative, is in keeping with life as narrative, a reality that has a beginning, middle, and an end. Brueggemann more fully develops this concept in his classic *Finally Comes the Poet* by stating that

> the event of preaching is an event in transformed imagination. Poets, in the moment of preaching, are permitted to perceive and voice the world differently, to dare a new phrase, a new picture, a fresh juxtaposition of matters long known . . . because finally church people are like other people: we are not changed by new rules. The deep places in our lives— places of resistance and embrace—are not ultimately reached by instruction. Those places of resistance and embrace are reached only by stories, by images, metaphors and phrases that line out the world differently, apart from our fear and hurt (Brueggemann 1989, 110).

Paul Ricoeur wrote of metaphors: "Finally, if all language, all symbolism, consists in 'remaking reality,' there is no place in language where this work is more plainly or fully demonstrated" (Ricoeur 1977, 237). All symbols and images serve as metaphors, words that characterize a person, event, or idea in vivid graphics. Jesus referred to Herod as "that fox," and Churchill designated Mussolini the "utensil." Metaphor is visual language that effective communication cannot do without. The effectiveness and affectiveness of the metaphor is highly relative to culture, age, and personal history. One student preacher referred to Jesus as the "roadrunner," because He was always able to escape from the Pharisees. But a seminary audience of students and faculty may have perceived that the image subtracted more than it added: "Beep, beep" hardly translates into "Woe, Woe."

All of us, if we are willing to risk culturally relevant language, will come up short at least some of the time. There are only degrees of success, and all metaphors only approximate the aspect of a truth or object that they are attempting to communicate. These graphic objects invade our consciousness, enabling preaching to become phenomenological, an experience rather than just a hearing. If the following from the linguist James Edie is true, then coming up with the right object that incarnates an explanation or argument will be worth our best effort: "I certainly will save my readers from rehearsal of yet another taxonomy of theories of metaphor, mainly because, like theories and aesthetics, they are so abstract, each one so one sided, so boring in their intentions and so unfruitful in their consequences, that anyone of us would gladly sacrifice them all for one good piece of art, for one good poem, for an epigram, for a metaphor" (Edie 1976, 189).

Metaphor is as essential to preaching as hardness is to a diamond. As gas requires oxygen to burn, imagination employs metaphor for communication, so much so that David Buttrick states, "Inescapably, preaching is a work of metaphor." The sermon offers new images freshly informing consciousness, spiritual software for running the human machine. Buttrick concludes that "preaching is a means of grace because it speaks the images, symbols, myths, and meanings, which are saving, and are hermeneutic for God's self-disclosure" (Buttrick 1987, 116). Metaphorically speaking, I would mortgage my right arm for one good metaphor that would turn stony ground into fertile soil, and trade beauty for ashes. "In the Last Leaf," the O'Henry short story, the alcoholic artist painted a leaf on the wall so that the tree outside of the patient's window would never be barren. O'Henry's metaphor—the artist—gave life even as he desired salvation for his alcohol-saturated existence.

discovering biblical metaphors

Many texts graciously supply metaphors. First Kings 14:25–27 states that King Rehoboam replaced the stolen gold shields with shields of brass. Henry Sloan Coffin interpreted the shields of brass as going on in life although we have only second best. Haddon Robinson reminds us that the serpent that was lifted up in the wilderness became an idol to the Hebrew people. Thus, in his sermon "Good Snakes Gone Bad," he suggests that any object or method, once advantageous and redemptive, can become a fetish, having lost its original purpose. Means often become ends, objects of worship rather than worshiping the God who gave them.

Preachers who are recorded in Scripture abounded in metaphors. Listeners took home images that had been branded into their consciousness. A traveler through the minor prophets encounters images that assault and assure, rebuke and redeem. Hosea labels Israel a harlot, an unfaithful bride unfit for marriage, yet the object of God's relentless love. How can she return to God? "By breaking up her fallow ground," preparing herself for the seed of God's faithfulness, the watering of God's grace (see 10:12). God explains His communication method with Israel: "I have also spoken with the prophets, and I gave numerous visions, and through the prophets I gave parables" (12:10, NASB). As an image is an object that represents a truth, a parable is a story that represents a truth, literally meaning "alongside of." Parables almost always consist of images. John Milbank refers to the prophet as "a kind of concrete exegesis of God to his people" (Milbank 1997, 131).

The message of Joel is "urgency," though that word is never used. "Blow a trumpet in Zion and sound an alarm on My holy mountain" (2:1, NASB). And what will persons who respond to the alarm, do? "Return to me with all your heart and with fasting, weeping, and mourning; and rend your heart and not your garments" (vv. 12-13, NASB). How urgent is repentance for Israel? It is so critical that the bridegroom "come out of his room and the bride out of her bridal chamber" (v. 16, NASB). A newly married couple will dispense with what they normally do on their first night of marriage. A person would have to mine his or her image depository for a long time before bettering Joel's scenario. The situation couldn't be more urgent. A right relationship with God is to be Israel's top priority.

Amos does not declare, "God is going to evaluate his people," but rather, "I am about to put a plumb line in the midst of My people" (7:8, NASB). Micah does not say, "God is going to interrupt your agenda," an agenda that is feeble and transient. Instead, Micah declares, "The mountains will melt under Him, and the valleys will be split. Like wax before the fire, like water poured down a steep place" (1:4, NKJV). Micah doesn't sound like a kind grandmother refereeing the squabbling of her snotty-nosed grandchildren with the moral platitude "play pretty, children." Micah lets the Israelites know that they weren't much interested in playing pretty. "Hear now heads of Jacob and rulers of the house of Israel is it not for you to know justice? You who hate good and love evil, who tear off their skin from them and their flesh from their bones, who eat the flesh of my people, strip off their skin from them, break their bones and chop them up as for the pot and as meat in a kettle" (3:1-3, NASB). We should not gather from this indictment that the Israelites had turned to cannibalism but that greed, hatred, and exploitation of others were cannibalistic. It would take nothing less than "imaginative shock" to get Israel's attention. Words acted as a "slap in the face" providing a "rapid and pitiless review" with a dazzling and horrifying vision that things will either get better or worse (Riegert 1990, 9).

The minor prophets do not restrict themselves to negative images. Preaching is, at least sometimes, something other than dropping firebrands on the heads of the Israelites. "But for you who fear My name, the sun of righteousness will rise with healing in its wings, and you will go forth and skip about like calves in the stall" (Mal. 4:2, NASB). Norman Ward, a fellow Bible school student preached on "calves in the stall." God's care and provision were made vivid by Norman's ability to describe a calf, caressed and petted by its owner. The calf exuded security and freedom, the confidence of resting in the arms of constant and faithful care. This calf flaunted the newness of life granted by a liberating God. The calf, for the first time in its brief life, had been loosed from its constricting stall, allowed to explore the pastures of God's gracious promises. As the calf leaped, ran, and frolicked on hills blanketed with clover, I think I heard it say, "I've got the best owner in the world."

heaven to earth

Imaginative speech moves an idea from tacit understanding to tactile comprehension. In short, faith language of the heart gives people something on to which they can hold. Most people desire a rock or an oak tree, two compelling images in Ps. 1, rather than a theory, no matter how compelling the theory might be. Images intensify perception and enable memory. An abstract idea is encompassed or bolstered by something specific and concrete. What is specific and concrete comes from the everyday experiences of the listener. David mastered the everydayness of language when he contrasted a righteous man as a tree with the wicked man who has the stability of chaff. These metaphors also demonstrate the need for context specificity, since the meaning of chaff would be lost on most urban dwellers.

The sermon as a communication medium has displayed remarkable staying power throughout the centuries. Its constancy is no doubt first due to God's ordering of preaching as a perennial instrument of good news. But second, preachers throughout the centuries have displayed an ingenuity for pulling heaven and earth together, for bringing the Word of God to bear on the world of emergencies and celebrations, adolescence and old age, city and country, stagecoach and jet travel, marriage and death. The limitless gospel has been transported by way of contemporary idioms, images of relevancy that convey eternal truth. Henry Clay Morrison, founder of Asbury Theological Seminary, developed what he called his elevator sermon, at that time the newest technology. On the elevator he took his listeners down into hell to meet the residents. The imagery worked. I am told that persons throughout the congregation could be seen pulling their arms into their sides, as they "descended into Hell," so they wouldn't get the cinders on them.

Even as Jesus experientially and sensually interacted with this world, so must our speech if it is going to make a difference to our congregations. In the hermeneutics of imagination, words become birthing rooms of creation, that paradoxical and profane starting block for life that begins a course forever bouncing between nausea and exhilaration. Speech that is continuous with life is the only type of speech that will provide sufficient spiritual oxygen for those suffocated by the stress of everyday existence. Charles Bartow wrote in *God's Human Speech,*

> The divine reality itself, that is to say, directs our quest for understanding and obedience, for the words of Scripture are not unearthy and magical. They have not descended to us from heaven on angel's wings. They are not seemingly human, docetic. Instead, they are really human through and through. God picked the words of Scripture right off the streets of our often mean and mundane life (Bartow 1997, 38).

Preaching that connects never ignores the "mean and the mundane," lest it aim at nothing, which it is sure to hit. Preaching where people don't live is like fishing in Death Valley, a dry and monotonous business.

the sermon's critical image—incarnation

Christian theology consists of a central and critical image. As the words of the Hebrew prophets consisted of images, so the Word in the New Testament becomes an image, the parable of God. The God of Christianity is not a metaphysical concept, a fanciful notion, or an ethereal ideal. Christian theology is not other worldly, but is on a continuum with the created order and our sensual experiences of that created order. The writer to the Hebrews wrote, "God, after He spoke long ago to the fathers in the prophets in many portions and in many ways, in these last days has spoken to us in His Son whom He appointed heir of all things, through whom He also made the world. And He is the radiance of His glory and the exact representation of His nature, and upholds all things by the word of His power" (1:1-3, NASB).

The greatest act of imagination ever conceived incarnated God and brought heaven down to earth. The constant business of imagination is incarnation, "the Word became flesh" (John 1:14). The Word communicated imaginatively can be seen, heard, felt, smelled, and tasted. No effective communication has ever bypassed the sensuality of life. Highly theoretical, conceptual, abstract thinking falls on deaf ears if void of the Word that can be sensately received. Who needs a lecture when they see the "handwriting on the wall"? Visual speech translates precept into percept. I will always remember one of my Bible school professor's sermons on the three legs of our faith—the Word of God, the blood of Christ, and our obedience—because he had the congregation picture a three-legged stool. If one of the legs of the three-legged stool breaks, the stool collapses and whatever or whoever is sitting on it, with it.

A theology of incarnation ponders the God who took on himself the form of man, a hot, dusty, oily body. Jesus does not leave us simply to speculate about the exact image of God but is constantly enabling us to latch on to His image of everydayness: "I am the bread that came down from heaven" (John 6:41). "I am the light of the world" (8:12). "I am the door of the sheep" (10:7, KJV). "I am the good shepherd" (10:11). "I am the true vine" (15:1). No wonder Augustine said, "The study of the New Testament begins with that of its tropes" (Wilder 1964, 126). Tropes consist of figures of speech, analogies, metaphors and symbols that turn our attention to a visual object in order to understand an idea or precept. Eberhard Jungel argues for metaphor as a specific instance of trope (taken from the Greek word *trepein*, to turn away from the original content of the word to a different content). "This 'turn' was understood as the artistic alteration of a word or phrase from its proper meaning to another" (Jungel 1989, 21). (Coincidentally the word *advertise* is derived from the Latin *adverter*, meaning "to turn to." Never has preaching had more competing images.)

Incarnational speech, "the word became flesh," claims symbols, images, and metaphors not simply as good communication techniques but as the essence of the gospel itself. The incarnational gospel employs an incarnational methodology of communication. The incarnation of our God is so complex, paradoxical, and mysterious that only images and symbols that allow for the same paradox and mysteriousness will do. Depth of faith is not provided by easy answers but by metaphorical language that allows for reflection and ponderment. The solution to human predicament is not an explanation, but a God to whom we can relate, and even more importantly who knows

how to relate to us. Too often our preaching resembles technicalities, the kind of tired answers, formulas for living, proffered by Job's friends. Eugene Peterson observes, "But it is the 'technical' that ruins them. They are answers without personal relationship, intellect without intimacy. The answers are slapped onto Job's ravished life, like labels on a specimen bottle" (Peterson 2002, 840).

Christ revealed himself through images, images that explore and enhance relational perception. Images open for us dimensions of relational depth and conceptual faith that serve as archetypes for endless contemplation. Christ as a preacher models for us word images that are absolutely necessary for receiving the gift of faith. Why would faith need eyes to see if there is nothing to see? In Christian preaching, images and concepts always exist in a symbiotic relationship. Without this interdependency preaching comes across as dry cotton balls offered for the main course at a welcome-home dinner. Such was the observation of George Santayana living as a boy in Boston:

> If later I was taken to some Unitarian Church, it didn't matter. It seemed a little ridiculous, all those good people in their Sunday clothes, so demure, so conscious of one another, not needing in the least to pray or to be prayed for, not inclined to sing, but liking to flock together once a week, as people in Spain flock to the *paseo*, and glad to hear a sermon like the leading article in some superior newspaper, calculated to confirm the conviction already in them that their bourgeois virtues were quite sufficient and that perhaps in time poor backward races and nations might be led to acquire them (Santayana 1963, 165).

comparing images and symbols

While an image is a device for seeing something through something else, a symbol is more comprehensive and centrist for theological thinking. A symbol attaches itself to an actual historical event, while an image may or may not be part of historical narrative. Images are indirectly indispensable in giving context to the Christian faith and are of infinite variety. The cultures of time and place determine relevancy. John Bunyan and John Milton demand lexical overhauls for all but the most literary anglophiles. Bunyan's *Pilgrim's Progress*, written by a man who had almost no formal education, towers as a monument to spiritual imagination. "Vanity Fair and "The Slough of Despondency" merit analogical reinterpretations for every generation, which Sherwood Wirt attempts in *Passport to Life City*.

While the images of Christian communication are cued by relevancy, the symbols of Christianity are nonnegotiable. The manger and the Cross are indispensable to the story of Christ. They are the substance of the Jesus story, leaving no doubt as to their meaning. That is not to say that the manger at the inn can't become the cab of a semi at a truck stop, or the Cross can't become the witch's rock of sacrifice in C. S. Lewis's *The Lion, the Witch, and the Wardrobe*. In fact, the preacher for every generation will make sure that his or her people have handled and inspected these symbols from every angle possible. As David Bryant clarifies, "Symbols possess more meaning than any interpretation can articulate (they are multivalent), so that their precise meaning for a situation becomes evident only through the art of living interpretation" (Bryant 1989, 147).

Image reflects, while symbol represents. The mystery of symbol is less explainable, thus serving as archetypes that often appear in dreams, induced from complex systems of thoughts and experiences. They are less created than they are induced or intuited. In contrast to symbols, images are objects that are similar to other objects or things, abbreviated similes that serve as mirrors. All people possess symbols by wearing them, driving them, flaunting them, and living in them. Symbols represent worlds of hope, faith, and commitment whether they be a swoosh or a cross. Images resemble the idea or object to which they are analogous. Symbols signify an idea rooted in a historical ideology, whether that ideology be supported by fact or mythology.

Objects often may serve as both an image and a symbol. If I had created for my dad, a World War II Navy veteran, a replica of a ship on which he served, the scaled model would serve as both symbol and image. The replica would symbolize his sacrifice and represent a flood of memories, some good and some bad. The copy of the original would also serve as an image, more or less according to faithfulness to detail. Thus, there is a carryover between image and symbol. However, the rainbow and Jacob's ladder best serve as symbols, representing God's faithfulness and accessibility or immanence, since Jacob said, "Surely the LORD is in this place, and I did not know it" (Gen. 28:16, NKJV). In contrast, the potter in Jeremiah images the sovereignty of God, and the harlot in Hosea mirrors the waywardness in Israel. The symbol represents unusual historical circumstances, which had never before occurred, whereas the images draw from and reflect everyday life. Pots and prostitutes are common. I suspect that in the years after the flood, when Noah saw a rainbow, a tear may have come to his eye. Jeremiah made no such emotional connection when he viewed a pot. Clyde Holbrook explains the difference between a symbol and an image:

Symbols impinge the past on the present, whereas images rely for their effect on spontaneous recognition in the moment. . . . Symbols develop their power over time; images simply occur compelling assent and understanding. The sharpness of detail in the image catches the imagination of the reader or listener; the symbol, deeply embedded in the traditions of the religious community, incites reflective interpretation and emotional attachment. . . . But no Christian symbol ever exhibits humor as an image may. For example, there is a world of difference between the direct appeal made by Jesus' humorous image of the rich man's failure to enter the kingdom (like the camel trying to go through the eye of a needle) and the symbol of Jesus on the cross (Holbrook 1984, 61).

the images of parable and hyperbole

Parables serve as living interpretations, the rhetorical device Jesus most used to relay an essential truth for Kingdom living. The parables almost always contain images: seed, ground, pigs, barns, camels, sheep, coins, and so on. These stories are often told for their shock value: battering rams knocking down false walls of security. As McFague says, "A parable is, in this analysis, an assault on the accepted conventional way of viewing reality. It is an assault on the social, economic and mythic structures people build for their own comfort and security" (McFague 1982, 47). Parables suggest that there are other ways of viewing the world than the American myths, which almost always end in disillusionment. As in John Crossan's words, "You have built a lovely home, myth assures us; but, whispers parable, you are right above an earthquake fault" (McFague 1982, 47).

No communicator has ever excelled more in hyperbolic images than did Jesus. Hyperbole makes logic look like it's dropping an anchor encased in cement. All populist communicators follow Jesus' lead in getting the point across. "If thy . . . eye offend thee, pluck it out, . . . if thy . . . hand offend thee, cut it off" (Matt. 5:29-30, KJV). "Whoso shall offend one of these little ones . . . it would be better for him that a millstone were hanged around his neck, and that he were drowned in the depths of the sea" (18:6, KJV). Hyperbole, taken from the Greek, means literally to go through, beyond, or over. The point is more than just gotten across; it is hurled far enough to leave no doubt. The truth of the matter is found in overkill or in over objectifying an idea. To see the idea in gargantuan dimensions is the point of hyperbole. In making the point that cigarettes destroy teeth, Frank McCourt's father said

that he "had holes in his teeth big enough for a sparrow to raise a family in" (McCourt 1996, 138). Rick Bragg's mother cleaned his ears for church so deep "I thought she would gouge all the way through and pull the wash rag out the other side of my head and dusted with so much talcum I was chemically unable to sweat" (Bragg 1997, 85). The lawyer who prosecuted the mammoth utility company on behalf of a smaller one, stated to the jury, "So now we see what it is. They got us where they want us. They holding us up with one hand, their good sharp fishin' knife in the other, and they sayin', 'you jes set still, little catfish, we're jes going to gut ya'" (Riegert 1990, 69). He won the case.

the difficulties of visual speech

One must be careful that the image does not overcome the truth or overwhelm the congregation to the point of subverting the truth. The image may be so gargantuan and grotesque that it rules out the subtle nuances of theological reflection. Thus, the immensity of the image paradoxically reduces the truth that one attempts to communicate. A long illustration from an athletic event, movie, or novel, which some of my seminary students tell, reminds me of the reverend who took his son Stanley to view a newly painted mural of a train in a local school auditorium. The preacher explained that the picture was of "the future coming towards us, the train is this country's unity far off but bearing down on us." Stanley responded to his dad's metaphorical explanation with, "No, it's a train." All of this varies with age and culture. If a child hears a sentence "Wherever it slithers, the slimy slug of sin leaves its 'uck,'" he or she may be left only with a slug.

The preacher experiments with objects, lending visuality to the text or idea being stressed. In conveying the concept of Christ's resurrection power invading the walking, talking, sitting, and eating of everydayness (Luke 24), I place a softball on the altar. I close the message by telling how God used a softball game (everydayness) as a medium for spiritually reaching out to a person in crisis. This is one of the few times I use a tangible object for theological communication. My assessment is that visual aids often subtract more than they add. A preacher recently held up a teflon frying pan to illustrate how we can resist temptation, even as teflon doesn't allow food to stick to a cooking surface. I didn't learn much about resisting temptation, but I did learn something about frying an egg.

Language, mostly because it is preserved in books, is conservative in nature. Thus, it tends to make cognition static and immobile. Language has to be stretched over both time and space by creating idioms that connect with the present. The following from D. G. Hart serves as an example: "Asking evangelicals to recover tradition is like coaxing a thirteen-year-old who steadily drinks Mountain Dew to taste wine. The facial reaction will not likely indicate pleasure" (Hart 2004, 183). The statement works for most persons living in 2005. Whether it will work in 2025 is anybody's guess. The reference to Mountain Dew is far more temporal than the reference to wine. Because a college president was away from campus for such long periods of time, some imaginative students drew his picture on cafeteria milk cartons. The accusatory cartoon would be lost on anyone who does not remember missing children being pictured on milk cartons in the 1980s. This demonstrates both the bane and blessing of contemporary language.

images as analogical speech

Dorothy Sayers has written, "All language including visual language about God must, as St. Thomas Aquinas pointed out, necessarily be analogical" (Sayers 1987, 22-23). The truth is that all language about anything is analogical; we think in a series of metaphors. We can explain nothing in terms of itself, only in terms of other things. Dennis Kinlaw references the analogies of the forensic, the familial, and the nuptial as pedagogical lessons employed by God. Jesus began His ministry in Cana of Galilee turning water into wine not as a lesson on being the competent party host but as a nuptial sign pointing to His larger purpose of redeeming a bride. Kinlaw refers to God as the "supreme 3rd grade teacher, master of the object lesson" (Kinlaw, *Let's Start with Jesus*).

The apostle Paul often used the functional similarities between two entities that are substantially unalike. He referred to sin as "a body of death," intelligible speech as the "clear call of a trumpet," the Christian journey as "an athletic race," those that are blameless and pure as "shining stars of the universe," spiritual preparation as the full military defense of "swords, shields, and helmets." No communication thirsts more for analogy than the unseen of spiritual truth. We connect the objects of the world around us with the spiritual data accumulated from biblical reading, worship attending, prayer, and theological dialogue. Theological imagination gives form to that which is previously unseen so that it might be better understood. In *A Midsummer Night's Dream,* Shakespeare declared that fantasies rather than cool reason are able to see devils:

The poet's eye, in a fine frenzy rolling,
Doth glance from heaven to earth, from earth to heaven;
And, imagination bodies forth
The forms of things unknown, the poet's pen
Turns them to shapes, and gives to airy nothing
A local habitation and a name.
(Shakespeare 1918, 64).

Webster defines an analogy as "a similarity or likeness between things in some circumstances or effects when the things are otherwise entirely different." Notice the number of times Jesus said, "The kingdom of heaven is like . . ." Christ's parabolic analogies always grabbed everyday images such as mustard seeds, treasures, merchants, nets, homeowners, kings, and foundations for houses. Jesus was the master of what biblical scholar James Sanders calls "dynamic analogies," interpretative equivalents that would allow hearers today to be challenged as were the first hearers of the sayings or parables (Sanders 1984, 70-71). Finding images or situations parallel to those in the mind of the original speaker or listener enables the text to come alive for 21st-century congregations. As Stephen Farris says to his students, "Don't leave your text in the first century" (Farris 1998, 13).

Even though congregational personalities largely determine analogies that the preacher will use, one must be cautious of feeding hearers a steady diet of Krispy Kreme doughnuts. There is always the temptation to boil the gospel down into sound bytes, lapel buttons, bumper stickers, and slogans. David Buttrick warns against domesticating God and trivializing the gospel: "The obvious danger in analogy is that it can paint our image on the face of God, scale down God's revelation to our conventional wisdom" (Farris 1998, 17).

There is the danger not only of reductionism but also of using analogies that don't connect. I illustrated Rom. 8:20, "The creation was subjected to futility [vanity, emptiness, meaninglessness, angst, frustration]," by reference to my children on a roller coaster at a theme park, who asked, "Dad, what are we going to do tomorrow?" Isn't the moment ever good enough? Isn't there pure joy in anything? (I can't vouch that they ever asked me while actually on the roller coaster, but certainly during the course of the day at the theme park.) As I used this feeble analogy, a family got up and walked out. They probably possessed some theological conviction against attending theme parks.

While preaching in Japan, I attempted to explain that a relationship with God is not a scientific formula but an enthralling romance: "Before I married my wife, I didn't check her family genealogy, her transcripts at the University of Kentucky, her medical records, her credit rating, or the number of awards she had won in high school. I simply fell in love with her." After the sermon, one of the Japanese leaders said to me, "We do all of those things in our country." My attempt at sharpening the application had been bludgeoned by a cultural faux pas.

But I am not alone in my analogical miscues. A preacher tried to make a major point out of the disciples washing and mending their nets: "This was a waste of time. They should have been casting their nets into the deep." Any net fisherman knows that preparation of equipment comes before using it. Nevertheless, we attempt to fish for appropriate tropes that will relay brazen serpents to suburbanites who have never seen a garden snake. Thus, we humbly accept Stephen Farris's challenge, while recognizing that we will never fully succeed because all analogies in the end are limited: "We need, then, in our preaching a way of liking the world of the Biblical text and the world in which we live and preach, that which affirms similarity and respects dissimilarity" (Farris 1998, 7-8).

images as dynamic equivalents

The seminary chapel coordinator recently assigned me the task of preaching on Ash Wednesday, the first day of Lent. I chose the archetypical text from which we derive the Lenten 40 days, the temptation of Christ in the wilderness. Out of the three Synoptics, I chose Luke 4, because I am partial to Luke as a historian (I count myself an amateur historian), and I favor his theological arrangement surrounding the temptation. I approach this text with fear and trembling and profound doubt that I can translate this cosmic battle between God and Satan in any way that resembles what mere mortals experience as temptation. Somebody who has never fasted 40 days (and I haven't) and who does not have the power to turn the finest flour into biscuits (and I don't) is not going to be tempted to turn stones into bread. Did Satan convert the ovens of hell into a giant Panera Bread factory so that the aroma would fill the universe? Did the saliva glands stimulated by the fragrance of fresh bread cause Christ's mouth to stab with pain?

The three surrounding sections of Scripture enable me to understand the text. For the baptismal scene, 3:21-22, Luke portrays Jesus standing in line with all the others, poor and prostitutes, orderly adults and squirrelly children, with the words "Jesus also" (NKJV). In Matthew's version, there is a huge debate between John the Baptizer and the Son of God: "But John tried to deter him, saying, 'I need to be baptized by you, and do you come to me?'" (Matt. 3:14). Matthew singled Jesus out as the special person that He was. Luke has Jesus simply get in line with all the rest.

After the baptism, Luke gives the long genealogy, which is again quite different from Matthew's. In Matthew's genealogy, we go 12 words and we are to David; 16 words bring us to Abraham. Matthew makes sure that his readers know Jesus as a Hebrew blueblood, a royal insider, a connected favorite son to any and everybody that really matters in Israel's history. In Lukan genealogy, we go 40 generations before we get to anyone we have ever heard of. Luke's genealogy is full of nobodies, people who day after day got up, went to work, came home, and went to bed. Luke's account of Jesus' ancestry sounds a lot like mine. I researched my family, and there is nobody that ever made a ripple beyond spitting in the wind while standing on the bank of Mud Creek. My English ancestors settled in the marshlands of eastern North Carolina and hardly ventured beyond where they landed. I identify with the long line in Luke's baptism and the long line in the genealogy, both precede the wilderness temptation.

Following the wilderness passage, Luke narrates Christ's returning to Nazareth, His hometown, where His first congregation responds, "Isn't this Joseph's son?" (4:22). Jesus returned to the place where everything He said and did would be refracted through the kid who had grown up playing in the streets, as far as we know, little different than any other kid. What all these passages have in common is the word "no." No to priority, no to privilege, no to power, and—in particular—no to playing the Deity card, the card of omniscience and omnipotence, when Christ had every right to do just that, as God in the flesh. Don't you think that Jesus every once in a while was tempted to say, "You know, I'm not really Joseph's son"?

I am still left searching for a dynamic equivalent: an image that raises the question, what does the temptation of Christ look like for a seminary student inaugurating his or her ministry. Is there a similarity? My sermon sends the seminary graduate to Morningside Church of the Nazarene (a fictional church depicted in the integrated senior seminar as a case study). Abandoned buildings, overgrown lots, vacated homes, boarded-up windows, crack houses, liquor stores, and trash-strewn streets provide the demographics for Morningside. As the freshly minted pastor sits in his office, he reflects on last Sunday's sermon, which would have made the drone of a mosquito on a hot, sultry night seem inviting. A ringing phone pierces the gloom of this pastor's dreary hopelessness. The owner of the bread factory several blocks over (the only reputable business that hasn't left the community) wants to buy the church's property and use it for a bread store. The pastor calls the district superintendent hoping for his consent, because this would be the perfect way out. The ecclesiastical higher-up says that he will consult with the advisory board and get back with the pastor later.

On another dreary day, maybe in March when Ash Wednesday sometimes falls (Garrison Keillor says that March is God's invention to let those of us who do not drink know what a hangover is like), the phone rings again. The largest church in the denomination wants this young graduate to be their pastor. He won't have to jump through all the ecclesiastical hoops, working his way through mean appointments with cranky people. He will go straight to the top of the ecclesiastical heap, not having to endure the tedium of small churches. But again, the district superintendent is not nearly as excited as the Morningside pastor had hoped. The church superior reminds the novice that he hasn't even been at Morningside six months, and he wouldn't want to communicate that he was just using these poor, abandoned people to get to a better place.

A couple of months later, the new pastor was at his lowest point of despondency. Every thought was a complaint that God had not fully rewarded him for his seminary preparation. He had "grown" the church from 70 to 40 average attendance, several of the main families had left, the church finances had fallen off, two key board members were going through a divorce, and it seemed as if he was preaching a funeral once a week. He deserved a better vocational opportunity, and it was time to spill his guts to the district superintendent. But no sooner had he started his tirade, when the D. S. interrupted him: "Now is the time to tell you that you haven't been pastoring an actual church but a 'virtual church.' Virtual Church is a program produced by a new company called Ecclesio Games. This particular game is titled 'How to tell if your seminarian really has it,' or 'Will you stand the test instead of putting the Lord, thy God, to the test?'" The district superintendent firmly but gently declared, "Sorry. You have failed."

The sermon would be a real downer if it ended on that negative note. The good news of the text is that Jesus was, at all points, tempted as we are, yet He has defeated Satan for us, so that our strength is in Him, not in ourselves. The writer to the Hebrews declared, "For since He Himself was tempted in that which He has suffered, He is able to come to the aid of those who are tempted" (Heb. 2:18, NASB). Jesus refused to play the "I deserve better than this" card, so that we might have better than we deserve, life in Him. Jesus said no so that He might say yes. You can't have a resurrection without having a crucifixion. You can't say yes without saying no.

Father Edmund LaPoint (d. 1932) was the priest at Santa Ysabel, 50 miles inland from San Diego, California. A priest came to California in 1769, declaring the territory "a barren land, sterile, covered with rocks, without green grass or water." This describes Santa Ysabel, not 1 of the 21 stately missions that line the coast of California. It is a forgotten inland post, what must have seemed to Father LaPoint like light years from the cool breezes blowing off the Pacific in southern California. Father LaPoint walked from Canada to Santa Ysabel and stayed there for 29 years, never leaving. When he lay down at night, listening to coyotes yelp, wolves howl, and the wind whipping around the corners of his adobe hut, he must have been tempted, at least once in a while, to seek greener pastures. He said no that he might say yes to the hundreds of dwarf-sized Indians (they seemed very short gathered around his over-six-foot frame) who depended on him for spiritual care. Father LaPoint was buried beside the door of the church where he gave the entirety of his ministerial career.

Is there any way to say no in an ecclesiastical culture that touts the person who pastors the biggest church, reaches the highest church office, seeks the status symbols of success, rather than offers the sacrifice of servanthood? Is there any way that Christ's no can become my no so that His yes might become my yes? Here is the best news of the text: "Jesus, full of the Holy Spirit, returned from the Jordan, and was led by the Spirit in the desert." Can I depend on the infilling of the Holy Spirit in the same way Christ did? This is not best answered with a facile yes but with a living witness, a living parable who says no through the power of the Spirit so that his or her life might become a divine yes to the power of God.

Samuel Logan Brengle experienced saying no to himself and yes to the Holy Spirit as a student at the Boston School of Theology. He planned, as a very bright student and a master of elocution (he had been a debate champion in college), a career in the Methodist Church. Instead, William Booth, general of the Salvation Army, came through Boston on a storming, preaching tour, and Brengle became enamored by Booth's fiery spirit. Brengle perceived God was telling him no to the Methodist Church and yes to the lowly Salvation Army, which consisted of ministering to the poor. In those days, all aspiring candidates went to England and appeared before the general himself for admission as a cadet. Booth looked down at Brengle's credentials and back up at the youthful, hopeful face. Booth said, "Young man, you can't submit to our authority, you have too much education; you're of the dangerous kind." Brengle pleaded with the general by saying, "But sir, I have been filled with the Holy Spirit." Booth rescinded his rejection, and Brengle was allowed into the Salvation Army.

The Army appointed Brengle to a dysfunctional corps in Danbury, Connecticut. "I inherited a three-foot, six-inch dwarfed, hunch-back girl, and a six-foot, three-inch former slave named George Washington. I also had as my first assistant, a lieutenant who had a lame leg which he drug behind him." In those days, the Salvation Army marched and played a band to the extent that anyone was capable of performing. Captain Brengle, with his hunch-backed girl, former slave, and lame-legged lieutenant marched through the streets of Danbury, beating their drums, shaking timbrels, and blowing a horn. When they passed a large, imposing Methodist Church, Satan said, "You fool! You could have been pastor of that church." Sam Brengle said no so that he might say yes, as the army's most prolific author and best-loved preacher in its history.

The above homiletical sample attempts to reconcile impressionistic and propositional preaching. The students have experienced the drama of Christ's temptation while being given a clear proposition. Experiencing the sermon phenomenologically need not rule out a single, pivotal idea. The sermon transposes the cosmic wilderness battle of Christ to a 21st-century pastor's battle with temptations that range from expediency and utilitarianism to the self-serving "I deserve better than this" attitude. Risking reductionism (and how would any attempt at a dynamic equivalent not fall short of what Christ really experienced?), I have drawn from both commercial and technological arsenals without sacrificing a theological theme. Hopefully, the lighter moments of contemporary imagery allowed us to move to a deeper theological imagination. Satan tested Jesus by saying to Him, "Prove yourself—if You are the Son of God—play the Deity card." The greatest temptation that I will overcome is the temptation to prove myself to family, friends, and colleagues. Could Jesus continue to live in the security of His Father's affirmation, "This is my beloved Son, in whom I am well pleased" (Matt. 3:17, KJV)? Holiness theology has long understood that a yes always demands an equally important no, a no to myself and its exaltation.

The sermon was preached to an academic community, exam-oriented, and technologically savvy. The very relevancy that cued the message limits it. It would have to be reworked for other congregational settings. Edmund

Steimle reminds us that the timeless sermon is a poor sermon. The sermon cannot be relevant without secularization. To secularize the sermon is to use the images found in the everydayness of 21st-century Americans, or of whatever culture in which one happens to be ministering. Christ lived in a very different culture than we do. Plows and sheep do not readily translate into everyday images for a group of adolescents, maybe even urban adults, who have seen neither. Jesus' invitation to take up His yoke would be lost on most moderns. I, myself, did not comprehend what the "sheep before his shearers is silent" (Isa. 53:7) actually looks like until I watched a sheep go limp and docile as it was being sheared in Australia. Thus, the preacher is constantly asking, "What are the specifics of this text that can be transported to the 21st century?" What would this look like if it took place today, rather than 2,000 years ago? As Steimle argues, "The fabric of the biblical witness is completely and thoroughly secular, even when it sounds just the opposite in our twentieth-century ears. . . . The story of God's dealings with His people is studded with battles, sex, and death, and shady deals, with the plight of poverty-stricken widows and the suffering of the innocent, with markets and temples and idols and courts and deserts and cities" (Steimle 1980, 165).

using images already in the text

The purpose of preaching is not to teach Scripture, but to focus on life through the lens of Scripture. This axiom is not for the purpose of denigrating the importance of knowing the biblical story. In fact, the proper use of the Bible's images and rightly identifying their connective tissue with everyday life calls for a constant rereading of the biblical narrative and reapplication to an everchanging world. Thus, we identify those archetypical images that are the stuff of an ancient time and place and retransplant them to our day: Exodus, wilderness, light, darkness, rock, body, bride, sackcloth, and ashes (I recently showed a piece of burlap to a group of children, as I tried to communicate the concept of sackcloth and ashes). Thus, we try to accomplish exactly what the biblical writers attempted, to speak and write in language that could be seen. The image is only appropriate to the extent that it magnifies the truth, not subtracts from it by magnifying itself. G. B. Caird writes, "When we look at an object through a lens, we concentrate on the object and ignore the lens. Metaphor is a lens; it is as though the speaker were saying, 'Look through this and see what I have seen, something you would never have noticed without the lens'" (Caird 1997, 152).

The above sermon on the temptation of Christ demonstrated a way to bring contemporary images to the text. However, there are a multitude of biblical images that can be transported straight to our culture, with little or no interpretation other than the biblical context in which they are used. They present possibilities for the one-image sermon, in which a dimension of the physical evokes or reflects a spiritual problem or spiritual potential. The word "gate" is such an object. In the context of the rich man and Lazarus, the gate represents a barrier, prejudice, or exclusion. But in the description of the New Jerusalem, the gate symbolizes the inclusion of grace. There are two words for gate in the New Testament: *thura,* which denotes an ordinary gate or door, and *pulon,* which connotes a gate of grandeur, splendor, and significance. A *pulon* is a gate that makes a statement. A *pulon* separated the rich man and Lazarus, a gate of nonempathy, a gate of economic disparity, a gate of holier-than-thou spirituality. Lazarus's condition, in the Jewish mentality, was certainly due to his having sinned. You can't be on welfare, unless you have done something wrong. Lazarus's condition must have been Lazarus's fault. (I was alerted to the importance of the gate by David Buttrick.)

My parents, good people that they were, effectively taught me to build gates between clean and unclean (we were poor, but we were clean), between the advantaged and disadvantaged (make something out of yourself, son), the white collar and blue collar (get a good education), between those who work with their hands and those who work with their minds (you don't want to get a manual labor job). All of these moralisms enabled me to build gates, and I have been building them ever since. Getting ahead, distancing oneself from the poor, is good old American theology but is rather damnable business if one desires to be a citizen in the kingdom of God. "Christian America" continues to be a nation divided by racial prejudice, economic stratification, and superiority over anyone who doesn't dress, act, and talk like us. Segregated fault lines demarcate every American city, waiting to erupt into earthquakes, as is currently the case in Durham, North Carolina, between Duke University's lacrosse players and those who live on the other side of the tracks. Town and gown is only a small part of the equation. The tension represents generations of gate building.

A church experienced white flight but had the foresight to donate the church to their denomination, which would, in turn, install a black pastor to minister to the African-American neighborhood. One day as the pastor was home, he heard a ruckus outside the parsonage. He couldn't recall that he had ordered any maintenance or repairs, so he stepped outside to investigate.

He confronted two white men who were removing the air conditioner from the parsonage window. When he asked them what they had in mind, they responded, "We gave this air-conditioner to the church; we're not leaving it here for the _____." I am ashamed to confess that happened in my denomination. The gate in Lazarus's story is the dark crevice in every person's soul.

The rich man and Lazarus found themselves on the opposite sides of an unbridgeable, uncrossable chasm. Gates of separation always become chasms; there is no hell like separation. Separation is forever, unless we allow Christ to be our peace, to "destroy . . . the barrier, the dividing wall of hostility" (Eph. 2:14). Jesus has let us in on a scary thought: gates erected here and now remain erected forever, and those who think they are on the right side may be forever on the wrong side. The gate image provides a visual urgency for identifying and tearing down walls between us and others.

We find more positive and inviting images in Ezek. 48 and Rev. 21, where we encounter 12 gates, each with a name of one of Jacob's sons written on it. "On no day will its gates ever be shut, for there will be no night there" (Rev. 21:25). The gates call for a rehearsal of some very dysfunctional family history. Never were gene pools more critical to a family's relational dynamic. Rachel and Leah entered into a baby production contest, with Leah the clear winner. The infertile Rachel entered the fray by offering her maidservant to bear children sired by her husband. After the genetic dust had settled on the family squabble, Leah had six children; Bilhah and Zilpah, two each; and Rachel finally ended up with Joseph and Benjamin. Remember that when Jacob was returning to encounter his brother, Esau, whom he had beguiled out of the family inheritance (Gen. 33), he sent the first 10 of his children with their mothers as a human shield to protect Joseph and Rachel (Benjamin was not yet born). All of this favoritism harvested deep hostility between Joseph and the 10—a hostility that ultimately spewed out on Joseph, the tattletale. These brothers, full of deceit, treachery, hatred, and revenge, will forever have their names written on the doors to the New Jerusalem.

The gates to the heavenly city symbolize grace, grace sufficient for the deepest scars, misgivings, and shame, the kind of events that forever scream, "You're not fit for a rundown flat, much less a city whose gates are 'twelve pearls, each gate made of a single pearl. The great street of the city was of pure gold, like transparent glass'" (Rev. 21: 21). God's great gig is irony. He certainly has a sense of humor. The scoundrels who sold their sibling into slavery will forever have their names engraved in pearl. I suspect one of the dominant sounds of eternity will be laughter, and one of the most frequent comments in the celestial city will be, "You made it, I can't believe it!" Remember that Jacob said to at least some of his sons, "You've made my name stink to high heaven" (Gen. 34:30, TM). Does God have enough grace to transform the stench of life into a fragrance forever floating through the corridors of eternal life? Can that transformation start here and now?

All of us have closed doors in our lives, gates that we would rather not open because something in our past stinks. We would rather forget about it, but completely compartmentalizing life is impossible. Just when we think the room of managed sins and shameful regrets is cordoned off, its contents seep out at inappropriate moments no matter how hard we squelch or repress them. Nothing in our lives is ever over when it is over. The only solution to haunting memories is to open the door to God's healing grace.

Allow me to reference my own life by way of the gate of God's redeeming love. My genealogy consists of two family stories, vastly different. On my father's side one discovers a happy, congenial family, a hospitable home on an island, Portsmouth, North Carolina. The family was hardworking, food and clothing were at the subsistence level, and there was always room at the large table for someone else. The family, though not particularly religious, abounded in life's basic virtues. My aunts and uncles always made me feel special, and I am left with fond memories.

My mother's story was quite different; she was born out of wedlock—the only child of a father and mother who divorced before she came into the world. Being raised by an overly protective mother, she saw her father only once in her life. Until my mother died, her past remained a closed door, at least to me. Research of my mother's family revealed grace-drenched data. My great-grandfather, on a Sunday evening in 1897, was fishing in Nelson Bay off of Sea Level, North Carolina. Upon hearing the sounds of a revival at Mann's chapel, a Methodist Church, the six fishermen, wet, barefoot, smelling like fish, left their skiffs and attended the closing service. When an invitation was given, all six went forward and confessed Christ as their Savior. Three years later, the same six men were drowned in one of the most devastating hurricanes that ever hit North Carolina. Because the psalmist wrote, "But from everlasting to everlasting, the LORD's love is with those who fear him, and their righteousness with their children's children (Ps. 103:17), I believe I am the direct descendant of the grace that flowed to my great-grandfather. Though his physical life was cut short, his spiritual influence continues to live. I suspect that for all of us, no matter how forbidding the door with all of life's "pile" behind it, if we allow God to open it, we'll find a gate with our name written on it.

What I have attempted to do in both of these passages is what Elizabeth Achtemeier calls exchanging one set of images for another. Images represent frames of reference, worlds of reality by which we live and define ourselves. I sought to make the rich man's gate, ornate and prestigious, as hideous and destructive to human relationships as possible. The exclusiveness of gates, walls of separation, can be transformed into covenants committed by the grace of God to counting others better than ourselves. In the second sermon, I use the gates of the Holy City to serve as what Bruce Salmon calls "positive upheavals, a momentous inbreaking of blessing" (Rose 1997, 78), a new reality of living, shameful shut doors traded for open gates of grace! God is not into skeletons in the closets, but testimonies to dysfunctionalisms that have been redeemed. Such is the story of those who have been given a future not dictated by their past.

four

PREACHING as IRONY

the irony of the biblical narrative

The heart of Christianity beats with an irony: God became man. Even more ironical, men killed Him. God majors in inappropriateness. The ultimate taboo God gave Israel was the injunction against sacrificing their children to pagan gods. God broke His own command. He sacrificed His Son on our behalf. The Cross stands at the center of God's plan to confound the normality of life. In the biblical story, hardly anything goes as expected. Why would it when the meek inherit the earth, when conquering comes through surrendering, and when the only route to exaltation is humiliation? Irony is a disjuncture between cause and effect, a contradiction between intention and outcome or an incongruity between setting and event. What is expected does not take place. What is unexpected does take place. A man bites a dog, a fire truck catches on fire, and God dies. The apotheosis of irony occurred on Golgatha, a contradiction that the religious somebodies reduced to mockery. "He saved others; He cannot save Himself" (Matt. 27:42, NASB).

God leaves people muttering, "It ought to be different than this." When Noah was inside a makeshift boat (it was the first boat he had built) and faced the proverbial problem of life, can't stand the stench on the inside or the storm on the outside, he must have said, "It ought to be different than this." When Sarah had a baby at age 90, she probably said to Abraham, "We should have tried this a little sooner." When Joseph was walking across hot, burning sand, feet manacled and eyes fastened on the rear end of a camel, he thought to himself, "This isn't going according to plan." According to plan hardly ever matches God's plan. For that reason, the "preacher" wrote: "I again saw under the sun that the race is not to the swift and the battle is not to the warriors, neither is bread to the wise nor wealth to the discerning nor favor to men of ability; for time and chance overtake them all" (Eccles. 9:11, NASB). For the writer of Ecclesiastes, neither life nor God can be contained or explained in a rational formula. Old Testament literary scholar Thomas Jemi=lity sums up the sermon in Ecclesiastes by simply saying, "Irony is the believer's necessary mode of being" (Jemielity 1992, 111).

God's irony cuts across the grain of life, deconstructs conventional wisdom, and often leaves us dumbfounded. Hardly anything in the biblical narrative goes as expected. And because we often overlay the biblical text with our American middle-class assumptions, we miss the reversals that undermine those assumptions. Folk theology, evangelical paradigms, and cultural biases serve as fog banks between us and God's perspective on life. We misinterpret the acts of God because we ignore God's explicit reminder to Isaiah that "My thoughts are not your thoughts, nor are your ways My ways. . . . For as the heavens are higher than the earth, so are My ways higher than your ways and My thoughts than your thoughts" (Isa. 55:8-9, NASB).

Rarely does God take the route I would have taken to accomplish His purpose as I understand that purpose. I would have kept snakes out of the garden. I would have taken a more direct route across the Sinai desert, and were I David, I would have had Saul taken out. Thus, Scripture constantly sets me up, causing my propensities to expediency and self-gratification to boomerang and cripple my best-laid plans. God batters and smashes my ego defenses, my wrong perceptions, that at the time seemed so right but from God's perception were so wrong. Jeremiah wrote, "I know, O LORD, that a man's way is not in himself, Nor is it in a man who walks to direct his steps" (Jer. 10:23, NASB). At almost every step in the biblical narrative, God reverses human tendencies.

Both ancient and modern literature of lasting value have majored in irony. They have highlighted the futility of human endeavors, life's agonizing attempts to secure the glory of immortality or, at the very least, comfort and significance. Again, the Old Testament preacher testified, "I have seen all the works which have been done under the sun, and behold, all is vanity and striving after wind. What is crooked cannot be straightened and what is lacking cannot be counted" (Eccles. 1:14-15, NASB). Irony, from God's perspective, summarizes life's ultimate truths: when we are full we are empty; when we are strong we are weak; when we believe ourselves to be resting in the lap of security, we are most susceptible to powers beyond our control. Irony mocks our courage, trumps our boasting, and undermines our fondest aspirations.

The taunting and mocking Sennacherib surrounded Jerusalem with the mightiest army in the world, confident that the tiny fortress would open its gate to his 185,000 troops. Israel responded: "Whom have you reproached and blasphemed? And against whom have you raised your voice, and haughtily lifted up your eyes? Against the Holy One of Israel!" (2 Kings 19:22, NASB). The army of Judah didn't have to lift a sword. By daybreak of Israel's confrontation, the angel of God slew all 185,000, and Sennacherib scampered home, only to be executed by compatriots who gave his throne to another. But the greatest irony of God's miraculous intervention is that Israel could never get the irony. They continued to rely on their own strength in spite of God saying, "The king is not saved by a mighty army; a warrior is not delivered by great strength. A horse is a false hope for victory; nor does it deliver anyone by its great strength" (Ps. 33:16-17, NASB).

Irony has the last laugh. The predictability of formulas comes up short against the unruly forces that disrupt a fill-in-the-blank approach to life. Irony laughs at all of us who would reduce life to cause-and-effect analysis. Pickpockets have their pockets picked, scammers are scammed, and Haman is hanged on the very gallows that he had built for Mordecai's lynching. No one ever had the tables more definitively turned on him than did Haman (see Esther 6:6-12). All of us, at least once in a while, are trapped in our own devices. Balaam desiring to compromise prophetical integrity, pleasing both Moses and Balak, securing the favor of both Yahweh and Baal, got stopped in his tracks by the angel of the Lord. Balaam's jackass saved him from destruction; the dumb beast of burden spoke words of wisdom to its owner, who was too dumb to see the path to perdition. The dictum that God always uses persons as His mouthpiece isn't entirely true. In a pinch, a jackass will do. (See Num. 22.)

irony as upsetting the equilibrium

What Eugene Lowry refers to as "upsetting the equilibrium," I designate as escaping the evangelical paradigm. The evangelical paradigm comes to the text with the same old interpretations and hackneyed translations, never plummeting the multiple layers that often escape our superficial examination. The suspicion that the text holds a greater depth than suggested in Sunday School will cause me to ask, "What was it really like to slay all the men, women, and children of five villages in southern Canaan" (see Josh. 10)? What would it really be like as a pastor to marry a prostitute and move her into the parsonage (see Hos. 3)? What would it really be like to have a brother who got everything and I got nothing (Joseph, in Gen. 37)? What would it really be like to be sent as an evangelist to a people who had raped, maimed, and gouged out the eyes of my ancestors (Jonah)?

All the above biblical situations represent ambiguities, conflicts, and tensions in our thinking. We don't know with whom to side, the Israelites or the Canaanites, Joseph or his brothers. Lowry argues that a sermon works best when it opens with an ambiguity, a problem, contradiction, or discrepancy to be solved. The sermon is plotted by beginning it with a disequilibrium, such as Phillips Brooks's opening line, "It is not easy to decide just what the apostles expected with reference to the second coming" (Lowry 1980, 36). Lowry explains:

The homiletical vision expressed in this writing assumes that ambiguity and its resolution is the basic form-ingredient to any sermon, whether life-situational, expository, doctrinal, etc., in content. There is always one major discrepancy, bind, or problem which is the issue. The central task of any sermon, therefore, is the resolution of that particular central ambiguity" (Lowry 1980, 31).

Irony thrives on the reversal of fortune. God roots for the underdog. The scrawny David killed the giant. Joseph knew more than all the Egyptian magicians. Daniel and the Hebrew children were more buff eating kale and drinking water than the children of the Babylonian ruling class who ate beef and drank milkshakes. Nehemiah won the showdown with the kings that surrounded Jerusalem by declaring, "The God of heaven will give us success; therefore we His servants will arise and build, but you have no portion, right or memorial to Jerusalem" (Neh. 2:20, NASB). The prostitute Rahab, who lived on the wall of Jericho, fully grasped the implications of an encroaching army commanded by no less than God:

> I know that the LORD has given you this land, and that the terror of you
> has fallen on us, and that all the inhabitants of the land have melted be-
> fore you. For we have heard how the LORD dried up the water of the Red
> Sea before you when you came out of Egypt, what you did to the two kings
> of the Amorites who were beyond the Jordan, to Sihon and Og, whom you
> utterly destroyed. When we heard it, our hearts melted and no courage re-
> mained in any man any longer because of you; for the LORD your God, He
> is God in heaven above and on earth beneath (Josh. 2:9-11, NASB).

In that the harlot Rahab is one of two women who made it to God's hall of fame (see Heb. 11), the story is worth a double take (Sarah is the other woman—having a baby at age 90 meets the criterion for anybody's hall of fame). As one reads the story about the conquering of Jericho, a critical question surfaces: Why did God send two spies to gather intelligence from someone who lived in the city? The spy endeavor had failed 40 years earlier. What if one or both of these spies returned with a negative report: "They've got enough ammo in that place to blow us back to the Sinai desert!" We're certain that one of them did not carry a listening device while the other sat in a van recording military strategy leaked by government insiders. Why did Israel need information from the inside of the city when Jericho would fall by simply marching around it? God's actions are never superfluous; thus the deployment of intelligence agents cues God's intention: God came not to sack a city but to save a sinner. Thus, playful speculation discovers that God's ultimate purpose is never destruction, but always redemption. Possible title for a Rahab narrative sermon: "The mole on the wall who made it to the hall."

irony as the key to tragedy and radical grace

The above may lead one to believe that God's irony always produces happy endings. To the contrary, humankind is often its own worst enemy. Edwin Good, in his *Irony in the Old Testament,* reminds us of irony's underside. Humanity, which wants to become like God, becomes less than human. The couple who were assigned to rule the earth became slaves of the soil. Grasping for everything, Adam and Eve lost everything. The tower meant to unite earth's inhabitants fragmented humankind. But all of this is not without its humorous elements. Fleeing from fire and brimstone, Lot argued about the escape route. He would have rather not gone through the hill country. Misplaced priorities and values demonstrate confusion, the ludicrous disjunctions easily seen by us who know the whole story, in contrast to the person caught in a fragmented experience. Persons clutching household items have been discovered in the lava that spewed out of Vesuvius and swallowed Pompeii. Those of us who know the rest of the story smile at the person painting the deck chairs on the Titanic.

Genesis 49 provides the classic example of God's action hardly ever aligning itself with human perception. The blessing of the patriarch Jacob miscues at several points. The tribe of Levi became priests for the nation of Israel, the most prestigious function in the Hebrew economy. Yet Jacob says, "Cursed be their anger, for it is fierce; and their wrath, for it is cruel. I will despise them in Jacob and scatter them in Israel" (49:7, NASB). Logic calls for Judah to serve as the high priest, since he is the one who interceded to Joseph for his brothers, and Joseph should be in the lineage of Christ, since he functioned as the redemptive link for the Jacob clan. But neither of these assumptions was to prove true.

Of all people to preserve the Messianic line, to produce the Lion who would offer salvation to all of humankind, Judah was the least likely of the 12 brothers. He was a case in point for egregious and impetuous decision making. Homiletical intrigue can be had with speculation as to why Judah produced the blood lineage that gave birth to the Messiah. He must have read bedtime stories to his children. His must have been a model Rotarian. Did he coach Little League baseball? Was he a troop master for the Boy Scouts? The truth is, we do not know of anything that Judah did right as father, husband, or civic leader. What we do know, is that Judah entered into a bad marriage with a Canaanite woman. We know that his sons were so evil that God slew them. After his wife died, he was without sexual fulfillment. Instead of remarrying, he sought out a prostitute, or one whom he thought was a prostitute. Tamar, wife of his deceased son Er, dressing as a harlot and positioning herself in the red-light district, deceived her father-in-law, either as revenge or mockery for failing to provide her a husband. When Judah attempted to retrieve his staff and family seal, left in payment for Tamar's sexual favor, she was nowhere to be found. Rather than pressing the matter, Judah stated, "Let her keep them, otherwise we will become a laughingstock" (Gen. 38:23, NASB).

As they say, the rest is history. To the above illicit tryst were born twin boys, Zerah and Perez. Three verses into Matthew, we find Perez in the lineage of Christ. "Laughingstock" does not seem to be very suitable material out of which to construct a Messianic throne. (Irony is further heightened because, as mentioned earlier, Perez represents the reversal of the status of the first born, a consistent theme throughout Genesis.) That Perez, a bastard son, conceived in a burning passion of incestuous lust, would serve as a genetic link to the pure and holy Son of God is, indeed, a grotesque irony. We might forthrightly ask God, "Is this the best You could do to produce a Savior? Why didn't You start over?" A careful reading of the Pentateuch reminds us that God was often tempted to start over, to destroy the nation of Israel, and begin anew with another people. Steven McCutchan suggests the following dialogue between God and Moses:

GOD: Look what your people are doing!

MOSES: Uh, I AM, it is a long way down the mountain; I am not able to see as far as your are, I AM.

GOD: Oh, yeah, sorry about that.

MOSES: Besides, what is this "my people" bit? A little while ago they were "your people." Don't forget, I was quite happy tending my sheep in the desert. It was your idea to bring them out of Egypt.

GOD: Moses, when they obey they are *my* people; when they disobey they are your people, and right now they are *disobeying.*

MOSES: I am not sure I like those terms, but I am not sure I have any choice. Oh, well, let me have the worst: what are they doing?

GOD: They are building a golden calf! And they are dancing and playing ribald games.

MOSES: Oh, God!

GOD: What's that?

MOSES: Nothing, it is just an expression. It is a little easier than saying, Oh, I AM.

GOD: I see.

MOSES: Listen, I AM. Maybe they are just making a gift for you.

GOD: It is very clearly stated right here in paragraph two: Thou shalt not make unto thyself any graven image.

MOSES: Well, maybe they misunderstood. You know, people don't speak that King James Hebrew anymore.

GOD: Do not make excuses for them, Moses. Yours are a stiff-necked people. Now, therefore, let me alone that my wrath may burn hot against them and I may consume them.

MOSES: Listen, I AM. I do not think that is a very good idea.

GOD: Why not?

MOSES: Well, it is not very good PR, that's all.

GOD: PR?

MOSES: Sure. You have to think of the Egyptian press. I can just see the headlines now: RADICAL GOD LOSES TEMPER, CONSUMES PEOPLE WITH HOT WRATH. Who's going to want to join a community with a God like that? (Adams 1997, 106-7).

Certainly God could have discovered more trustworthy people to model and spread the message of radical monotheism than the dim-witted Hebrews, so called because of their always being covered with the dust stirred up by the sheep, goats, and camels they tended. The good news of the infortuitous events in Judah's life: God has never started over, and He never will. He will take us right where we are, transforming sordid lives and deeds, in order to glorify himself. God never changes our story. Instead, He clothes it with redeeming grace that constantly reminds us that no past is so dark it cannot be brought to the light of God's salvation. If God chose only those with a perfect past, what hope would there be for you and me? It is only through the discovery of irony that we begin to perceive the depth of the human problem and the radical nature of grace.

choosing an ironic rather than a self-evident text

An ironic text occurs in Joshua's final speech to the Hebrew people: "You will not be able to serve the LORD, for He is a holy God. He is a jealous God; He will not forgive your transgression or your sins" (Josh. 24:19, NASB). The deductive text, four verses earlier, beckons to us: "But as for me and my house, we will serve the LORD" (v. 15, NASB). We resist the temptation to preach on 24:15 because it is a self-evident proposition. In contrast, Joshua's negative prediction (24:19) intrigues us because it upsets the equilibrium of

God's economy. The irony of Joshua's negativism is that there was every reason for valediction and no cause for malediction. Before Joshua's last will
and testament, 13 victories occurred under his military command against 1
defeat. The second irony is that telling people they cannot do something creates a sure formula for failure, or so we think. Telling Israel they can't be holy
goes against everything we believe about God's expectations for His people.
The nations that stood before Joshua cried out in rebuttal, "No, but we will
serve the LORD" (v. 21, NASB). Guess who was right? The next chapter, Judges
1, narrates a litany of Israel's failures to liquidate the Canaanites and to follow God's law of holiness, noncontamination and nonaccommodation. "It
came about when Israel became strong, that they put the Canaanites to
forced labor, but they did not drive them out completely" (Judg. 1:28, NASB).
Israel's half measures evolved into dire circumstances: "Then the Amorites
forced the sons of Dan into the hill country, for they did not allow them to
come down into the valley" (v. 34, NASB).

The holiness code "Be Ye Holy for I am Holy," the no-compromise law of
separation, is stated three times in the Old Testament, each time in a noncontamination context (Lev. 11:45; 19:2; 20:26). "You can eat an animal
that chews the cud and divides the hoof, but don't eat an animal that does
one or the other" (see 11:3-4). "Don't sow a field with two kinds of seed,
weave a garment of two kinds of fibers or mate two kinds of animals" (see
19:19). "Any man from the sons of Israel or from the aliens sojourning in Israel who gives any of his offspring to Molech, shall surely be put to death;
the people of the land shall stone him with stones" (20:2, NASB). Child sacrifice was the ultimate taboo, a horrifying sin that the Israelites would later
commit. The point is that nonaccommodationism is impossible, unless we
join some monastic order or live the life of a hermit; we eventually take on
the hues that surround us. Compromise is so subtle, we hardly know when it
takes place. The desires for legitimation, inclusion, and acceptance eventually
trump the command to be separate from the world's values. Joshua was exactly right; we are not able to be holy, at least in our own strength.

A humanistic effort at holiness is akin to a self-removal gall bladder kit.
Even though it can be bought for only $14.95, it's messy, painful, and down-
right impossible. Transforming holiness into a herculean effort reduces one
to the pathetic central character in Flannery O'Connor's *Wise Blood*, who kept
pieces of glass and rock in his shoes, put his eyes out with acid, and wrapped
his chest with barbed wire to atone for his sins, all which led to a hopeless
and tragic death. Many of our attempts at righteousness fall into the trap of

Benjamin Franklin's "Pull yourself up by your own bootstraps" theology. As
Franklin was conquering the virtues of life, working on a separate one each
week (12 of them including temperance, orderliness, and frugality), a Quaker
friend said to him, "Ben, you are known to be a proud man." Thus, Franklin
added a 13th virtue to his list: humility. After giving extended effort to attain-
ing humility, Franklin confessed: "I discovered nothing was so difficult to ex-
tract from the human condition as pride, and if I did overcome my pride, I
would probably be proud of my humility." Achieving holiness is a losing
proposition. In fact, it is a contradiction in terms.

Quite surprisingly, the holiness code is quoted only once in the New Testament and even more amazing, it is quoted by Peter, hardly the model for
moral courage. Peter's braggadocian claims to stalwart faithfulness in following Christ consistently ended in disasters. Jesus becomes so exasperated
with him that at one point He virtually levels him with unequivocal condemnation: "Get behind Me, Satan! You are a stumbling block to Me; for you are
not setting your mind on God's interest, but man's" (Matt. 16:23, NASB). The
comical event already alluded to in chapter 2, the cutting off Malchus's ear,
again highlighted Peter's blundering attempt to play the hero. For him to be
carrying one of the two swords in the disciples possession (Luke 22:38), did
Peter claim that he had taken fencing lessons or that he had trained as a
gladiator? Peter was to prove no exception to the rule that fishermen make
poor swordsmen. Standing behind Malchus, meaning to run him through,
Peter can only manage to catch his ear. Another failure!

Peter would go down in New Testament history as a blowhard—one who
talked a better game than he played. He betrayed his loyalty to Jesus with a
shameful denial. A person who could not stand up to the accusations of a
servant girl doesn't seem to be a logical exponent for the holiness code,
which is the whole point. Peter's failures brought him to the realization of his
own moral bankruptcy. He discovered the truth of Joshua's summation of
the human condition. No amount of effort will achieve holiness. Holiness is
not a moral effort. It is a gift from God. "Be ye holy; for I am holy" (1 Pet.
1:16, KJV) is not primarily a command, standard, or moral obligation. It is a
promise and a provision. The only way a person can be holy is to receive it as
a gift. Holiness is not primarily what I do, but what God does. No, I can't be
holy, but there is One who can make me holy and keep me holy through His
shed blood. Why else would Peter have written,

Seeing that His divine power has granted to us everything pertaining
to life and godliness, through the true knowledge of Him who called us by

His own glory and excellence. For by these He has granted to us His precious and magnificent promises, so that by them you might become partakers of the divine nature, having escaped the corruption that is in the world by lust" *(2 Pet. 1:3-4, NASB)*.

hosea as archetypical irony

Hosea masters both irony and analogy. Outrageous love stalks the prostitute, who has indiscriminately sold herself, like a jackass in heat, braying in a field to whoever will pay attention. How could Israel have been so unfaithful in the light of God's covenant of faithfulness? God's blessing ironically resulted in Israel both cursing and biting the very hand that fed it. "Israel is a luxuriant vine; He produces fruit for himself the more his fruit, the more he made; the richer his land, the better he made the sacred pillars. Their heart is faithless" (10:1-2, NASB). Israel's faithless fickleness affects mood swings in a Father who doesn't know whether to scorn or console, love or reject, banish or embrace. Not that God is inconsistent but the sins of a wayward wife challenged the emotions of even deity. If they didn't, He would be a cold dictator rather than a loving husband. God as the wounded husband was hurt, frustrated, bewildered, jealous, angry, and perplexed as to what would assure Israel of His covenant love. "What shall I do with you, O Ephraim? What shall I do with you, O Judah? For your loyalty is like a morning cloud and like the dew which goes away early" (Hos. 6:4, NASB). Jemielity comments: "With Hosea we enter an ironic world like Samuel Beckett's *Waiting for Godot* or (Evelyn) Waugh's *Vile Bodies*. The text itself is a jumble of foreign content, almost that very parody of form, of fragmented, incomplete utterance which accidently or deliberately appears repeatedly in the tradition of satire and irony" (Jemielity 1992, 112).

Wicked and wanton disregard for God's unfailing love and provision demands a radical and absurd response. God commands Hosea not only to marry a prostitute but also, after betrothal when she has spurned his love, to marry her again. The three children born to the marriage are given names that represent the self-destructiveness and dysfunctionalism that mar, mock, and cripple the family: "Delayed Damnation," "No More Mercy," and "Illegitimate." No hope for health and happiness in this home. Imagine the conversational love and intimacy when Dad barks, "Delayed Damnation, do the dishes"; or Mom commands No More Mercy to mow the lawn or Illegitimate to take out the trash. The vibes intensify the shame and guilt for people who hardly ever know a joyful moment.

I choose a contemporary setting to enable both my hearers and me to grasp the intensity of God's unfailing love. A pastor, who longs to enable his congregation to fall in love with Christ, is commanded by God to visit the red-light district of his city and bring home a prostitute. Wow! Did the church ever wake up when he brought his red-light district prize to church the next morning. Instead of a yawn, there was a scowl. Instead of dozing, the congregation disdained. Instead of wide-open arms welcoming the pastor's new wife, there was gossip. Well, at least the preacher had their attention. When Gomer forsook the family for her old lifestyle, there were plenty of "I told you so's" and an abundance of Scripture quotations such as, "You can't cast pearls before swine" (see Matt. 7:6), or that American aphorism, "You can't make a silk purse out of a sow's ear." Deep depression consumed the pastor. What was he going to do with three children while he pastored a church? Perhaps he misunderstood God's call on his life. His old job at J. C. Penney's was looking better all the time.

No one was more surprised than Hosea when God told him to marry Gomer for the second time. No need going into the sordid details, but this time Gomer's situation was far more desperate. She was enslaved to her pimp to the tune of $15,000. That was every cent Hosea had in the bank, a retirement fund with which he would one day buy a small retirement home down in the Ozarks. With no little doubt and a whole lot of reservation, he withdrew the entire amount and bought Gomer's freedom. The church was so embarrassed that they called for a congregational meeting with the ex-pressed intention of voting out the pastor. Doctor Simon Saint chaired the meeting with Gomer and Hosea sitting on the front pew. "Birds of a feather flock together" was proof enough that the pastor had disgraced the church, and it would never be able to recover its reputation in the community as a holy church, a congregation with high standards and strict entrance requirements. Even if there was not much joy in the church, it would be a place of punctilious order and righteous indignation. It was said of Si Saint, "If heaven wasn't ready when he got there, it soon would be."

Hosea answered the bell. Looking Si Saint in the eyes with both empathy and sincerity he said, "You know, I didn't have to pastor this church. Just out of seminary I received a call to a church three times the size of this church. They had a magnificent new parsonage, quite unlike the three-bedroom, one-bathroom rundown flat that you put me in. They offered me a new Mercedes; instead, I have been driving a 1985 Hyundai. Their salary was five times as much as I am getting paid. But I didn't want to pastor a church that was so prosperous that it no longer had to depend on God. I wanted to lead a group of people that were more concerned about others than themselves; who spent more energy on the outside of the church than the inside; who were constantly longing to seek and save the lost; who were more concerned about ministering than being ministered to. I could have married the cover girl on *Vogue* magazine. But instead, I chose to be married to a prostitute, you!"

It got so quiet in the church that you could hear the electricity running through the wires. God overwhelmed us with His love on that day. The real miracle is we received it. God rescued us from our self-serving agendas. Preoccupation with ourselves melted in the warmth of God's transforming grace. Ladies gathered around Gomer, consumed her with compassion, and let her know that she was the best thing that had ever happened to that church. I don't know why Gomer had sold her body to men who would only abuse her. I do know that there are only two kinds of people in the world, those who have been loved and those who haven't. I also know that good things happen when persons receive compassion rather than condemnation.

The name of the church was changed from "We're the Elect" to the "Church of the Wedding." We would celebrate the marriage of Hosea and Gomer. I have never seen a bride so radiant, a bridegroom so majestic. "Wow" and "Oh my" were heard as the bride and her attendants, dressed in dazzling white, stood at the front of the church. When the bridegroom came down the aisle on a white horse, instead of standing, the wedding party and all of the congregation fell on their faces crying out, "Hallelujah," "Amen," and ascriptions of praise crescendoing to "Worthy is the Lamb that was slain to receive power and riches and wisdom and might and honor and glory and blessing" (Rev. 5:12, NASB).

Did I forget to tell you that the names of all of the family members were changed? Hosea's name was changed to "Savior." Gomer became "Perfection." Delayed Damnation was forever referred to as "Already Redeemed." We started calling No More Mercy "Plenty of Grace"; and Illegitimate became "Belongs to God." Every Sunday since the Wedding we have celebrated a marriage between Savior and Perfection. Every worship service is a wedding celebrating the Bridegroom's love for His Bride. People from miles around come to our church. No matter who they are, they are received with rejoicing, and no matter how many come, there is always room. And the church has sent me to invite you: "The Spirit and the bride say, 'Come' and let the one who hears say, 'Come' and let the one who is thirsty come; let the one who wishes take the water of life without cost" (Rev. 22:17, NASB). The promise of

God was fulfilled:
>   I will heal their apostasy,
>>   I will love them freely,
>>   For My anger has turned away from them.
>
>   I will be like the dew to Israel;
>>   He will blossom like the lily,
>>   And he will take root like cedars of Lebanon.
>
>   His shoots will sprout,
>>   And his beauty will be like the olive tree
>>   And his fragrance like the cedars of Lebanon.
>
>   Those who live in his shadow
>>   Will again raise grain,
>>   And they will blossom like the vine (Hos. 14:4-7, NASB).

More than any other Old Testament prophet Hosea championed irony with an archetypical metaphor for God's relationship to humanity. At no place do we look deeper into the heart of God than when we contemplate God's relentless love for someone who least deserved it. No sin is so deep, no shame so embarrassing, no history so dark that it cannot be redeemed with God's love. Hosea proclaims that there is room at the Cross for even you and me.

christ's use of irony

No communicator ever employed the rhetoric of irony, satire, and sarcasm more than did Jesus. Hardly anything He said or did corresponded with the conventional wisdom that defined the ruling theology. What the religious leaders touted as wisdom, Jesus referred to as blindness, a smug detachment from what really matters. The Gospel of John contrasts the blind ignorance of the Pharisees with the wisdom of God's intention and redemptive plan for all peoples. This contrast ascends to comedic levels when a blind man who has received his sight says to the religious leaders, "Well, here is an amazing thing, that you do not know where He is from, and yet He opened my eyes" (9:30, NASB). The Pharisees condemned Jesus for healing on the Sabbath rather than praising Him for giving 20/20 vision to a man who had never looked into a woman's face, had never understood what a cloud looks like, and did not have the foggiest notion how the drab barrenness of winter looks different from the budding green of springtime. Indeed, the reigning theology, "Strain at a gnat and swallow a camel" (see Matt. 23:24), led to professors of ethics forgetting to remove the beam from their own eye before removing a speck of dust from someone else's (see Matt. 7:3). They occupied themselves with arranging the cups in the cupboard, in the path of a tornado packing 200-mile-an-hour winds.

Immediately after saying, "For judgment I came into this world, so that those who do not see may see, and that those who see may become blind. . . . If you were blind, you would have no sin; but since you say, 'We see,' your sin remains" (John 9:39, 41, NASB). Jesus gave a discourse on sheep. Sheep are dumb by any estimation. Sheep thrive on bewilderment and confusion. Dogs herding sheep is the most intriguing interaction I have ever witnessed between different species of animals. The dog scurries back and forth across the back of the sheep, intermittently jumping off to nip and bark at their heels. The dogs comprehend a plan and purpose that are unknown to the sheep. Sheep are dumber than dogs, yet the sheep know more than the brightest and educated of the day; the sheep know the voice of the shepherd, the door of the sheep, and, most importantly, the shepherd himself. "He who is a hired hand, and not a shepherd, who is not the owner of the sheep, sees the wolf coming, and leaves the sheep and flees, and the wolf snatches them and scatters them" (10:12, NASB). The Pharisees had been tried and condemned and didn't know it. But maybe they did. "I told you, and you do not believe; the works that I do in *My Father's* name, these testify of Me. But you do not believe, because you are not of *My* sheep" (vv. 25-26, NASB, emphasis added).

Jesus deals out a theology of the absurd. Those that work the most are paid the same as those who work the least; the person who secures his future has no future; the person who gives the least has a verbal memorial erected in her honor and all of this is underlined with Jesus' declaration that "whoever saves his life will lose it" (see Matt. 16:24; Mark 8:35; Luke 9:24; 17:33). Jesus has come to construct an upside-down kingdom, undermining an ethical house constructed of pious platitudes. Hypocrisy would be exposed for what it was, vain self-promotion that posed in the guises of ostentatious alms giving, pretentious asceticism, and repetitious ritual. Christ's assessment of trying to impress God as well as one's peers is as unsettling now as it was then. "If you receive a reward in this life, don't expect one in the next" (see Matt. 6:1-4). Christ reminded us that the motive behind the deed is more critical than the deed itself. In other words, the real problem of life is not doing good, it is doing good without others knowing it. Christ used irony, satire, and, above all, parable to enable all of us to comb our souls for the infectious lice of self-aggrandizement.

In *The Humor of Christ*, Elton Trueblood wrote, "Though Christ employed several types of humor, the most common type which he used is irony, i.e., a holding up to public view of either vice or folly, but without a note of bitterness or the attempt to harm" (Trueblood 1964, 55). Christ majored in irony that could be seen. "Thus, when you give alms, sound no trumpet before you, as the hypocrites do in the synagogues and in the street, that they may be praised by men" (Matt. 6:2, RSV). If you want to catch the full effect of this ludicrous disjuncture, stand up and blow a trumpet as you drop your tithe in the offering plate next Sunday.

After Jesus warned against the kind of sensationalism that gets up a crowd (Matt 24:26) and the difficulty of localizing God (24:27), He stated: "Wherever the corpse is, there the vultures will gather" (24:28, NASB). Was Jesus saying, "Don't boast about numbers. All you need to get up a crowd is something that stinks"? Imagine a megapastor standing up before the Sunday morning crowd that has gathered to hear some movie star or other celebrity giving their testimony (I find nothing much more entertaining than the Saturday newspaper advertisements for Sunday church) and saying, "You people have about the same mentality as vultures."

Jesus must have smiled to himself when he nicknamed Peter "Rocky," that paragon of restraint and stability. Peter stuck his foot in his mouth so many times that for his first meal of the day he put ketchup on his shoelaces. Sort of like calling Muhammad Ali a shining example of meekness. Trueblood observes that "If this was the 'Rock' on which the redemptive fellowship had to be built, it certainly seemed to be a shaky foundation" (Trueblood 1964, 63). Christ's use of parody underscores the inherent truth of His irony. Shakiness is all that God has to work with when it comes to building the unshakable Kingdom. After all, concrete begins with shifting sand.

The essence of Christ's teaching was, "You have heard, but I say." True religion, if it was going to be more substantial than hay, wood, and stubble, would have to totally infiltrate and integrate attitudes and motivations; all would have to be directed to God's glory instead of self-seeking. What was so upsetting in this new teaching was that it exposed us for who we truly are in the light of God's perspective, the only assessment that really counts. Robert Tannehill claims that the sayings of Jesus act as jolts, challenging and disrupting the fixed structures of meaning that inhere in the nature of reality itself. He argues that forceful and imaginative language operates in the religious dimension of life in ways that rational language finds itself inept and impotent. Attitudes, customs, and bias are so deeply ingrained that Jesus means His words to act as megaphones shouting, "The problem is much bigger than you think." Words must invade the conscience, an almost inpregnable fortress built of rationalization and all other ego defenses that make up the walls of both self-presentation and self-preservation. The persons of a society obsessed with image and impression will not easily submit to a gospel that calls for transparency. Tannehill writes, "If the text has its weapons we have our armor. We are not inclined to allow tampering with the depth of our personal existence" (Tannehill 1975, 56). This inversion of values disrupts the status quo. Jesus means to disturb; thus there is almost always fallout.

No symbolism in the life of Christ escapes the ironic: the manger, the towel and basin, the donkey that Christ rode into Jerusalem, and ultimately the Cross. When Jacques-Louis David painted *Napoleon Crossing the Alps,* he placed the French general, later to have himself crowned emperor, on a magnificent steed. Actually, Napoleon crossed the rugged and perilous mountainous range on a mule, the only animal sure-footed enough to carry him. No aspiring emancipator should be seen riding on a mule. No conqueror other than Jesus has ever entered a city riding a donkey. The apostle Paul biographically sketched the absurdities that the Incarnation entailed: He "emptied Himself, taking the form of a bond-servant, and being made in the likeness of men. . . . He humbled Himself by becoming obedient to the point of death, even death on the cross" (Phil. 2:7-8, NASB).

christ's life as irony

No man ever left more ironic contradictions in His wake than did Jesus. "He came to His own, and His own did not receive Him" (John 1:11, NKJV). He founded the world's most numerically populated religion, but the religious rejected Him. Salvation was of the Jews, but the Jews did not accept Him as their Messiah. The included were excluded and the excluded were included. Right off the bat, Jesus let the somebodies know that they were nobodies. When He reminded His first congregation that Elijah visited only a Sidonian widow and Elisha healed only a Syrian commander, "All the people in the synagogue were filled with rage as they heard these things; and they got up and drove Him out of the city, and led Him to the brow of the hill on which their city had been built, in order to throw Him down the cliff" (Luke 4:28-29, NASB). No parish ever turned on a pastor quicker than the synagogue crowd in Jesus' hometown.

Christ opposed those who live in a house of moral certitude. The Pharisees were His favorite target, because they, unlike the Sadducees, based salvation on the strict observance of the Mishnah, the moral law that had accreted around the Levitical code. Moral minutia was so obtuse and complicated that only professionals could interpret it, and often they did not agree. Jesus lashed out at the oppressive bondage in a manner that, no doubt, made His disciples cringe: "Woe to you lawyers as well! For you weigh men down with burdens hard to bear, while you yourselves will not even touch the burdens with one of your fingers" (11:46, NASB). This statement of Christ reveals a double irony. The Law of Moses, which was meant to usher in Jubilee, rest, and freedom, had led only to bondage, and second, what the religious teachers demanded of others, they somehow felt themselves exempt. Only iconoclastic language bordering on insult would break through such blindness. Jesus had no patience with those that project on others higher standards than they require of themselves. At times Jesus allowed His listeners to draw their own conclusions; at other times there would be no doubt about His conclusion: "Now you Pharisees clean the outside of the cup and of the platter, but inside of you, you are full of robbery and wickedness" (v. 39, NASB). Here was more straightforward irony, untempered by civility, lest the point be missed, and it wasn't: "One of the lawyers said to Him in reply, 'Teacher, when You say this, You insult us too'" (v. 45, NASB). Jesus, the meek, mild Lamb of God. The King of insult! More irony!

irony as sarcasm

Not having been personally present, we have difficulty in identifying sarcasm in the sayings of Christ. If John Crossan is even partially correct in characterizing Jesus as a nomadic cynic, then Jesus must have used sarcasm, an indirect form of satire, a stroke of genius, deftly painting listeners into the picture without them knowing it. Sarcasm is intriguing for the interpreter because it may be individually and differently translated and applied by those who hear it. Sarcasm creates absurdities for the purpose of dislodging misperceptions that border on stupidity. Trueblood is convinced that Jesus was joking with the following statement: "And I tell you, make friends for yourselves by means of unrighteous mammon, so that when it fails they may receive you in eternal habitation" (Luke 16:9, RSV). Or in other words, "You think that the crooks and swindlers that you hang around are going to form the welcoming committee for heaven." Jesus did not caustically sneer at the stupidity of the "righteous" but did satirically expose falsehood with a ridiculous statement. Though Trueblood hesitates to use the word *sarcasm* because of its bitter tone, he interprets that Jesus "is making a statement so preposterous that the sensitive hearer is suppose to be able to see that the clear intent is the exact opposite of the literal statement" (Trueblood 1964, 102).

Jesus' instruction to His disciples to sell their coats and buy swords is ludicrous, unless one interprets it as sarcasm or, at least, irony. This command comes on the heels of Peter's declaring with sonorous bravado, "Lord, with you, I am ready to go to both prison and to death." Is Jesus saying, "If you are so brave, why don't you go ahead and buy a sword?" The whole passage is cued by the argument about who was to be regarded as the greatest. Again, the disciples misunderstood the essence of the Kingdom, "But it is not this way with you, but the one who is the greatest among you must become like the youngest, and the leader like the server" (Luke 22:26, NASB). Their thickheadedness, often akin to mine, may have left Jesus exasperated. "OK. You want to go the world's route? You want to establish an earthly kingdom? Go ahead and buy a sword." Obviously, they didn't get it. The disciples scrounged through their meager military depot and came up with two swords, to which Jesus responded. "It is enough." More sarcasm? Christ's "enough" may represent a sarcastic jest to fishermen being translated into gladiators. "It wouldn't make any difference if you had one thousand swords." At the bottom of this enigmatic exchange is the theological truth that Jesus could have well intended. One sword plus God equals God. Two swords plus God equals God. A million swords plus God equals God. The math is always the same. The only part of the equation that matters is God.

I am aware of other interpretations of this text. John Milbank opines that Christ is fulfilling the prophecy, "He was reckoned with the transgressors" (Milbank 1997, 145). Jesus would provide substantive evidence that He and His crowd possessed an unregistered weapon. "That will be enough to do us in." I am confident that my conjecture is no more on target than is Milbank's. Such is the freedom of biblical hermeneutics, a freedom that each of us allows the other.

The above multiple interpretations provide homiletical intrigue that should captivate both preacher and listener. No saying or incident has been more puzzling than Christ's encounter with the Syrophoenician woman. When she implored him to heal her demon-possessed daughter, Christ responded, "It is not good to take the children's bread and throw it to the dogs." Some biblical scholars have tried to get Jesus off the hook by pointing out that the Greek word used for dog in each of the Synoptics connotes a puppy. Yet because Jesus spoke in Aramaic, we are left in the dark as to the exact word that Jesus used. Thus, the word for dog is left to the Gospel writer's discretion.

Since inclusion is one of the salient themes of Christ's ministry, we suspect that the encounter was another opportunity to combat the prejudice of His disciples and whoever else may have been observing. Jesus' reference to the above lady as a dog leads me to believe that He was mouthing exactly what His disciples were thinking. They would have not only referred to the woman as a dog but were tempted to epithets even more insulting. It really must have dumbfounded the disciples when Christ allowed the woman to rebuke both Him and them. "Yes, Lord, but even the dogs feed on the crumbs which fall from their masters' table" (Matt. 15:27, NASB). Could Jesus have set up a more effective exchange for getting the disciples' attention? One wonders if Christ slowly looked around at His followers before He said, "Oh woman, your faith is great, it shall be done for you as you wish" (v. 28, NASB). If this woman was a dog, she had come out looking like a Great Dane groomed for first prize. Christ had allowed a pagan female to theologically trump mean-spirited, holier-than-thou, "we've got more important business to attend to," chauvinistic religion. Did the disciples leave muttering to themselves or simply say nothing for the next several hours?

the cursing of the fig tree

On the surface, Jesus' actions are a conundrum, out of character with the God who incarnates love of both neighbor and enemy. At first impression, Jesus laying waste to the Temple and cursing the fig tree seem little more than road rage. Yet these actions fulfill the divine image just as much as the placid Jesus who meekly enters Jerusalem on a donkey. Both the trashing and the cursing take place after the Triumphal Entry recorded by Matthew and Mark. Thus, the last week of Christ's life portrays a contradictory Savior, a person on whose wrong side we wouldn't want to get. These incidents provide the perfect opportunities to theologically explore the humanity of Christ in ways not henceforth revealed. These perplexing actions challenge our best psychological inquiry and imagination. The smiting of the fig tree may have indicated that Jesus was just simply hungry. But if one notices, the disciples and Jesus left from Bethphage, meaning "house of figs." Why didn't they fill up a knapsack with figs, devouring it at a midmorning stop? As Jesus trashed the Temple and cursed the fig tree, maybe He was spewing out the doom and gloom that overwhelmed Him as He faced the Cross. At one point He confessed, "My spirit is heavy within me" (John 12:27). This kind of homiletical peeling of layers off the narrative allows us to identify the humanity of Christ but not discover the heart of Jesus' actions.

The irony of Christ's cursing the fig tree is heightened by two facts given by the Gospel writers. Matthew tells us that the fig tree was by itself (21:19). In other words, the tree was an accident. A farmer doesn't plant a tree alone on the side of the hill to be beaten by the wind, scorched by the sun, and pelted by sand in shallow, rocky soil. There was no evidence that the tree was ever nurtured, fertilized, or cared for in any way. It must have looked over at the grove of olive trees and said to itself, "Well, look at them. They've got the comfort, care, and protection of one another. I'm right here by myself and no one cares a lick about what happens to me." This fig tree deserved far more pity than it did scorn.

The second ironic characteristic of the fig tree is that "it was not the season for figs" (Mark. 11:15). This particular observation accented Jesus' non-empathy and senseless condemnation. He was demanding that which is impossible, which is the very point of the narrative. The observation that the fig tree was withered from the roots up was followed by possibly the most preposterous promise that Christ ever made, "Truly I say to you, whoever says to this mountain, 'Be taken up and cast into the sea,' and does not doubt in his heart, but believes that what he says is going to happen, it will be granted to him" (v. 23, NASB). That improbability is no greater than fulfilling Christ's next command, "Forgive, if you have anything against anyone" (v. 25, NASB). All of these images represent human impossibilities outside the possibilities of grace. For any of them, within my own incapacities, it is always out of season. Whatever I say to God, when I stand before Him in the last day (of course I will be speechless), I better not say, "God, You don't understand, it was out of season." Or "You don't understand the circumstances I was in, the soil was shallow, the wind was blowing, the sun was scorching, and I was alone, all by myself." In the kingdom of God, no excuse is ever good enough for fruitlessness. Why? Because Jesus unequivocally stated that "I am the vine, you are the branches; he who abides in Me and I in him, he bears much fruit, for apart from Me you can do nothing" (John 15:5, NASB). Fruit bearing is a sure thing when one abides in Christ.

the gospel as postmodern irony

All of the above demonstrates the inverted kingdom of God. These twists and turns (we don't quite know where we are going) argue for inductive preaching, an exploratory approach both for sermon production and sermon delivery. Hardly any of us would read anything, a short story or novel, that doesn't hold a certain amount of suspense. Tolstoy knew this when he wrote "Six Feet of Land" and O'Henry, when he penned the "Gift of the Magi." The former story demonstrates the malevolence of life, and the latter, the benevolence. Both stories boast of irony, a turning of the tables on misguided but well-intentioned people, persons sort of like you and me. Thus, they boast of the gospel's ultimate truth: the foolishness of the Cross is the wisdom of God. Irony provides a surprise ending to the story. O'Henry wrote, "I have lamely related to you the uneventful chronicle of two foolish children in a flat who most unwisely sacrificed for each other the greatest treasures of their house" (O'Henry 1988, 7).

Preaching that maintains the irony of the gospel presents a valid and primary option for postmodern preaching. Christ's stories reverse fortune, make sinners out to be saints, convert the pious into scoundrels, exalt the insignificant, and reduce life's normative concerns to mean scampering for self-gratification and glorification. They confront and condemn the alignments and values of American society, no less than the stratification and class-consciousness that defined Israel and the surrounding culture. Jesus' parables portend Jeffrey Archer stories, which leave the pretentions of western society wallowing in the dust of disillusionment. Thomas Oden's comments on Kierkegaard sum up all story spinners, who serve up irony to the delicious delight of those of us who love a good yarn, even if it does leave us with ketchup and mustard on our faces. "In order to qualify as a parable in a literary sense, a story must have aesthetic balance, some trenchant elements of metaphorical imagination, brevity and economy, limited development of characterization, and a concentrated plot with a powerful 'twist' or reversal of insight" (Oden 1978, xvi). Nobody did it better than Jesus.

Though our hearers will not recognize us as literary geniuses, which we aren't, they will be able to participate in the divine sense of humor. They will discover that God has the last laugh and that the joke is always on us. Irony is always the ultimate truth. It isn't that postmodernity doesn't believe in truths. It simply believes that there is no single truth to be elevated above a cacophony of competing beliefs. Nowhere does Jesus emphatically state that everyone is equal in God's eyes. He simply told a story of a Samaritan who acted a whole lot more neighborly than did the spiritually elite. The "Who is my neighbor?" inquisitor was left with much to think about, which isn't a bad goal for any sermon.

five

PREACHING as cinematography

the images of cinema

Nothing exceeds cinematography in persuasion through iconography. Clark Gable wearing no T-shirt in *It Happened One Night* inflicted a curse upon the men's underwear industry, while James Dean smoking a cigarette blessed the tobacco industry. For better or worse we become what we watch. Paul Newman and Meryl Streep become larger-than-life figures, especially in a day of the personality cult. These popular icons overshadow Jesus and Paul, no matter how attractive we try to make both them and other biblical characters. No amount of vivid prose can resurrect 2,000-year-old persons from the graves of obscurity, much less demonstrate that they are more valuable life models than the suave, debonair, and physically attractive stars that fill giant screens. This is all the more reason why we need the Holy Spirit to release both the imagination of the speaker and the hearer. The eye is the camera of the brain, and without the brain recognizing, retrieving, and interpreting everything that is seen, the eye is superfluous. Thus, the job of preaching is not to compete with the cinema but to prepare sanctified minds and hearts to be the ultimate evaluators as to whether the images that are projected by all forms of media are redemptive, or need to be damned to an eternal hell with the rest of Satan's lies.

As the dominant art form of the 21st century, cinematography capitalizes on images to communicate the movie's major theme or message. As we have argued, preaching works best when it can be seen, not with film clips, but with metaphorical images that carry the message. Preaching and cinematography use metaphor, both as an organizing principle and a vehicle to carry the central idea of the film or sermon. Sermons and movies project on an inanimate object a theology or philosophy, or draw from objects characteristics that are analogous to or representative of an idea. These objects often carry the omnipresence of commonness, or everydayness, but at times depend on unique images such as the *Maltese Falcon* ("what dreams are made of") in the movie by the same name or "Rosebud" (lost childhood) in *Citizen Kane*. The movies *Chocolat* and *Babette's Feast* utilize food to deliver messages of liberating grace and the sacramental value of community. In the movie *Titanic*, the ship itself stands as an archetype of technological pride and the inability of humankind to secure its own fate. After the ship hits an iceberg, partly because it was attempting to set a speed record across the Atlantic, the captain poignantly and sarcastically said to Bruce Isbay, the owner of the ship, "You will get your headlines." Isbay's vanity was at the expense of over 1,500 lives being lost at sea.

In my opinion, one of the most moving and certainly most theological scenes to ever occur in a movie provides the conclusion for *Places in the Heart.* The movie, set in the early 20th-century Deep South, depicts racism, adultery, and the eking out of a living by the widow of a sheriff who was accidentally shot by an African-American boy. The accident leads to a lynching and the Ku Klux Klan antagonizing the widow (Sally Field), who hires a black man (Danny Glover) to tend her crops. For the closing scene, the camera moves across the faces of all the antagonists in the story: Klansmen, the widow, the black farmhand, the sheriff, and the boy who killed him, as they sit in church and pass the Eucharist to one another with the words "the peace of Christ." The symbol of the body and blood of Christ displaces the hatred and violence that have plagued the southern community.

the influence of cinema

Cinema attendance dropped off dramatically during the postwar years. John Belton argues that the decline was not so much due to the competition of television as it was America's increased affluence and discretionary income. Americans increasingly gave time to golf, hunting, fishing, spectator sports, and family vacations. Both television and competitive athletics challenged movies to become more participatory. Cinemascope, panavision, and in particular 3D were all introduced as options superior to more passive television viewing. Movies advertised themselves as a medium that would allow the viewer "to be there." Nondifferentiation between actors and viewers, both of them sharing the same space, became the goal of both movie production and projection. Cinemarama filmed with three cameras and projected with three cameras.

When these three images were projected in the theatre by three synchronized projectors onto a deeply curved screen that extended across the full width of most movie palaces, they engulfed audiences, producing a powerful illusion of depth by filling the spectator's field of view, including peripheral vision. Multitrack stereophonic sound, which originated from five speakers situated behind the screen from a battery of surround speakers, placed to the sides of and behind the audience reinforced the spectators illusion of engulfment, which was described in the press as audience "participation" (Belton 1994, 262).

Although the cost of attending a theater goes up, the decline of cinema attendance in America has been stabilized, if not reversed. Americans in 2002 spent $9.4 billion on movie tickets, a 10 percent increase over the previous year (Barsotti 2004, 13). In 2005, 81 percent of Americans identified themselves as frequent (at least once a month) or occasional (once in six months) moviegoers. The younger an adult is, the more likely he or she is to be influenced by cinema. Eighteen- to 20-year-olds are twice as likely to frequent the theater as those who are over 50.

The option of cinema over TV, even big screen TV, is because of several reasons that relate to preaching. Theaters offer sacred space not in a Christian or theistic sense but in terms of sanctuary. Movies are preluded with the reminder to turn off cell phones and to remove children from the theater if they become a distraction. Home does not afford this kind of seclusion. Second, buying a movie ticket is a far more selective process than mindless channel surfing. Attending a theater encompasses an intentionality that does not normally motivate grabbing the TV remote. Thus, a movie becomes an event. Not many persons remember the dates of *Bonanza* and *Dallas* episodes, but standing in line for the opening of a *Star Wars* or a *Lord of the Rings* film becomes a part of one's personal narrative. David Morley, in a perceptive article "Television: Not So Much a Visual Medium, More of a Visual Object," contrasts the "social architecture" of cinema offering relaxation, fun, and excitement with the bland utilitarianism of TV:

> In the darkness of the theatre we find the very source of the fascination exercised by film—consider on the other hand the opposite experience, the experience of television which also shows films. Nothing, no fascination. The darkness is dissolved, the space is organized by furniture and familiar objects, tamed . . . television condemns us to the familiar whose household utensil it has become, just as the hearth once was flanked by its predictable communal stewing pot, in times past (Morley 1995, 171).

But there is a far greater reason than the above observations why someone settles into the dark of a theater. Of the three distinct pleasures that Jon Boorstin delineates coming from movie watching, the voyeur, the vicarious, and visceral, the last belongs almost totally to cinematography. If I stand in the Louvre and stare at the Mona Lisa, I am participating in voyeurism. If I read the *Grapes of Wrath,* I may or may not vicariously attach myself to the Joads and their pathetic lives as they make their way to California. But nothing in those art forms can make me strain every muscle as does being chased by a boulder with Indiana Jones in *Raiders of the Lost Ark,* hanging with Jimmy Stewart from a tall building in *Vertigo,* or escaping a dinosaur in *Jurassic Park.*

The exigencies kick their way into the subconscious to depths that are beyond the reach of even staged theater. The blind Audrey Hepburn attempting to escape a murderous intruder, played by Alan Arkin, engulfs the viewer with palpable anxiety while watching *Wait Until Dark*. One senses relief exiting the theater with the realization that it was only a movie. Boorstin writes that the aim of the director is, "To create a particular gut reaction in the audience. And in order to achieve the effect the director must look deep inside, not to plumb the subtleties of emotion, but to re-create the way the world looks to a person under stress. The director comes face-to-face with the subjective quality of lived experience" (Boorstin 1995, 119).

cinematographic preaching as phenomenology

Propositional, deductive preaching views truth as a staid, fixed point of reference. Truth is like a rock, having no life of its own. Cinematographic preaching allows for different frames of reference, correctly presuming that truth is more than a logical construct, other than a sentence written in black and white. Living truth is a consciousness informed by events and relationships. "Remember the Sabbath to keep it holy" resurrects images of standing on the dock while my buddies went swimming or being rebuked by a saint for reading *Sports Illustrated* on Sunday. David Buttrick argues that cinematography is analogous to 20th-century consciousness, as "simultaneously perspectivial and complex." Sermons that assume hegemony of thought and perception preach to the choir. Cinematographic preaching allows for varying orientation or points of view.

The poverty in Kansas City can be represented by a fact or statistic or it can become the fatherless home with seven children, the utility company having cut the gas off on a very cold day. The year-old infant was born just before the elderly dad died with cancer. A preacher with a camera takes us into the cold, cockroach-infested house and joins the 200-pound, 13-year-old kid as he attempts to fix another can-emptied meal on a filthy, grease-covered stove. Lens depth demands involvement, where as "churchy" preaching often draws a sharp demarcation that states "we're in here, they're out there." Buttrick writes,

> To seize an analogy, think of film making. In an earlier era, movie directors worked with a fixed-location camera and movie actors walked around in front of the lens. . . . Today, directors use a camera on a moving boom so that camera angles change, lenses widen or narrow down,

distances vary, imitating the way in which we actual perceive reality (Buttrick 1987, 55).

Preaching is effective, not to the extent that it informs the understanding, but to the extent it forms the consciousness. Phenomenological preaching shifts reality by experiencing or inducing the reality that it represents. The reality construct of the sermon becomes the reality construct of the hearer. A sermon on grace encodes grace within the consciousness of the listener. The question for the phenomenological approach is not what is learned but "what happens when a preached sermon presses on the keyboard of the listener's mind" (Long 1988b, 108). Or to use another metaphor, preaching is like sharing a camera with the congregation. The camera leaves an exposure on the soul, symbols and images that fill the reality frame. Though Buttrick nowhere defines "phenomenological preaching" (that I can find), he uses phrases such as "angled modes of perspectual human consciousness," "perspectual shifts," and "world forming" (Buttrick 1983, 29). A sermon for Buttrick is not a discourse that is spoken but an event that takes place in the mind of the listener. If the furniture of the mind hasn't been replaced, it has at least been rearranged. The evaluative question for preaching is not "What did you hear?" but rather "What happened to you?"

Tex Sample labels media experience as immersion rather than absorption. Absorption means one takes in the media mix, in contrast with immersion, which means one enters into it. When Sample asked his grandson why he needed six speakers for his audio system, the answer was "so you can be in it, you feel like you are just in the music" (Sample 2005, 125). This is the argument made by Doug Pagitt for preaching as "progressional dialogue" rather than "speeching." The former allows persons on the inside of the sermon rather than holding them at the arms length of generic application. Implication differs from application in that the former asks

> how we fit into the story of God as opposed to what we are suppose to do with the story. In truth, implication is the more instinctive response to a powerful story. This is the sense people have when they see a movie. Scary movies are scary because viewers tend to see themselves as part of the story or believe the story could become a part of their lives. There is an entire generation of moviegoers who cannot enter the shower without thinking about the shower scene from *Psycho* (Pagitt 2005, 100).

Immersion communication requires an experiential atmosphere. A sermon on race relations, absent the opportunity to interface with other races, will fall on deaf ears. Sermons on repentance are efficacious only to the extent that repentance is modeled and allowed. In the context of Jesus stating that "no servant is greater than his master" (John 13:16), He washed His disciples' feet. "Do you understand what I have done for you" (v. 12)? The only opportunity for understanding was through Christ's audiovisual. He excelled at teaching because experience provided insight into His words. Christ immersed His message in both word and deed. No wonder that Marshall McLuhan stated that Christ represented the "only case in which the medium and the message are perfectly identical" (Babin 1991, 6).

What a preacher should fear most is indifference. Preaching that fails to get any kind of reaction from those who have intentionally chosen to give a half hour to someone leading them on a discovery of God, which is what all preaching is about, has miserably failed. Preaching creates in the hearts and minds of the listener love, fear, guilt, hope, grief, anger, generosity, and so on. In other words, the critical goal of preaching is preemption, the displacement of values, habits, and attitudes that are unlike Christ, the gods of self-sovereignty and the perennial and constant tendency to turn life in on itself rather than focus on the good of others. This can be done only by creating God's emotions in the listener's affections. Quite simply, the job of preaching is to enable the church to hate what God hates and love what God loves. If the preacher has created for the listener a picture of sin as horrifying as sin is to the heart of God, the preacher has accomplished his or her purpose. If the preacher has created a love for the most despicable sinner to the extent that God loves the sinner, the sermon has done its work.

preaching without preaching

The objection may be raised that preaching is very unlike acting, which is the staple of both stage and movie set. It is no accident, as Harry Stout narrates in *The Divine Dramatist,* that George Whitefield studied London stage, especially the acting of David Garrick, the leading actor of the day. But most of us would be put off by exaggerated oratory, melodramatic poses, and manufactured emotions. However, good acting is not acting; it is to become lost in the emotions and motions of the character being played. Identification closes the gap between actor and the person whom the actor represents. Forgetting that one is playing the part has become known in both screen and stage as "method acting." *Cinema Studies,* written by Susan Hayward and referred to as "the essential guide for anyone interested in film," defines method acting as "Completely natural, to so infuse oneself with the thoughts, emotions and personality of the character that one becomes that character" (Hayward 2000, 227-28).

Good preachers preach without preaching. Preaching that prescribes, moralizes, and badgers resembles the proverbial "old Dutch uncle" giving tips for making it in an ugly and desperate existence. Henry David Thoreau may have been right when he opined that "most men live lives of quiet desperation," but they will not rise above it by receiving hints for living. They will ascend above life's nagging strains, crippling circumstances, and hopeless dreariness not by being verbally tossed a manual of self-help but by being raptured by salvific grace. Persons can choose to change only as their consciousness is invaded by liberating affection for other than what they already are. Preaching at people only causes them to retrench into the excuses and defenses, if not outright disagreement, that enable them to continue to live in the paradigms and ideologies that have always defined them. Catherine Barsotti and Robert K. Johnston write in *Finding God in the Movies* that movies portray life; "they don't prescribe it, they are more like poetry than propositions, they present; they as stories preach" (Barsotti 2004, 28).

Any gestures, movements, or emotions that a speaker has to intentionally and consciously create while communicating come across as plastic and superficial. Inauthenticity creates dissonance between the preacher and his or her listeners. The only way that churchgoers are drawn into the sermon is for the preacher to be absorbed in and by his or her own material. Emotional authenticity can never be created. It has to naturally arise from the compatibility between the preacher and the text that he or she is proclaiming. The pastor is never ready to preach, unless he or she has placed himself or herself under the truth of the text. The amen of the congregation needs to be the echo of the amen that resonates deep within the preacher's character.

Self-doubt in the preacher is created by his or her lack of conviction that this exercise in proclamation is God's message for this hour. A person with momentous news, D-Day, victory in Europe, or the destruction of New York's World Trade Center, would never stop to think what gestures and emotions he or she was going to attach to the announcement, unless he or she was as hollow as a department store mannequin. Good preaching is essentially like good cinema in that both of them close emotional distance. Barsotti and Johnston argue, "Successful movies do not merely transport us somewhere new; they inspire us to become emotionally attached, to become one with the characters. . . . The emotional wallop might sneak up on the viewer as in *Smoke Signals*, but if it rings false or is missing, the movie simply fails" (Barsotti 2004, 27). Once in a while a pastor will preach a "gut-wrenching" sermon, from which it takes at least a few hours to recover or which at least momentarily curbs the relish for Sunday dinner. Would it be possible by way of the power of the Holy Spirit to preach in such a way that people would leave the church as they do the theater after seeing *Schindler's List* or *The World Trade Center*?

Paradoxically, even as good movies demand that the viewers become participants, they also create a safe distance. Movies don't present us with confrontational either-ors, "Got to make a decision now" alternatives. They allow us to reflect, ponder, and contemplate various responses. Al Gore's *An Inconvenient Truth* may elicit a whole range of responses, from buying a smaller vehicle to eschewing all carbon-dioxide-producing machinery and refusing to do business with anyone who uses such machinery. Whatever my response, any change will take place only through a gradual conviction that environmental stewardship is important to my Christian identity. Thus, change will take place both on a rational and affective level, as I digest facts, figures, and images that present evidence our planet is changing and I may be having a negative influence. Both movies and sermons may detonate as an explosive power obliterating false gods and enabling a new reality. They may also work as leaven that slowly expands into an expulsive power of a new affection, value, or conviction.

text as preaching script

Finding a good text is not unlike a director discovering a good script. Film scholar Louis Giannetti states that "it's doubtful that even a genius like Bergman or Kubrick could do much with the script or stars of *Abbot and Costello Meet the Mummy*. In other words, a director has got to have a fighting chance with the material. When the subject matter sinks beneath a certain potential the result is not tension, but artistic annihilation" (Giannetti 1999, 452). All Scripture is equally inspired but not equally inspiring. At least some of the biblical story translates into difficulty for 21st-century communication. God's attempt to kill Moses, the cursing of children by Elisha, and God's wrath poured out on Tyre are all cases in point. Deciphering the intention of these pericopes is highly controversial, if not impossible, and second, imposing theocracy or favoritism on the United States, at the expense of third-world countries or anyone else, self-destructs or is blindsided by theological contradictions.

A text should not be rescued by cleverness or inventions of an intent that was foreign to the original writer or God. The temptation is to make God politically correct or completely understandable or to presume that God never does anything bad from our perspective. I have witnessed preachers who "artistically annihilated" the text. (I have committed the crime myself, unwilling to accept the plain meaning of the text.) One preacher justified Cain's evil deed of murder by ignoring the plain verdict of 1 John 3:12, "Do not be like Cain, who belonged to the evil one and murdered his brother. Why did he murder him? Because his own actions were evil and his brothers were righteous." Another homiletician twisted and gerrymandered Matt. 22 until the person without a wedding garment was the object of God's salvation. Universalism was preached at the expense of ignoring the forthright judgment of the text. "The king commanded, 'Tie him hand and foot, and throw him outside, into the darkness, where there will be weeping and gnashing of teeth'" (v. 13).

The above does not preclude choosing difficult texts, but they should never be done at the expense of honesty and integrity. Often, the greater the complexity of the text the greater the potential for sermonic intrigue. Thus, the parable of the 10 virgins, 5 of whom had little oil in their lamps, necessitates a reevaluation of normative interpretation. Those caught short on oil expected the imminent return of the Bridegroom. Shouldn't they be rewarded for their expectancy? Perhaps their expectancy of the soon return is the essence of their "foolishness." The real question of life is not "If you die tonight will you go to heaven?" but "If God allows you to spend 20 more years on earth, what difference will it make?" Christ's parable challenges me with interpreting what it means to be married to the "Bridegroom" in the here and now rather than the by-and-by.

the vernacular texture of sermonic language

Sermonic language and screenwriting find commonality in oral communication, speech that uses vernacular language rather than formal prose. My students' paraphrasing of Scripture almost always results in language more stilted and structured then the way we talk or think. Sermonic script is not for the purpose of spitting out polished prose but inviting the listener into fragmented thought processes behind the script. Good screenwriting evidences the way people think and act when they are caught in the pressures and stresses of everyday life. Dialogue is halting, hesitating, fearful, hopeful, doubting, and interjected with pauses that represent both self-incrimination and suspicion of others. Linda Quanstrom provides a staccato, agonizing texture for the speech and thoughts of the man who was beaten and robbed on the Jericho Road:

"Oh, God, let me die. Please let me die."

It was high noon when he awoke. Sweat drenched his forehead and clouded his eyes. He tried to move, but the pain was too great.

Then he heard them—bells. The soft jingle got louder and distinct. "I'm saved. I'm saved. A priest." He tried to call out, but his tongue wouldn't move. He waited. The bells stopped. Silence. When he heard them again, they clanged and jangled in erratic staccato and then faded. Silence.

"No, no. He's gone. How could he leave? How could he . . . he thought that I was dead. He thought I was dead. He couldn't touch a dead body. O, God, sometimes Your law is so hard."

"I must move. I must sit up. I must yell out" (Quanstrom 1994, 37).

Notice all that could have gone on in Gen. 22:3: "Early the next morning Abraham got up and saddled his donkey." What's it like for a man 110 years old to pull himself out of bed? A man stiff in the joints? A man facing the crisis of his life? A man with a divine mandate to murder his son? Was his donkey a personal pet? What did he call the donkey? You can trust a donkey. Dependable, not like a capricious God. A fickle God. A God who mocks by giving and taking away.

"It's dark," thought Isaac. "The old man is nuts cutting wood at 3 A.M. Can't sleep for him cutting wood and he wants me to go. The last time Dad got up this early Ishmael went with him. Ishmael is gone forever. Never saw him again. I don't want to go."

The flap of the tent flew open. Isaac peered over the top of the blanket. Saw the stooped figure. His quiet, pathetic-looking dad, standing at the door: "Get up Isaac. Isaac, Isaac, get up." Tough on a kid, a 110-year-old dad with weird ideas. "What am I going to tell my friends? They've asked me so many times before, 'Is that your great-grandfather?'"

"Dad, let me sleep a few more minutes. I'll get up. Not now, Dad. Come back later. Where's Mom, Dad?" Isaac drug himself out of bed.

The above hardly measures up to the conversation between the Malloy brothers in *On the Waterfront* (Rod Steiger and Marlon Brando) or Rick Blaine's parting words to Ilsa Lazlo (Humphrey Bogart and Ingrid Bergman) in *Casablanca*. But the point is not to come up with a memorable line such as Brando's poignant and tragic regret, "I could have been a contender," or Bogart's flippant and yet heart-wrenching good-bye, "Here's looking at you, kid." What is at stake is honest and realistic language that is true to the situation. Preaching is less about literary excellence as it is the raw materials of life. Expressive language is neither crude nor vulgar but demonstrates emotional depth congruent with the crisis or tension being depicted. Stephen King, who has probably had more novels converted to cinema than any other author, writes,

> Book buyers aren't attracted, by and large, by the literary merits of a novel; book buyers want a good story to take with them on the airplane, something that will first fascinate them, then pull them in and keep them turning the pages. This happens, I think, when readers recognize the people in a book, their behaviors, their surroundings, and their talk. When the reader hears strong echoes of his or her own life and beliefs, he or she is apt to become more invested in the story (King 2000, 156).

the preacher and the director

The more creative the work of art, the less it can be captured by how-tos. To the extent that preaching and cinema arouse and evoke, the less they are explainable. Both directors and preachers project their personalities on to their art form to the extent that sermons and movies are extensions of the artist. A borrowed sermon is a contradiction in terms; perhaps a borrowed presentation of a sermon but never a borrowed sermon. Sermons reflect the preacher's personality, gifts, idiosyncrasies, and, above all, his or her relationship to God. To present a congregation with someone else's material (though we are all thieves stealing from other thieves) is to cheat God's people out of God's word for such a time and place as this, a moment that has never occurred and will never occur again. When Robert Altman was asked why he gave such little direction to actors, he responded, "How can I tell them what I want when I am looking for something I have never seen?" This is not to say that Altman did not engrave his films with his personality as an anti-Hollywood iconoclast. Altman was known for "overlapping dialogue, meandering camera and improvisational feel" (*Newsweek,* Dec. 25, 2006, 106).

"Auteur theory" emphasizes a director stamping the film with his "own personal vision, style, and thematic obsession" (Giannetti 1999, 509). Style and thematic obsession correspond to Phillips Brooks's definition of preaching as "truth spoken through personality." Having served as a director of an international organization that paraded the best preachers they could find across its platform, I was constantly amazed at their uniqueness. Whatever it is that makes preaching great can never be simply transferred as technique from one person to another. It can be cultivated only through a lifetime of hard work, devotion to God, and a passion for preaching well. Thus, after all the critics have had their say (and no professions elicit more criticism than do preachers and movie directors), the artist is the final judge. He or she journeys within the shadowlands of marshy bogs and treacherous terrain that lie between preaching as entertainment and preaching as faithfulness to God and His Word.

All creativity is stamped with the artist's idiosyncrasies, eccentricities, and those propensities buried who knows where in the preacher's inner psyche. Irregularities of personality provide spontaneity and innovation beyond lecture and textbook. The stories of movies are the stories of directors; the stories of sermons are the stories of preachers. For Jimmy Stewart's filibuster in *Mr. Smith Goes to Washington*, Frank Capra swabbed Stewart's throat with a vile tasting solution. Capra, rather than make Stewart seem like he was hoarse, actually made him hoarse. When John Ford was told by the studio that he was behind a day in his shooting, he asked the messenger how much script was normally shot in a day. "About eight pages" the messenger replied. Ford immediately grabbed the script and tore eight pages into shreds, "You can go back and tell the studio we are back on schedule."

culturally transcendent preaching

Preaching has long served as a popular medium for dispensing truth or what its listeners perceive to be the truth. In spite of Hollywood's fabrication of myth and propagation of stereotypes, it also at times has taken itself seriously as a vehicle of truth that attempts social transformation and even in some cases the triumph of justice. Errol Morris's documentary *The Thin Blue Line* served to free Randall Dale Adams who had been wrongly convicted of killing a policeman. Even more fictionalized accounts of injustice and bigotry, such as *Mississippi Burning*, have served to readdress the racism of the '60s and '70s. *The Ghosts of Mississippi*, which retold the story of Medgar Evers and his murder, reopened the case against Byron De La Beckwith. In 2004 De La Beckwith was convicted for a murder that he had committed as a Ku Klux Klansman 40 years earlier.

Both films and sermons represent ideologies and both often peddle erroneous myths. Fundamentalist preaching that demeans this life at the expense of the next, promotes racism and escapism, and severs the social gospel from individual salvation is as theologically amiss as the western that depicted white hats against black and glorified the rugged frontiersmen who killed Indians before they scalped the frontiersmen's golden-haired, blue-eyed daughters. Both preaching and cinema can represent the viewpoint of the dominant sociological group at the expense of minorities, the poor, and those with little to no clout in a world where monetary might makes right. No sermon or movie ever fully represents truth; they are only approximations to the reality as found in Jesus Christ, the only person who perfectly embodied truth, justice, and mercy.

Unfortunately, both the Church and Hollywood have often been co-opted by the prevailing social order. Charles Marsh honestly and painfully tells the story of his preacher dad who was called on to honor Clifford Wilson, winner of the Jaycee Man of the Year award in Laurel, Mississippi, 1968. Wilson was indeed a civic leader, coaching a Little League baseball team and heading up a Cub Scout pack. Pastor Marsh touted Wilson as one who was exemplary of a good community: "People who relate to their fellow man and take an active interest in civic affairs, people who have a constructive influence on society, whose lives are driven by an intangible, invisible force that emanates from their personality" (Marsh 2001, 151). After the speech and presentation of the award, Clifford Wilson and Bob Marsh were photographed, smiling and shaking hands. Within an hour of the photograph Wilson was arrested by the FBI for being the hitman in the Ku Klux Klan killing of Vernon Dahmer. Years later Bob Marsh wrote to his son saying, "I thank God I went through this hell so I can see it for what it was." Unfortunately it often requires blindsiding, cataclysmic events to give us such clear vision. Charles referred to the confounding event as "redemption's comedy . . . the hilarity of grace, the way it sometimes hits you in the gut like a punch line. But God, if I may say so myself, outdid himself here" (Marsh 2001, 188).

Sermons that aspire to the moral awakenings of *To Kill a Mockingbird, Sophie's Choice, Philadelphia,* and *The Apostle,* which I admit often represent Hollywood idealism, will by the Holy Spirit make parishioners aware of the evil that not only daily assaults but also lurks behind our fondest intentions. Both movies and sermons act as mirrors for seeing ourselves. By watching the persons who inhabit Atticus Finch's town *(To Kill a Mockingbird),* I see people I don't like. As I am repulsed by them, I am alarmed at the same characteristics that I find deep down within my own soul. Sermons work best as visions, causing me to inwardly cry out as did Isaiah, "Woe is me, . . . I am a man of unclean lips, and I dwell in the midst of people of unclean lips" (Isa. 6:5, NKJV).

sermon editing

Only a fraction of shot film makes it to the theater. Thus, the editor, to whom an Oscar is given, is as important as the person who runs the camera. The editor's job is to choose the film most essential to the story, to transition as smoothly as possible, and to make sure there are no major incongruities in the splicing of the film, such as an actor wearing a red tie and a blue tie in the same scene. The editor is consumed with continuity as opposed to jumping: the glass was just full but is now empty, or it just looked as though it was seven o'clock but now appears to be six o'clock. In other words, there must be a chronological, topical, emotional flow that matches reality. An unbelievable scene takes place in *Speed,* a movie that depicts a bus programmed to explode if its speed falls below 50 miles per hour. Anxiety for the viewers is created by following the bus turning corners, running intersections, and jumping drawbridges without slowing down. All of a sudden, this hysteria is reduced to a falling in love dialogue between the driver (Keanu Reeves) and a pretty city employee (Sandra Bullock). This love scene is so supercilious and incongruent with the film's idiom that whatever credulity the plight attempts to create is completely undermined.

John Boorstin argues that editing is often a trial-and-error process. Sermonizing would best be served by rearranging material, repositioning illustrations, explanations, quotations, and portions of the narrative to test for flow, continuity, and transition. In the healing of the woman with the issue of blood, I work through the reasons as to why Jesus stopped and embarrassed her. I spend 3 to 4 minutes in a 30-minute sermon setting the scene of the woman finally touching Christ's robe after several failed attempts, the social impropriety of Jesus embarrassing her, and the awkwardness of the lady coming forward. But then I have to theologically and psychologically get into the mind of Christ, like a sleuth working through a maze. This demands experimentation, speculation about the reason for an encounter that could have been bypassed, working from least important motive to most important.

Jairus must have been a type A personality, hypertension flowing through his arteries, blood spurting out of his ears, as he tried to hurry Jesus along. Interjected at this point is a scene of me trying to find the shortest line at Wal-Mart, where invariably the computer shuts down, the person in front of me needs a price check on an item 300 yards away, or something is wrong with his or her credit card. This juxtaposition between the tension felt by Jairus and my dilemma at Wal-Mart provides a contemporary idiom and offers relief from theological speculation by interjecting an everyday experience. This brief humor prepares my listeners to theologically explore Jesus' social impropriety at a deeper level. I verbalized this several times before I was satisfied with the transition between ideas, that I had not overwhelmed the hearer with a close-up shot without backing away for a lighter moment.

Branigan observes that normal editing attempts to eliminate jumps between shots so that the spectator will "experience a smooth, rapid movement that is faster than an object of interest" (Branigan 2006, 163). This means that the preacher allows the hearer to dominate the material and not the other way around. Never shoot a scene, or race through material, too fast for the congregation. On the other hand, pace at times needs to be quickened to prevent boredom. Movies seldom show someone walking from car to house but compress the transition. I tend to err on the side of compression, quickening pace, since I don't want my sermon to resemble a security camera fixed on a diamond ring case in a jewelry store.

For the above reason, I discourage students from giving introductory or transitional remarks such as "this is illustrated by" or "this is like" or "we will now make application" or "I one time heard the story." All of these transitional phrases serve not as bridges but as walls between thoughts and moves. Relationships between sermon moves should be readily apparent, and if not, they should provide a clue or enlightenment that makes perfect sense in retrospect. Good editing cuts out all material that does not carry its own weight. Weight is assessed by several questions: Is it interesting in and of itself? Does it add to the force of impression and penetration? Does it carry God's truth in a manner that accents the central idea of the message rather than reduces it? Was the anecdote only for entertainment purposes or did it carry the message forward? Does the scholarly insight really help the listener focus on the message or does it slow down the sermon's movement?

Technical exegesis has no place in the sermon, unless it readily closes the gap between the sermon and hearer. In John 7:15, the question is asked, "How did this man get such learning without having studied?" Literally the text says "having never studied letters." The Greek word for letters, *grammata,* provides the etymology for our English word *grammar.* I make brief allusion to this only because my audience is able to readily connect. In Luke 5, we are told that Matthew Levi put on a "megabanquet" for his guests. The qualifier *mega* carries directly over into English. McDonald's was not the first institution to come up with a "megameal." In Matt. 2, the Greek word for star, which the magi followed, *astera,* from which we get the word *astrology* or *astronomer,* provides a clue to the identity of the "wise men." This popular kind of exegesis provides a bit of intellectual stimulus but needs to be kept on the light side. I rarely ever prepare a message without studying the text in an interlinear Bible that gives an exact and grammatical translation of the Greek/Hebrew text. This study is for my illumination, not for obtuse and pedantic explanations that hold interest for only esoteric minds.

Pacing is critical to holding attention, getting on with the story and compressing the elements that are not essential to either holding interest or increasing understanding. Progression is essential if congregants are not going to drift forward to the NFL game that awaits them at home. The first time I preach a message, I almost always have too much material, a quote I don't need, one too many stories, a scripture that expands the parameters of the text beyond being helpful. What feels far away, is not relevant to everyday life, and carries little to no contemporary application has a deadening effect. Humor is theology's closest friend because it saves both preacher and listener from being overwhelmed. The preacher is much like the film editor, because he or she learns over time what really works, what carries an emotional wallop, what pulls the listener into the text, and what part of the text carries the idea of the message. The following from Jon Boorstin could apply to editing sermons: "The act of editing is in large part sensing the difference—feeling how much less of something is required on screen, feeling that edge where we teeter into boredom. There is no formula for this. It is a function of many variables, the editor's internal clock, the exact composition of the shot, what proceeds and follows it, the overall rhythms of the film, even the size of the screen" (Boorstin, 1995, 48).

The editing maxim that best applies to preaching is that more is often less. Preaching will exhibit both courage and humility by confessing that just because I had a thought, it really wasn't all that inspired. I often work under the foolish presumption that my sermons are made better by expanding them. Being concise, comprehensive, and clear are homiletical gifts that will endear the preacher to his or her congregation. Stephen King suggests the 10 percent formula: the second draft of a manuscript (sermon) should be 10 percent shorter than the first draft. An editor responded to one of King's manuscripts, "not bad, but puffy." Detecting "puff," though not a spiritual gift listed by the apostle Paul, demands heavenly wisdom and earthly cunning.

the homiletical *mise en scene*

One of the reasons that biblical events are accessible to film is that many of the Bible's settings have changed little over the last 2,000 years. Bedouins still live in tents, streets are made of stone, rock houses are still the architecture of choice, and urbanism has failed to claim much of the Middle East's rocky and arid terrain. When visiting an open-air market in old Jerusalem or Amman, Jordan, one gets the idea that he or she is stepping back into the New Testament. The *mise en scene* (French, literally "placing on stage") needs to become as critical for preaching as it is for filming. Louis Giannetti explains that the *mise en scene* is always in three dimensions: "Objects and people are arranged in actual space which has depth as well as height and width. This space is also a continuation of the same space that the audience occupies, no matter how much a theatre director tries to suggest a separate 'world' on the stage" (Giannetti 1999, 42). Film directors excel in enabling their viewers to be there, as did Alfred Hitchcock who utilized windows as movie frames, "allowing audiences to pry into the intimate details of the characters' lives" (Giannetti 1999, 46).

Normally several *mise en scenes* define a movie, such as both the dance at Tara and the overview shot of ravaged Atlanta in *Gone with the Wind*. In *The Nativity,* the village of Nazareth is authentically represented in its stark simplicity and the subsistent impoverishment of its inhabitants. In narrative sermons, time limitations will allow for a detailed description of only one setting. Thomas Troeger argues that Jesus' parables worked in his culture in the way that movies do for us today. For the parable of the "great feast" Troeger constructs the unforgettable dinner party, "a lavish banquet of roasted quail and pheasant, triple chocolate cakes, with quadruple chocolate icing." Chauffeured limousines, after having been turned down by persons occupied with business, vacations, and honeymoons, pick up the homeless in wheelchairs, frayed coats, and moth-eaten sock hats (Troeger 1996, 48-57).

Obviously, the preacher will have to stand imaginatively within the physical space of a specific text. No one did this better than the Scottish preacher Peter Marshall, who pastored New York Avenue's First Presbyterian Church in Washington, D.C., and was chaplain of the United States Senate:

> The morning sun had been up for some hours over the city of David. Already pilgrims and visitors were pouring in through the gates, mingling with merchants from the villages round about, with shepherds coming down from the hills, and the gnarled streets were crowded.
>
> There were the aged, stooped with years, muttering to themselves as they pushed through the throngs, and there were children playing in the streets, calling to each other in shrill voices. There were men and women too, carrying burdens, baskets of vegetables, casks of wine, water bags.

And there were tradesmen with their tools. Here a donkey stood sleepily beneath his burden in the sunlight. . . .

It was not easy to make one's way through the crowd. But it was especially difficult for a procession that started out from the governor's palace. At its head rode a Roman centurion, disdainful and aloof, scorn for the like of child or cripple who might be in his way. His lips curled in thin lines of contempt as he watched through half-shut eyes the shouting, jeering crowd.

Before him went two legionnaires, clearing the crowd aside as best they could with curses and careless blows. . . . The sunlight glanced on the spears and helmets of the soldiers. There was a rhythmic clanking of steel as their shields touched their belt buckles and the scabbards of their swords (Denison 2006, 29-30).

The following characteristics apply to both preaching and cinematography. Even more importantly, they describe God's methods of communication as found in Scripture.

A. Graphic Speech*

Attentive Bible reading is synonymous with a course in graphic arts. God employs real-life situations rather than "how to manuals." All sermon preparation requires three-dimensional glasses that allow flat-line perception to be transposed into hurling objects. At least once in a while both preacher and people need to feel like ducking, rather than politely listening. The Bible does not proposition its listeners; it shocks, scares, arrests, and awakens them with smoke, fire, stones, swords, brides, prostitutes, gardens, gates, snakes, and bones. These images allow sermons to become love affairs, battlefields, and courtroom dramas. Abraham Heschel states that God's images "must not shine, they must burn" (Heschel 1962, 7).

In Luke 22:19, Jesus states to His disciples, "Just as my father gave to me a Kingdom, I give a kingdom to you" (author's translation). A short while later, the crowd who gathered at Pilate's judgment hall (what would that look like on a movie set?) chose between two kingdoms. Would they choose the lowly Nazarene or the insurrectionist and murderer, Barabbas? I want my lis-

---

*Remainder of chapter excerpted and adapted from Darius Salter, "Preaching as God Encounter," in *The Pastor's Guide to Effective Preaching* (Kansas City: Beacon Hill Press of Kansas City, 2003), 89-104. Used by permission.

teners to see, smell, and hear Barabbas. Barabbas reeks of body odor, glistens with sweat, snarls with obscenities, and foams at the mouth. This barbaric savage is unshaven, filthy, and bulging with muscles, which are restrained by chains and manacles. After describing Barabbas, I return to Jesus' declaration of the Kingdom gift. What kind of domain was Jesus offering? A four-bedroom house on a corner lot? Employment with fringe benefits and a good retirement plan?

Before I answer the above, I return to Barabbas, whom we have typecast and miscast. I believe that we would need to choose Sean Connery, the original 007, to play Barabbas: "My name is Bond, James Bond." Barabbas was chisel-faced, steel-eyed, square-jawed, and dapperly draped in an Armani suit. As an insurrectionist, he was a champion of the people, an avenger of justice, the hope of the enslaved Jews to free them from the Roman government. Barabbas had much to offer: profit-sharing, linear security, and entitlement to one's fair share of the Israeli (American) pie. All Jesus has to offer is the Cross. The fringe benefits are not all that inviting. The choice the crowd made on that day between two kingdoms clues me in on the kind of kingdom Jesus was offering His disciples, the same kingdom that He offers you and me: "You can have all of the turf you want, as long as its boundaries are defined by the Cross."

Jeremiah earned an A for sermon illustration. His illustrations were a tangible, observable, acting out of the spoken word. God not only gave the Word but also gave instructions for acting it out. "Take the waistband that you have bought . . . and arise, go to the Euphrates and hide it there in a crevice of the rock" (13:4, NASB). "Arise and go down to the potter's house, and there I shall announce My words to you" (18:2, NASB). "Go and buy a potter's earthenware jar" (19:1, NASB). "The LORD showed me: behold, two baskets of figs set before the Temple of the LORD" (24:1, NASB). "Buy for yourself my field which is at Anathoth, for you have the right of redemption to buy it" (32:7, NASB). "Go to the house of the Rechabites and speak to them, and bring them into the house of the LORD, into one of the chambers, and give them wine to drink" (35:2, NASB). All of these tendentious activities addressed God's relationship with Judah—His holy faithfulness that would carry out His righteous justice as opposed to Judah's stubborn self-sovereignty. It would get worse before it got better.

God contextualizes communication. It behooves His messengers to do the same. Words are vessels; the vessels change as the communication context changes. It is not only that a pottery illustration may not hold the attention

of a suburban congregation, but that my pottery craftsmanship or lack thereof would only demonstrate that God is making a mess of things. Sermons
must be within the media matrix that is most meaningful. That does not
mean we are to substitute cinematography for a Spirit-filled sermon embodied and proclaimed via a Spirit-anointed personality. But it perhaps does
mean that our sermons need to be Spirit-anointed cinematography. Preaching that consists simply of syllogistic logic and propositional persuasion will
increasingly fall on the deaf ears of postmoderns. If the Enlightenment has
run out of fuel, pulpit communication will need to be more in the form of a
visual imaginative encounter than a rational construct. Sermons will consist
of plots, scenes, and characters with which listeners can identify because
there is a mutuality of plight and solution.

The Bible is a story offering a flood of light on the human predicament.
This spotlight leaves all of us found out, if not by others, at least by God. The
biblical floodlight is not for the purpose of stripping us for full disclosure by
onlookers, but that we might be able to perceive ourselves within the flow of
God's transforming grace. Scripture is the story of God's proffer of grace to
the greedy, lustful, deceitful, proud, immoral, and anxious—in other words,
to us. Though the context of life is different, the essential character is the
same. Jacob is everyman and Mary Magdalene is everywoman.

When sermons become imagologies, they enter into cyberspace, becoming accessible to people of all ages and all places. But they do not carry the
sanitized, abstract, detached quality of cyberspace. Preaching is injected with
sights, sounds, feelings, and attitudes that catch the attention of the archetypical formation that is a part of every consciousness or unconsciousness.
These images elicit latent emotions, reveal enslaving attitudes, expose crippling scars, and above all inspire hope.

We have the events and the emotions, but we lack scriptwriters, people
with imagination, people who can readdress the biblical drama in a contemporary idiom. There probably never has been a better scriptwriter than was
Robert G. Lee, pastor of the Bellevue Baptist Church in Memphis. Note his
description of Jezebel, who laid the plot for her husband to kill Naboth, owner of a coveted vineyard:

> Hear her derisive laugh as it rings out in the palace like the shrill crack-
> le of a wild owl that has returned to its nest and has found a serpent
> therein! With her tongue, sharp as a razor, she prods Ahab as an ox driver
> prods with sharp goad the ox which does not want to press his neck into
> the yoke, or as one whips with a rawhide a stubborn mule. With profuse

and harsh laughter this old gay gaudy guinea of Satan derided this king of hers for a cowardly buffoon and sordid jester. What hornetlike sting in her sarcasm! What wolf-mouth taunts she hurled at him for his scrupulous timidity! Her bosom with anger was heaving! Her eyes were flashing with rage under the surge of hot anger that swept over her (Lee 1957, 9).

For Robert G. Lee and those who heard him, the sermon was something not only to be heard but also to be seen and felt. The camera had zeroed in on jealousy personified in all of its grotesque manifestations. Certainly we would not want to live with her, which is precisely the point. Then "Why do we?" is the apt question. But the question deserves to be asked only if the script has sufficiently completed its task. If not, we are only left with a moralism: "Don't be jealous." Such sermons never work.

But the question deserves to be asked, "Must every sermon be a grotesque caricature of the sordid traits of life? Do we have to follow the present trend of cinematography, that is, blood and guts to attract viewers (listeners)? Does every sermon have to be a narrative about murder, theft, and God's revenge?" The staple, if not overwhelming, may become a bit tiring. Hopefully all cinematography does not have to go the way of Jezebel's demise. "These men put their strong men's fingers into her soft feminine flesh and picked her up, tired head and all, painted face and all, bejeweled fingers and all—and threw her down. Her body hit the street and burst open" (Lee 1957, 31).

Note the correlating scene from Jeremiah, "Then I will make to cease from the cities of Judah and from the streets of Jerusalem the voice of joy and the voice of gladness, the voice of the bridegroom and the voice of the bride; for the land will become a ruin" (7:34, NASB). The phrase "voice of the bridegroom and the voice of the bride" is unique to Jeremiah. He uses the phrase four times: 7:34; 16:9; 25:10; 33:11. The scene is of newlyweds. There is vibrancy in their speech, mirth in their words, excitement in their body language, radiance in their countenances, and sheer enjoyment over the presence of the other. The honeymoon is still on. The encounter is both enrapturing and intoxicating. These people are really in love. They really do like each other. Yes, it is idealistic. Most of us have experienced moments of it, animated moments that we hoped would last forever.

But the moments of invigorating reciprocity and mutual devotion did not last forever. The scene has changed. The room is dark and foreboding. The atmosphere is sullen and even bitter. Instead of kindness, there is harshness; instead of a smile, a scowl; instead of affection, animosity. How did we switch scenes? Things became more important than relationships, giving was replaced by getting; lust displaced love; hurry and worry obscured the good, the beautiful, and the truly rewarding. Vows of trust and fidelity were pre-empted by cultural mores, distrust, and unfaithfulness. How can we get back? Not easily. Spiteful and abusive spirits are not easy to transform. But there is good news. God can bring healing to the home. "Heal me, O LORD, and I will be healed; save me and I will be saved, for You are my praise" (17:14, NASB).

The characters of cinematography do not consist of propositional constructs but of flesh and blood persons. The Scriptures introduce traits, attitudes, virtues, ambitions, desires, and sins to us through persons. Most often these persons actually lived, that is, walked planet earth. At other times, they simply were representative figures, composite profiles who depict characteristics the speaker desired to highlight. It is an intriguing question but not crucial whether Jesus actually knew the people of whom He spoke, "a certain rich man and a certain poor man." More importantly, they bear symbolic significance; imaginatively described and highly suggestive of quintessential qualities and particularities that transcend time and space. The whore of Babylon always has been and always will exist, at least until her destruction. Her manifestations are no doubt more alluring in some ages than in others:

For all the nations have drunk of the wine of the passion of her immorality, and the kings of the earth have committed acts of immorality with her, and the merchants of the earth have become rich by the wealth of her sensuality. . . . Woe, Woe, the great city, she who was clothed in fine linen and purple and scarlet, and adorned with gold and precious stones and pearls" *(Rev. 18:3, 16, NASB)*.

Movie cameras never have done justice to Scripture. Its images are so graphic, passionate, and panoramic that representation by way of celluloid is impossible. The only thing that will work is cinematography by way of words. As Charles Bartow states in his chapter "Turning Ink into Blood," "Sensory experience is not a plus to thought, it is the stuff of it" (Bartow 1997, 73). Only words can convey and stimulate unlimited imagination. Pictures fail, because they are limited by the eye. In contrast, scriptural images are without limit—unlimited sin, unlimited love, and unlimited grace. The pastor prays, "God don't let my limited, stained-glassed, bland, sanitized, sterilized words, limit what You want to do in the human predicament." Jeremiah was not guilty of defining preaching as only polite speech.

B. Empathetic Speech

God is anthropathic, that is, He exhibits the same emotions as do humans, or more accurately, we exhibit or should exhibit the same emotions as does God. God's character remains unchanging but His emotions don't. God's emotions are always in keeping with the circumstance of His creation. Had I laughed when I was holding down my two-year old daughter while a doctor sewed a piece of flesh back into her lip, my emotional state would have been ludicrous. The placid toleration of my wife having an affair would indicate a flaw in both my character and hers. For that reason, lack of passion in preaching is more a theological issue than an emotional one. Dead and dull preaching lacks God's perspective on life. Lack of pathos is a failure to perceive what is at stake when one stands before a congregation of hungering souls. Heschel states, "An analysis of prophetic utterances shows that the fundamental experience of the prophet is a fellowship with the feelings of God, a *sympathy with the divine pathos*, a communion with the divine consciousness which comes about through the prophet's reflection of, or participation in, the divine pathos" (Heschel 1962, 26).

God perception elicits God emotion in the preacher: love, anger, jealousy, disappointment, and pleasure. Emotions that are trumped up by the preacher are deceitful and manipulative. Emotions that are masked because of false ideas of objectivity or the notion that sermon delivery is no more than a classroom lecture are cheating parishioners of what they need most—transformation.

Webster defines empathy as "The projection of one's own personality into the personality of another in order to understand him better." Empathetic words travel "with feeling." Someone has defined empathy as "your problem becoming the ache in my heart." An empathetic word is not a disengaged, unattached, uncaring, "take it or leave it" word. The prophetical word knows nothing of neutrality. The word spoken by God's prophet is passionately affective and consequential for both speaker and hearer. There is intense resonance because the plight of the hearer is also the plight of the speaker. The prophetical working code presupposes that "your future is inextricably bound up with mine."

No prophet demonstrated more pathos than did Jeremiah. At times his grief was overwhelming and the pressure almost unbearable. "My sorrow is beyond healing, my heart is faint within me" (8:18, NASB). The mental and physical stress was so intense that Jeremiah longed for cathartic release. "Oh that my head were waters and my eyes a fountain of tears, that I might weep day and night for the slain of the daughter of my people!" (9:1, NASB). The bereaved hired professional mourners who would catalyze the collective catharsis during a time of death or calamity. "Thus says the LORD of hosts, 'Consider and call for the mourning women, that they may come; and send for the wailing women, that they may come! Let them make haste and take up a wailing for us, that our eyes may shed tears and our eyelids flow with water'" (vv. 17-18, NASB).

Jeremiah's ministry did not practice a detached professionalism. As he spoke, he wept. Unfortunately, such grotesque melancholy today would be assumed to be a neurosis of major proportions brought on by an infantile rage deeply imbedded in the unconscious. "Certainly Jeremiah must have had a hypercritical father and an overwhelming anal-retentive mother." It is difficult for us to understand that what really affected Jeremiah was not a deterministic event in his past, but a foreboding future that he saw all too clearly.

Jeremiah proclaimed with passion. His words were emotively and imaginatively driven. They were objective in that he had insight into Judah's true condition. They were subjective in that he himself was Judean, an identity with his hearers that he could not escape. He could not escape this identification with his flock anymore than any responsible parent can say to his or her child, "Go ahead and try drugs and alcohol and see if I care." The proclamation of the gospel is enclosed with deep passionate caring that cannot be shrugged off.

The cavalier manner in which contemporary preaching takes place is rendering the pulpit ineffective. The Word has to be affective to be effective. Cool rational constructs will not change people. Urgent words that rain down like torrents are needed to wake drowsy parishioners anesthetized by trivial pursuits. The prophet speaks as if God means to be heard. God's message cloaked in a dry pedantic discourse represents an incongruity. Prophetic communication is intensely hot. "Is not My word like fire?" declares the LORD, "and like a hammer which shatters a rock?" (23:29, NASB). James Crenshaw writes in *Trembling at the Threshold of a Biblical Text,* "Only the person who trembles before God and others can expect to convince others that he or she realizes the gravity of trafficking in matters holy" (Crenshaw 1994, 129).

The prophet/priestly message tells a story that includes characters represented by people within the congregation. These people are not called out by name but rather are composite profiles that depict the essential characteristics of both individual and collective humanity. These composite profiles will vary from culture to culture and call for the pastor to be an astute observer of

the fears, anxieties, guilt, and escapisms of a particular people. The congregation is the pastor's extended family whom he or she attempts to know inti-
mately. The pastor is well aware of the skeletons in the closet and the family
events that are embarrassing, if not outright shameful. This astute, open-eyed
confession does not shrink from the truth: "And their nobles have sent their
servants for water, they have come to the cisterns and found no water. They
have returned with their vessels empty; they have been put to shame and hu-
miliated, and they cover their heads" (14:3, NASB). Church should be the last
place a person covers his or her head and hides from things as they really are.
"Do not trust in deceptive words, saying, 'This is the temple of the LORD, the
temple of the LORD, the temple of the LORD'" (7:4, NASB).

The sermon is the pastor telling his or her family story within the Christological drama. James Baldwin does this so effectively in *Go Tell It on the Mountain* that anguish, despair, fear, and hope leap from the pages. Gabriel, the
would-do-good preacher, in a moment of lust fathered a child. After banish-
ing both mother and child who meet tragic ends, Gabriel lives a life of denial
and guilt. Unattractive Deborah, his faithful first wife, who was molested
as a child, wants to believe the best of her husband, though she knows of
his adulterous affair and bastard son. Deborah dies young and childless.
Gabriel's sister Florence, who experienced marriage and divorce from an alcoholic husband, wants to believe in grace, but her faith is obscured by the
prevailing hypocrisy not only of Gabriel but also of a church unable to effect
lasting change for the good.

Elizabeth, who is now Gabriel's second wife, is forever haunted by the
memory of her first love, Richard, who was falsely arrested by white men, sav-
agely beaten, and who in his despair committed suicide. But during their
courtship, she conceived a son who was born after Richard's death. The son,
John, is rejected by Gabriel who has placed all of his hopes and dreams in
Roy, his true biological posterity. Roy is rebellious and violent, while John is
pensive and searching. In spite of rejection by his father and the resultant psychological twistedness, John finds redemption in the darkness of a dysfunctional family. But John's plight represents more than his own family; he is a
composite of the rejection of the black race and the darkness of the Harlem
Ghetto. Never was the longing for redemption so graphically depicted:

> It was a sound of rage and weeping, which filled the grace, rage, and
> weeping from time set free, but bound now in eternity; rage that had no
> language, weeping with no voice—which yet spoke now, to John's startled
> soul, of boundless melancholy, of the bitterest patience, and the longest

night; of the deepest water, the strongest chains, the most cruel lash; of humility most wretched, the dungeon most absolute, of love's bed defiled, and birth dishonored, and most bloody, unspeakable, sudden death. Yes, the darkness hummed with murder, the body in the water, the body in the fire, the body on the tree. John looked down the line of these armies of darkness, army upon army, and his soul whispered: *Who are these? Who are they?* And wondered: *Where shall I go?* (Baldwin 1953, 200-201).

Both Jeremiah's and Baldwin's passions were fueled by the perception of plight, the plight of their own people. The plight does not appear so desperate when camouflaged by the accumulation of "stuff" and the pursuit of middle-class aspirations. But the question needs to be asked, "Is the sting of sin any less for contemporary middle-class Americans than it was for the seventh-century B.C. Judeans or for the 1940 Harlem Blacks?" One would think not, if he or she reads current headlines and listens to the heartbeats of those who sit in our pews. Any insightful and caring physician would become gravely concerned, perhaps even weep.

C. Relevant Speech

As we earlier noted in chapter 1, the word *relevant* is derived from the Latin *relevare,* "to lift up again." That which is relevant treads on familiar territory. Theology for most Americans is not familiar territory, unless it attaches itself to contemporary concerns, idioms, and landmarks. We visually encounter these landmarks on a daily basis: McDonald's, Nike, traffic jams, cell phones, sports, and TV. On the other hand, they present themselves more abstractly but even more forcefully as fear, stress, panic, depression, exhaustion, anxiety, and danger. Preaching that does not embrace life as it is daily lived falls on deaf ears. Life must be worked out in details and so must preaching. Good cinematography excels in depicting life as it was or is, the way Broadway looked in 1937 or the way a Harlem high school looks today. Authenticity in both preaching and cinematography is validated by matching art to reality.

No book has ever been more realistic than the Bible. Its timelessness is preserved by its rawness. The book of beginnings is a treasure trove of predicaments that often seem hopelessly outside of God's sovereign grace. Adam, with salty sweat in his eyes and blisters on his hands, pines for the days of leisure back in the garden (with a lake full of bass). Noah's head throbs with a hangover as he remembers being at the helm of a ship (Willis 1989, 42). A 100-year-old husband and a 90-year-old wife attend Lamaze classes, enduring the stares and gossip that penetrate their dignity. The stories that we find in Scripture are no more ideal than my story, your story, and the stories of those who hear us. Greed, lust, envy, treachery, deceit, avarice, malice, as well as forgiveness, love, and kindness are the stuff of life. The archetypical currents of life flow through good sermons and good movies. A failure to recognize these currents is a reductionism of the highest order.

Some may think that to preach graphically, empathetically, and relevantly, one must possess either some innate talent or take an infinite number of preaching courses. Both may be helpful but not essential. Throughout history, effective preachers have employed plain language for plain people, using metaphors, symbols, and idioms that define everyday life. The incarnated Christ, who spoke of farms, treasures, banquets, and weddings, is our prime example.

Ironically, the absence of technical training can be an asset to preaching. In speaking of the prophet, Heschel states, "The gift he is blessed with is not a skill, but rather the gift of being guided and restrained, of being moved and curbed" (Heschel 1962, 22). Such was the recognition of the congregation in William Faulkner's *The Sound and the Fury* regarding the preacher brought down from St. Louis to preach the Easter sermon. The first impression drew comparison to a small-aged monkey undersized in a shabby alpaca coat. The consternation and unbelief of the congregation was articulated in the whisper of a small boy to his mother, "En dey brung dat all de way fum Saint Looey" (Faulkner 1984, 311). The 'dat' began slowly and methodically but gradually became like

> a worn small rock whelmed by the successive waves of his voice. With his body he seemed to feed the voice that, succubus like, had fleshed its teeth in him. And the congregation seemed to watch with its own eyes while the voice consumed him, until he was nothing and they were nothing and there was not even a voice, but instead their hearts were speaking toward one another in chanting measures beyond the need for words, so that when he came to rest against the reading desk, his monkey face lifted and his whole attitude, that of a serene tortured crucifix that transcended its shabbiness and insignificance and made it of no moment, a long moaning expulsion of breath rose from them, and a woman's single soprano: "Yes, Jesus!" (Faulkner 1984, 367-68).

For the oppressed and outcast race, the imagery was not lost. The "monkey" had trumpeted a blast of transcendent hope to those who had discovered through the experiences of life that only one hope really can be trusted.

"Whut I see? Whut I see, O sinner? I sees resurrection in de light: sees de meek Jesus sayin Dey kilt me dat ye shall live again. I died dat dem what sees and believe shall never die" (Faulkner 1984, 370). On the way home, a mother weeping tears of joy, as she walked in the noonday sun, heard the words of her accompanying boy, "He sho a preacher man! He didn't look like much at first, but hush!? He seed de power in de glory. Yes, suh. He seed hit, face to face, he seed it" (Faulkner 1984, 371).

Could it be that today's pastoral office is more concerned with "looks," appearance, than it is with substance? Samuel Chadwick reminded us who would be prophets that "indifference to religion is impossible where the preacher is a flame of fire . . . fire is self-evident. So is power!" (Chadwick 1972, 18). It is up to the pastor to see to it that there is abundant fuel. The world has the right to ministry ignited by a transcendent source. The fueling and the firing will have to be done on a daily basis. If not, it will be as disappointing as the leftovers from yesterday's breakfast. It is almost impossible to fool the guests. "God encounter" preachers must be "God encountered" preachers. Encounter is the stuff of both cinematography and preaching.

six

PREACHING

that

sees

GOD

a god after our own image

Tom Bodett when touting Motel 6 promised to "leave the light on" for us. The previous chapters have attempted to turn on the light for those of us who still believe that preaching can illuminate life. The visual rhetoric provided by images, irony, and story has, thus far, been workable. But now we come to preaching's most difficult and central task. How do we leave the light on for a God who likes to sit in the dark? Who doesn't want to be seen. He seems squeamish about showing up at office parties. He has not conceded that He and I should get together at least once a month at Starbucks so that I can ask Him about what stock to buy. Maybe He could let me in on the best motel rates, you know, something not listed in my California AAA book. It seems to me that God could use His omniscience much more effectively.

In spite of God not morphing himself at convenient moments on my behalf (remember Him telling the Samaritan women, "God is Spirit"), we all have images of God. On any given Sunday morning, we picture God as a financial planner, a physician, a counselor, and so on. The temptation is to visualize God according to my need at the moment. A god created by human desire would have to go through endless costume changes, dictated by roles I assign him multiplied by the six billion roles the rest of the world assigns Him. All of this sounds quite innocent, until we meditate on the second commandment: "You shall not make for yourself an idol, or any likeness of what is in heaven above or on the earth beneath or on the water under the earth" (Exod. 20:4, NASB). Since most of us haven't set up an idol shrine in our home (not even a graven image of Elvis), we check off the second commandment like we just picked up pants from the dry cleaners, "Now what was I supposed to do next?" Remember, God commanded the Israelites to destroy the Canaanites because that would be the only way to destroy their idols, gods manufactured according to need. Fertility, rain, harvest, and all the natural order (for them there was no distinction between natural and supernatural) could not function without the appropriate god; god appropriateness was dictated by the need of the moment. The second commandment could be paraphrased, "Don't be like the surrounding nations by fashioning gods after your own needs."

Every sermon is a theological treatise, attempting to get God right, exchanging false images of God for the God who is represented in Jesus Christ. This will be no easy task since Jesus, according to Stephen Prothero, is a "national icon" fashioned after our own image. "Jesus became a major personal-

ity in the United States because of the ability of religious insiders to make
Him culturally inescapable" (Prothero 2003, 6). Indeed, we are a "Jesus nation" with Christ functioning as a "common cultural icon," a Savior who for
many is a "buddy, smiling, winking, and giving life the thumbs up." The
American Church has bent over backward to make Jesus likeable, civil, polite,
and domesticated; to put as little distance as possible between Him and a
good American citizen. Prothero writes, "To hold Jesus up to the mirror of
American culture is to conduct a Rorschach test of ever-changing national
sensibilities. What Americans have seen in Him has been an expression of
their own hopes and fears—a reflection not simply of some 'Holy Other' divinity but also of themselves and their nation" (Prothero 2003, 9).

The American pulpit has demonstrated difficulty distinguishing the God
of the Hebrew and Christian Scriptures from a god who is America's No. 1
cheerleader and, when not cheerleading, driving the pace car for the great
American race. Neil Postman suggests that Jesus appearing in a wine commercial is the next step for America's consumer mad blasphemy. Jesus, holding a bottle of California Chardonnay in His hand, His robe caressed with a
gentle breeze, soft Middle-Eastern music playing in the background, proclaims, "When I transformed water into wine at Cana, this is what I had in
mind. Try it today. You'll become a believer" (Postman 1993, 164).

Gerhard Forde sums up American theology when he succinctly observes
that we have traded in a theology for a Jesusology: "Jesus is important reli-
giously for us because He is such a nice and important person, or perhaps
someone with whom we can identify and not because He is the son of God
who was crucified and yet raised" (Forde 1990, 88). Forde challenges the
preacher to discern what God is doing in the text and give permission for
God to do it. Texts grant authority for the Church to be the Church, to carry
out God's promise to claim the territory that the text ropes off, to translate
the intention of the text into the intention of the Church. "The texts do not
leave us in the dark. The people were shocked, incensed, amazed, offended;
they took up stones to kill. Or [the texts] comforted, healed and gave life.
The words drive inexorably to cross and resurrection; indeed they are the
word of the cross" (Forde 1990, 156).

Before we become arrogantly iconoclastic, all of us possess images of
God that are misshapen by culture, narcissism, and, in particular, the sins
that cloud the beatific vision. Our images are like someone, something, some
story, or some event. God can be pictured as our worst fear or best hope, our
worst enemy or best friend. For many He is simply a benign figure who does

little for good or evil. C. S. Lewis described the God of modernity as a congenial, bearded grandfather who at the end of the day yawns, smiles, and says a "good time was had by all." For all of us, God sits on a continuum that stretches between fidelity and self-absorbing narcissism or between perfect submission and self-escaping projection. (Freud was correct and wrong. Wish fulfillment dictates popular conceptions of God. He was wrong to conclude that this particular neurosis invalidates the existence of God. Since when did an imperfect desire invalidate the object of the desire?) David Greenshaw writes,

> God, in as much as God is known to us, is God as known to us. The notion of God abstracted from our knowing God, even in itself is wholly held within our notion of the abstraction. Imagine God if you can, as not imagined by humans. It is like the dentist who puts two hands in your mouth, nearly tickling your tonsils and says, 'Now relax.' It is impossible because the very act of imaging God as not imagined is already an act of imagining (Greenshaw 1996, 8).

seeing god in others

The American Church attempts to deal with false images, not by smashing them, but by ignoring them. The aphorism often goes something like this, "Don't look at people, look at Jesus." This works as well as saying to your friend during a walk at the zoo, "Don't look now, but that gorilla just got out of his cage." There is a very good reason why we attempt to find the image of God in persons; because, that's where He placed it. God made persons in His image because, first, He desired fellowship with someone other than himself and, second, so that we would remind one another of God. God made us to be sacraments to one another, channels of grace, reflections of divinity, fully human creations of God. Full humanity as incarnated in Jesus Christ is the gift of God to every creature who realizes that the goal of life is not to become like God but to become like the persons God intended us to be, exemplified and fully recovered in Jesus Christ as He walked the earth. Allan Coppedge writes,

> Since God is not like the heaven, the earth, the storm, the river, or the sky, He is not represented by any of these things. He is the creator who transcends all that He has made. Yet, He has not left Himself without some representation of His likeness in the created order, and that representation is found in men and women. It is the humanity that reflects the

image of the creator in the universe so that the New Testament can declare that man "is the image and glory of God" (Coppedge 2001, 69-70).

At least the above was God's plan. The amazement in a sin-cursed world is not that there are so many hypocrites in the church, persons who claim to represent God but don't. The wonder is that there are those who claim so little and yet nonpresumably and nonassumingly enjoy such close fellowship with God, that we can know God because we know one of His friends. Such was the experience of Tony Hendra, a future editor of *National Lampoon,* when he first met Father Joe:

> Father Joe didn't appear to need the clerical metal ruler of do-it-or-I'll-tell-your father. The "he" of his God was gentle, generous, endlessly creative, musical, artistic, an engineer, an architecture of genius, a "he" who felt his joy and your joy deeply, who could be hurt just as deeply but would never give up on you, showered you with gifts and opportunities whether you acknowledged them or not, who set your tasks, but didn't abandon you if you failed them (Hendra 2004, 67).

Indeed God has left visible witness to himself in divine surprises, persons who exemplify our understanding of what it means to be a God follower. I recently attended a court session in which a judge responded to an endless string of persons whose lives were saturated with problems. Her gracious, tender attitude made me want to ask her, "Are you a Christian? You sure act like one."

The Church is God made visible to the world. The Christian community alive in Christ is the visible attestation that the Holy Spirit continues to incarnate Christ in the lives of His followers. As John Webster argues, the Church is the Holy Spirit's visibility. The concealed God becomes unhidden in the life of the believer giving public testimony to the life of God. Though the believer may be an undercover agent for Jesus Christ, the Christian cannot help but blow his own cover. Though Christianity is a subversive activity, it believes a "private Christian" to be a contradiction in terms. It was this conviction that drove Dietrich Bonhoeffer from the safe confines of Union Theological Seminary in New York City back to his native Germany in 1939, a choice that led to his death. He wrote, "To flee into invisibility is to deny the call. Any community which wants to be invisible is no longer a community that follows Him." The Church is about the business of granting physical and visible "space for Christ" in the world (Webster 2005, 97-98).

Though God may use incidents to get our attention, His most frequent visible communication media are people, portable living tabernacles that are God's vessels. God's agents provide snapshots of the Kingdom, incarnational models of God's activity in the world. Denny Noland, a plumber, provides water all over the world. He has been to Albania eight times and Katrina-devastated New Orleans seven times. A couple, whose names I have forgotten, made their way down a nursing home corridor touching, hugging, and giving cookies to the warehoused elderly who have little to look forward to other than death. They eventually came to my Dad's room, sang a song, read Scripture, and prayed. If we are attuned to the vibes of God, we will encounter a constant stream of persons who bring heaven down to earth.

Lillian Mahorny, crippled by arthritis, transcended her pain by offering encouragement to a young wobbly pastor trying to find his ministerial legs. I never encountered Lillian when she did not have a smile on her face, when she wasn't more concerned about my needs than her needs, when she wasn't more than willing to play the organ or to fix a meal for me and my family. Thomas Long refers to these incarnations of grace as intrinsic analogies, people who experience and exemplify the concept we are inducting from the Scripture (as opposed to an extrinsic analogy that we draw from another medium such as a novel or a movie):

> If we are talking about forgiveness, we need to tell some piece of experience in which there is forgiveness. If we speak of grace then, what is the experience of grace in the lives of ordinary people? These do not need to be nice, packaged, preacher stories: in fact it is far better if they are not. We are trying to say what the Christian faith looks like when it is experienced by the couple on the front pew, the family mid-way back, the single person, the teenager in the balcony (Long 1988a, 13).

the blurred image

But many "Christians" remain private, not because of unwillingness to let their light shine, but because of some fear or perception of acceptance or lack thereof. God is not their commander. He has assigned them to the other side. If no one else wants me on their team, maybe God doesn't either.

Unfortunately, in spite of the Father Joes who may grace our lives, a condemning, criticizing, overbearing parent makes it impossible, outside of grace, to envision a God who is anything but the same. How we picture God picturing us determines how we picture God. What we think God thinks of us determines what we think about God. What we think about God is consistently formed by the significant others in our lives. If significant others are constantly disappointed in us, then we will believe God to be disappointed in us. If I need to work my fingers to the quick to earn my parents approval, I will be tempted to do the same for God, and of course, God will be even more difficult to impress. If relationships in my home were tallied with an account sheet, I will enter the church with the same ledger long after I've left home. And worse yet, for some persons nothing was ever good enough, no offering of social approval was accepted at the altar of "measure up."

Such was the case for Eva whose attempts to be accepted by her adopted mother were met with "you are beneath contempt" or "I can't stomach you." Likewise, Eva pictured God shaking her until her "teeth fell out" and exclaiming, "What in the world is the matter with you?" She thought of God responding to her sniffling self-pity with a "sick to death of her complaints" attitude. To her, everything she did displeased God, or simply came up short. Eva dwelled in a world of "black despair," an inner world tormented by demons who reminded her that she was sinful, bad, and beyond reform. Eva was victimized by the demon of "mommyism" that parasitically sucked the life out of her. In the process of therapy with a Christian psychologist, Eva had a nightmare. She dreamed that "she was possessed by her mother's spirit. She saw her mother in her own body, with long, clawlike fingers, clutching her vital organs, clinging on to Eva for dear life. . . . Eva was forced to carry this inner demon that sucked her life from her" (Hunsinger 1995, 171).

Eva overcame this tyrannical guilt by displacing images of her mother with images of Scripture. She lived in, reflected on, and appropriated Eph. 6:10-18: "Put on the whole armor of God that you may be able to stand against the wiles of the devil" (v. 11, NKJV). "Girding loins with truth" set her free from the lie that she was worthless. The ultimate truth of the gospel is that we can do nothing to merit or curry God's favor. We are infinitely loved, not because of what we do, but because we are His creation. The "breastplate of righteousness" was accepted as a gift that displaced self-righteousness. "Shod with . . . the gospel of peace" brought rest to a driven self, whose ceaseless busyness warded off accusations of laziness. "The shield of faith" protected her from the haunting accusations of Mommy and Daddy's fiery darts of attacking voices. "The helmet of salvation" protected her from the enemy's most fatal head wound, a cognitive distortion that believes good works will not only get you to heaven but also provide a nice obituary. The Word of God, otherwise known as the "sword of the Spirit," subdued demonic voices and severed false accusations from the affirmation that God's "strength is made perfect in weakness" (2 Cor. 12:9, NKJV).

the pastor as theologian

A pastor accepts the role of "theologian in residence." I tell seminary students that if they do not want to talk about God, they face a serious occupational hazard. God talk is paramount for preaching. But it is amazing how much preaching ignores God, skirts around Him, and fails to allow Him to speak to the critical issues of life. Preaching worth its salt (literally) acts as a means of grace, offering God to beggars when nothing less than God will do. With all of our talk about understanding our people, culturally and sociologically, the one assumption I need to make is that they are looking for God and they need God. Even better news, and more accurate, God is looking for them. The implicit or explicit introduction to every sermon is, "Let me introduce you to God."

Preaching acts as a means of pastoral care. I define pastoral care as applying the means of grace to the potentials and crises of human existence. Preaching is collective pastoral care that offers spiritual and emotional substance to embattled, weary pilgrims. Theological discernment in preaching knows what equipment and food to ration, never underestimating what it will take to win life's ultimate battle and arrive home safely. Preaching without theological depth not only mistakes the enemy but often doesn't know a battle is raging. Paul asked, "For if the bugle produces an indistinct sound, who will prepare himself for battle?" (1 Cor. 14:8, NASB). Preaching that does not offer theological preparation for living is like a military base commissary carrying only Little Debbie cakes or a military depot distributing only BB guns. They'll do in a pinch, but emptiness and defeat are not far behind.

the god of the text

Preaching invokes the name of God over all of life so that whatever we do, we do to the glory of God. It attempts to answer the question, "What is the relationship of God to this particular event or crisis?" How do the interests of God relate to my interests? Preaching constantly declares that "God is interested," allowing that His interest may be quite different from mine. God is not aloof from the human predicament. The Scriptures record God's interaction with the people who inhabit earth. As Paul Scott Wilson argues in *God Sense,* the central task of the sermon is to ask, "What is God doing?" Every text has a theology; every text makes a theological statement. Wilson writes, "The God sense of a Biblical text may be defined as those dimensions of it that speak of God's nature, acts, and relationship to humanity and creation, and that enable the Bible to be read as Scripture, the book of the church" (Wilson 2001, 68).

Reverence for God is directly proportional to respect for the text. Preaching without concentration on Scripture is like playing tennis without a ball—it leaves too much to the imagination. The pulpit cannot focus on God without giving sustained attention to the written record He has left of His connectedness with the material world. The Bible grants authority to the pulpit. The preacher places himself or herself under the text, absorbing the text, allowing the text to become the supreme rule of life. Preaching will rise only as high as the preacher's love for the Word and willingness to spend time in it. Conviction that the Scripture is normative for faith and practice provides certitude for its proclamation. The allowance for cultural relevance and application does not undermine the fact that the Scriptures belong as much to us as they did to Jesus and Paul. No one has more concisely and profoundly stated the dynamic of Scripture as normative for the pulpit than Donald G. Miller:

> The Bible is the unique record of the unique Act which creates, sustains, and controls the life of the church, and is as final and unrepeatable as that Act because it is really a part of the Act. If, then, preaching is to reproduce the effects of that Act in human lives now, it can normally do this only by so rooting itself in the Bible that the Deed there recorded is transfigured into living reality now (Miller 1954, 61).

preaching as witness to god's activity

The holy, transcendent God of the universe is anything but detached from His creation; He has created, is creating, and will continue to create. Personal involvement with His creation is God's foremost activity. Thus, preaching is witness to and affidavit for God's involvement with humankind. Be assured we are God's No. 1 project. Jeremiah promises that God will continue His plans in us (29:11), and Paul declared to the Philippian church that "I am confident of this very thing, that he who began a good work in you will perfect it until the day of Christ Jesus" (1:6, NASB). The Greek word for *confident* is taken from a family of words that connote belief, *pisteo*. Thus, every sermon is a creedal affirmation declaring the acts of God.

The foremost topic for the preaching of the prophets in the Old Testament and the apostles in the New Testament was God's involvement in the affairs of humankind. God's spokespersons do not leave life to the unruly forces of nature and to the unpredictability of sin-bent humanity. God's providences conquer chance, fate, and even natural law when they would stymie His purposes. History for both Hebrew monotheism and Christianity are the acts of God, without denying, and even emphasizing, that individuals play key roles in that history. Biblical theologian G. Ernest Wright argues that the key difference between ancient polytheism and the religion of Israel was that for the former there was an endless repetitive cycle dictated by the rhythms of nature. The only way to not be victimized by the capricious whims of nature was to appeal to the corresponding nature god. (This should be a lesson for all who would demand that God convert himself into a weather-man, a climatic magician who can prevent rain from falling on the kids' 10:30 A.M. Saturday baseball game, while generous precipitation provides much-needed moisture on the nearby wheat fields.) Wright states, "To be sure, there is an immediate awareness of God's presence in worship, in prayer, communion and confession; but the main emphasis of the Bible is certainly on His revelation of Himself in historical acts, and in definite 'words,' not in diffuse experience" (Wright 1958, 23). Wright defines biblical theology (and I would say biblical preaching) as "the confessional recital of the redemptive acts of God in a particular history, because history is the chief medium of revelation" (Wright 1958, 15).

The two apostolic sermons in the Book of Acts anchor themselves in the acts of God. Both Peter and Stephen knew that the only defense for following Christ was to be found in God's involvement. "God is responsible for what we are doing and what you are seeing" is the primary and supreme apolo-getic for Christianity. God is in on the scheme; He is the chief accomplice. Pe-ter states, "Therefore let all the house of Israel know for certain that God has made Him both Lord and Christ—this Jesus whom you crucified" (Acts 2:36, NASB). Stephen models historical recital as a structural form for preaching. Six times he refers to what God has said or done. No sermon has ever had a more dramatic or decisive conclusion: "Behold, I see the heavens opened up and the Son of Man standing at the right hand of God" (7:56, NASB). The Scottish preacher James Stewart rightly claimed that preaching for the Early Church was the "announcement of certain concrete facts of history, the heralding of real objective events. . . . The driving force of the early Christian mission was not propaganda of beautiful ideas of the brother-hood of man: it was proclamation of the mighty acts of God" (Stewart 1946, 63).

Explaining God's intervention in history is known in theological circles as theodicy. Theodicy attempts to reason why life does not go according to our plans, given the assumptions that God is both all powerful and all good. Theodicy presents preaching with its single greatest challenge, since either the events of life at times make no sense at all from our perspective or we impose our perspective on God no matter how selfish or warped our motives may be. Such was the case for preachers during the Civil War, which Harry Stout critically explores in his meticulously researched *Upon the Altar of the Nation: A Moral History of the American Civil War.* Most preachers converted God into a southern sympathizer or a northern abolitionist. After the South took Fort Sumter, James H. Eliot declared the capture at St. Michael's Church in Charleston, South Carolina, as nothing less than "the hand of God" (Stout 2006, 44). Discerning "the hand of God" is tricky business as demonstrated by the northern preacher who suggested that Lincoln's assassination was the providence of God, since Lincoln would not "have been equal to the harsh penalties that divine justice required on the beaten South, but instead would have been too lenient" (Stout 2006, 53).

Theological integrity demands that preaching grant permission to God to be God. American preaching has demonstrated considerable difficulty in allowing God to distance himself from its national agenda. For this reason, Stout refers to Lincoln's Gettysburg Address and Second Inaugural Address as the two greatest sermons ever preached on American soil. Both the North and South "read the same Bible and prayed to the same God." They both "invoked God's aid against the other" and then in perhaps the most poetic, profound, theological statement ever made in the United States, Lincoln confessed (in his Second Inaugural) God's transcendence, wisdom, and justice over the affairs of history:

Fondly do we hope—fervently do we pray—that this mighty scourge of war may speedily pass away. Yet, if God wills that it continue, until all the wealth piled by the bond-man's two hundred and fifty years of unrequited toil shall be sunk, and until every drop of blood drawn with the lash, shall be paid by another drawn with the sword, as was said three thousand years ago, so still it must be said "the judgments of the Lord, are true and righteous altogether (Stout 2006, 427).

Several days later, Lincoln, in a letter to Thurlow Reid, appraised his performance: "I believe it is not immediately popular. Men are not flattered by being shown that there has been a difference in purpose between the Almighty and them" (Stout 2006, 428). No statement that Lincoln ever uttered more concisely summed up the irony of America's deadliest war than the following: "It may seem strange that men would invoke the assistance of a just God in wringing their bread from the sweat of other men's faces."

the visible god of scripture

Throughout Scripture God consistently shows up, appearances that we refer to as epiphanies or theophanies, in the form of angels, human messengers, and burning bushes. Fire, smoke, clouds, thunder, and lightning were not only visible indicators that God had located himself in the midst of His people but also representations of the cosmic dimensions of His holiness and greatness. These overwhelming displays of presence called for one essential response, worship. What Rudolf Otto referred to as a "hushed trembling and speechless humility of the creature" (Otto 1958, 13).

God does not give a rational argument to convince Job of His justice and fairness. He simply points to the visible reminders of His creative power, examples from nature of the "sheer absolute wondrousness that transcends thought, as the mysterium, presented in its pure non-rational form" (Otto 1958, 13). The irony is that the luminous, ineffable, mysterious, and incomprehensible God constantly shows up in quite simple forms morphing into unmistakable evidence of His presence. William Dyrness in his book *Visual Faith* summarized that "throughout Scripture the visual experience of God's people was to accompany and elaborate God's word to them. A direct line extends from Abraham's experience in Gen. 18, through Moses' encounter on Sinai, and the cloud and fire in the wilderness, to the splendor of the Temple and the vision of Isaiah and Ezekiel, right through to the transfiguration, the crucifixion, Pentecost, and the Book of the Revelation" (Dyrness 2001, 84). It was Jacob who may have experienced the most physical, visible engagement with God of anyone in Scripture. Charles Wesley poetically captured Jacob's tussle with God in "Come, O Thou Traveler Unknown":

> I need not tell Thee who I am;
> My misery and sin declare.
> Thyself hast called me by my name;
> Look on Thy hands, and read it there.
> But who, I ask Thee, who art Thou?
> Tell me Thy Name, and tell me now.
> . . . . . .
>
> My prayer hath power with God; the grace
> Unspeakable I now receive;
> Through faith I see Thee face-to-face,
> I see Thee face-to-face, and live!
> In vain I have not wept and strove;
> Thy nature and Thy name is Love.
>   (Hildebrant 1963, 28)

the anthropomorphic god

Anthropomorphisms assign body parts to God. Visualizing God with hands, feet, arms, eyes, ears, and a face does not mean the Hebrews believed God possessed corporal existence. Poetic and figurative language emphasizes God's interaction with the world and affirms the personhood of God. The Hebrews would walk and talk with a God who was not an amorphous abstraction, but One who was capable of entering into the human experience. While God was holy and separate, He also risked the hurt and frustration of earthly involvement. True, God often gave assurance of His presence, guidance, and judgment by way of climatic revelation, such as clouds, whirlwinds, earthquakes, and lightning. But more importantly He revealed himself long before the Incarnation as a God of personal touch who longed for fellowship with His creation. The anthropomorphic God exhibited both tender mercy and vengeful retribution: "The eyes of the LORD are on the righteous and his ears are attentive to their cry; the face of the LORD is against those who do evil, to cut off the memory of them from the earth" (Ps. 34:15-16).

It may seem strange that a religion that so stringently forbade idolatrous images would so constantly communicate with images. The Hebrew prophets did not absolutize images. No one verbal image could contain the complexity and mystery of the God who refused to be captured in wood and stone. Wood and stone depersonalized, while the anthropomorphisms of the ancient poets attempted to represent a God who establishes a personal relationship with His creation. The prophets created images that represent a paradoxical God who at one moment is a "rod of anger" (see Isa. 10:5), and at another moment (both at the same time?) is a lover who has the "lips of lilies dripping with liquid myrrh" (see Song of Sol. 5:13). The Hebrew prophets understood that God was who He needed to be when He needed to be. The images of God are faithful but never frozen. Sallie McFague writes, "The Hebrew poet piled up and threw away metaphors of God, in the hope of both overwhelming the imagination with the divine richness and undercutting any idolatrous inclination to absolutize images" (McFague 1982, 43).

In 1951 Father Patrick Peyton wrote a book, *The Ear of God*. Peyton pictured a God who listened, who cared, and who carried on His heart the welfare of the nuclear family. He dedicated his ministerial career to the importance of prayer, popularizing the slogan "The family who prays together stays together." Throughout the '50s and '60s Peyton, more that any single person, made the ear of God available to hundreds of thousands of people throughout the world. He spoke at prayer rallies, often assembling as many as 50,000 people. A person of simple faith, healed from tuberculosis as a seminary student, Peyton enlisted dozens of Hollywood actors to participate in *Family Theater,* a radio program that ran from 1947 to 1969. *Family Theater,* which employed the voices of such luminaries as Bing Crosby, Bob Hope, Jane Wyatt, and Loretta Young, produced 550 shows. Bob Hope played a football star whose life is shattered by an automobile accident. He finds healing through the encouragement of a little girl who suggests that he try prayer. Peyton's conviction that God really does have an "ear" brought hope and healing to untold numbers.

The God of the Hebrews not only intervened for their well-being but even more importantly desired an intimate relationship with them. Before Moses reiterated the Ten Commandments as he stood between Mount Gerizim and Mount Ebal, as recorded in Deuteronomy, he reminded the Israelites that God spoke to them face-to-face at Mount Sinai. The uniqueness of Yahweh was not to be identified in what He required of Israel but by His attitude of love and concern that described a holistic and relational lifestyle. God wouldn't write life's job description with a stylus across the sky. He would communicate face-to-face, the only way to express loving concern, something remote sovereignty could not do. Biblical Hebrew apparently did not possess an abstract word to express "presence." The expression "the face of Yahweh" or the "face of Elohim" was used to designate the innermost being of God. To be face-to-face with God suggested the proximity of divine presence. The face, more than any other physical asset, is essential to identity. Identity formation by a child is gained by gazing into his or her mother's face. A personal God demands a facial identity in spite of His noncorporeal existence.

God's intimate, exclusive relationship would be communicated to Israel, not with a marriage contract, but with the gaze of a lover. The face communicates pleasure or displeasure, approval or rejection. We read one another by catching a smile, noting a smirk, and observing either affirmation or disdain. "Can I really trust this person?" is answered by observing the face more than listening to words. The prayer of the psalmist is "God be gracious to us and bless us, and cause His face to shine upon us" (67:1, NASB). If God "hides" His face, He is not simply withholding His presence; He is refusing to look at us, communicating disgust. The psalmist expressed this concern: "When You said, 'Seek My face' my heart said to You, 'Your face, O Lord, I will seek'; do not hide Your face from me. Do not turn Your servant away in anger" (27:8-9, NKJV).

God's face never betrays His true feelings, and His emotions are always congruent with a right relationship to us. An infinite smiley face belies the world of Darfur and the streets of South Chicago. Hot tears of anguish flow from a heart that agonizes over starving children, and spouses whose faces are no longer turned toward one another. No wonder Isaiah wrote of the Savior that His appearance would not be attractive because He was "A man of sorrows acquainted with grief; and like one from whom men hide their face He was despised, and we did not esteem Him" (53:3, NASB). Amy Carmichael rescued hundreds of Indian children from temple prostitution. Attempting to discipline an incorrigible child, she sat down with the girl before a mirror and read aloud from Isa. 53: "He was wounded for our transgressions, He was bruised for our iniquities." She then beat her arm with a strap conveying to the child that God's suffering is not only a consequence for our sin but also the power over its bondage.

Thomas Moore, Ireland's national poet, married a beautiful woman. Shortly after the wedding, Moore left for an extended trip during which his wife contracted smallpox. The dreaded disease left her face so scarred that she did not believe her new husband could bear looking at her. She requested the family's physician to meet Thomas upon his return, demanding that he forget about her, marry someone else, and start life over.

Upon returning home, Moore brushed the doctor aside and made his way up the stairs to his wife's bedroom. She stood behind the drapes in the darkened chamber and refused to disclose her ill fortune. Moore spent the night in prayer, and toward dawn penned the following words:

> Believe me, if all those endearing young charms,
>> Which I gaze on so fondly today,
> Were to change by tomorrow, and fleet in my arms,
>> Like fairy gifts fading away,
>
> Thou wouldst still be adored, as this moment thou art,
>> Let thy loveliness fade as it will,
> And around the dear ruin each wish of my heart
>> Would entwine itself verdantly still.

Just after daybreak, he stood again in his wife's bedroom and sang the poem, for which he has become most famous.

Thomas Moore's wife realized that she was not loved for her beauty, charm, or wealth. She was loved unconditionally. She threw open the drapes

and melted into her husband's arms.* Only God is able to love with no concern for return of that love on himself. Only God can enable us to do the
same. Self-interested love, something less than love, is a proposition that desires a return on ego investment. If love were a business deal, speculators
would place it on the stock market. And they have. No wonder we love-
starved fools continue to rush headlong into the cold, granite wall of disillusionment, rather than into the loving embrace of God's outstretched and
everlasting arms. Even when God is tempted to turn away His face, He fas-
tens on us a loving gaze.

a visual god—models, old and new

The images of God throughout the Old and New Testament provide both
themes and illustrations for preaching. Expositions of God as potter, vine-
dresser, cornerstone, shepherd, king, and father edify the Church. The analogy of faith, looking at God and applying aspects of His existence to our existence, mold us into His image through the power of the Holy Spirit. All
analogies in some aspect fail. God dwells on the threshold between accessibility and nonaccessibility, between comprehension and mysteriousness. A
sermon that likens our relationship to God as dialing 911 arrives at a truth
but a truth greatly reduced. Thus, the question must be asked, Does this
analogy or metaphor add more than it subtracts?

The metaphors of the Old Testament were distinct to a civilization and its
ways that have long died, at least to a 13-year-old boy living in New York City.
Biblical models for God are not constructed out of an alien world but out of
life as it was known. Models were taken from the categories of family (husband, mother), work and crafts (shepherd, potter), and politics (king, warrior).
Ian Ramsey cautions that all models at sometime lose relevance and fertility. So
we must always be contemplating new models, choosing models that are more
cosmic such as protector and guide, as constant as the pounding surf, and as
steady as Mount Ranier. To be eschewed are models that are quickly drained of
"disclosure possibilities" such as "fast as a Lamborghini" or "macho as a
Harley Davidson." The greater the novelty, the shorter the shelf life. Victorians
who spoke of railways to heaven lead Ramsey to quip, "There is little about the
British railroad to generate cosmic disclosure" (Ramsey 2007, 292).

---

*This may be an apocryphal account. The story is also told that Thomas Moore wrote
these words for the wife of the Duke of Wellington when her face was marred with the
scars of smallpox.

All models run the risk of limitation and the simplicity often disdained by academic theologians. The recent seminary student who was squeamish about the Bible being referred to as a "road map," and a theology professor who condemned Jesus being labeled the "all time champion of the world" need to hear the following from Ramsey: "At the moment it really does seem that we are all desperately afraid of leaving the well-trodden path of theological jargon and of claiming that measure of imaginative freedom which all the great preachers from Amos to Saint Paul assumed—not as a right, but as a pastoral necessity" (Ramsey 2007, 294). The poets have excelled in making God visible, as the following prayer from George MacDonald demonstrates:

> Be thou the well by which I lie and rest:
> Be thou my tree of life, my garden ground;
> Be thou my home, my fire, my chamber blest,
> My book of wisdom, loved of all the best;
> Oh, be my friend, each day still newer found,
> As the eternal days and nights go round!
> Nay, nay—thou art my God, in whom all loves are bound!*

In *Doing Theology with Huck and Jim,* Mark Shaw explores theology through "lordly lions and hassled husbands, Scrooge's and Huck Finn's, private investigators and perturbed insects" (Shaw 1993, 12). His most prevalent metaphor for God is that of "author," one who writes us into the "song of creation." Dickens rescued Scrooge from his evil self, and Mark Twain wept when Huck's drunken father beat his mother. Shaw imagines a conversation between Twain and Huck demonstrating the doctrine of freedom:

> Don't you understand—the only desires that exist in a character are "implanted" ones. I gave you the gift of freedom—the only kind of freedom that exists—the gifts of doing what you desire. There is no "you" apart from me. I give you life and breath and desire, and all I hear you say is that you, as a character, don't want character traits, you want to be the ultimate author (Shaw 1993, 118).

Shaw creates the god Pan living on Willow Island where "reeds sway like island dancers" and "grassy banks are filled with play and laughter." Pan with his flute "plays the music that creates and sustains the world of the river." Ratty explains to Mole after a lunch of cakes and melons, "We possess the powers to join in the music making with Pan. We can see the musical score as if it were all around us. The visible world is but the staff and notes of

*From *Diary of an Old Soul* by George MacDonald (p. 23) copyright © 1994 Augsburg Books. Used by permission of Augsburg Fortress Publishers.

the composition" (Shaw 1993, 140). Ratty confuses the cawing of the crows with the music from Pan's flute. "It must be Pan who is the source of the noise that is beating against my brain." Ratty stabs and kills Pan. Mole, even though he strikes the final blow into the still breathing Pan, testifies against his friend in court. The parable suggests aversion to God, alienation of others, and destruction of the environment, a rebellion cosmic in scope and intensely personal in its accusation. Sin is nothing less than theocide, the murder of God. If I choose sin, it would be better that God didn't exist.

Metaphors for God and our relationship to Him run the risk of both overstatement and understatement. This has been especially true of the Holiness Movement in which I have been fully immersed all of my Christian days. One of my former professors likened God entirely sanctifying us to his treatment of the poison ivy that grew in his backyard. He dug it up with a backhoe, poured gallons of gasoline in the trench, ignited the gasoline, scorched the trench, emptied bags of salt in the blackened hole, covered it back up with dirt, and then poured a concrete patio over the area. Obviously, a bit of overkill, a spiritual treatment that would not only sanctify but annihilate the recipient.

Codification, systemization, and analogical representation of God often come up short. Allegorical, metaphorical, and poetical theologies risk reductionism, which is why Sallie McFague and Amos Wilder argue that theology cannot abandon rational, conceptual modes of thought. It is at this very point that much tension has existed between the pulpit and academy. The incompatibility between the two is explored by Donald Wiebe in *The Irony of Theology and the Nature of Religious Thought*. Christianity has always had difficulties reconciling *mythos* and *logos*. Wiebe argues, I think overly so, that the nature of religious experience is incompatible with scientific rational attempts at plausibility. Such attempts have been "corrosive" to faith, since the temptation of rationality has always been to tame irrationality, to fine-sandpaper the unruly edges of our faith. We have never been quite able to explain God without capturing and manacling Him.

In *Ministry in the Image of God* Stephen Seamands confesses the paradox between God's simplicity and mystery. Though most analogies for the Trinity result in tritheism (three Gods) or modalism (a one-person God manifesting in three different ways), Seamands encourages visual aids for God's "complex simplicity": the three different states of water; the root, trunk and branches of a tree; or egg as white, yolk, and shell. In our attempts to give visual expression to God, we need to keep in mind the theological axiom of the 18th-century Gerhard Tersteegen whom Seamands quotes: "A God understood, a God comprehended, is no God" (Seamands 2005, 99). Capturing God on our mental celluloid is like the boy who kept trying to pour the Mediterranean Sea in a hole he had dug on the beach. The 4th-century bishop Augustine responded, "My dear boy, what an impossible thing to try to do. The sea is too vast and your hole is too small." A sobering and humbling observation for the theologian who had just given 15 years to writing a 500-page tome, *The Trinity*.

preaching as parousia

Preaching experiences its apotheosis in *parousia,* the coming of God. The ultimate desire for any sermon, the purpose of all preaching, is that God would come. Preaching consecrates itself as an instrument for the visitation of God. Preaching invites God to come, envisioning what life is like living in His presence. Parousia preaching imagines and describes specific situations where God overcomes evil, dispels darkness, transcends hatred, and speaks peace. What does a city invaded by God look like? What is the character of a God-directed marriage? What is conversation like in the presence of Christ? What kind of atmosphere would prevail in a public high school if a sizable minority of the students relied on the Holy Spirit to craft them into vessels transporting kindness and integrity?

The Book of the Revelation paints the most visual view of God not only in the Bible but in all of literature. Unfortunately, God in all His blinding beauty has been hidden behind the schemes of would-be clairvoyants who are bent on limiting the Book of the Revelation to time, place, and event. Relegating universal symbolism to my world in the 21st century, with ethnocentric interpretations, dulls vibrant symbolism meant to define all times and all places. Speculation, trading old conjecture for new relative to world events, obscures a tale as old as time, a prince is looking for a bride. His options are clear: He can marry a harlot who is beautiful, rich, seductive, and powerful or He can claim a woman whom He himself has made righteous, clean, and pure.

Bible scholars translate the Greek word *apokalypsis* as "revelation." Of course, the critical question for the Bible's last book is, "What does it reveal?" Because John opens the book with "The revelation of Jesus Christ," an expectant journey through its pages looks for signs and clues to the person and character of Jesus Christ. We come ultimately to a picture of the glorified living Christ: "His eyes are a flame of fire, and on His head are many diadems; and He has a name written on Him which no one knows except Himself. He is clothed with a robe dipped in blood, and His name is called The

Word of God" (19:12-13, NASB). If He showed up on Sunday morning, which He desires to do, two things would happen. First, He would get my attention. Second, I would do as the 24 elders—fall down before Him and worship.

As I write this, a newspaper article informs me that London scientists just yesterday moved the "Doomsday Clock" 2 minutes ahead to 11:57. We are on the brink of an "apocalypse," a nuclear or environmental disaster of cataclysmic proportions. This corruption of the word *apocalypse*—"All the bad things in the Bible," says Bruce Willis in *Armageddon*, as an asteroid is about to hit the earth—bypasses the ultimate revelation: "BEHOLD, HE IS COMING WITH THE CLOUDS, and every eye will see Him, even those who pierced Him; and all the tribes of the earth will mourn over Him" (1:7, NASB). Apocalyptic preaching is not a doomsday announcement; it is the Word of the stone rolling down the mountain, the sword out of His mouth, and the white horse galloping down the aisle of the church. Aidan Kavanaugh opines that receiving the Word of God "is not like receiving a telephone call, not like getting an idea. The Word of God is always a revelation: we stand before it always like Moses before the mystery of a burning bush, in awe, reverence—worshipfully" (Kavanaugh 1995, 132).

preaching as empowering sacrament

Sacramental preaching imparts the acts of God to the life of worship. Word and table, prophet and priest, are fused together because the Word becomes covenant, God's intention of gracious activity within the community of the gospel. As the priest offers the bread and cup, the prophet offers the death and resurrection of our Lord, not simply as historical events, but as experiential realities for 21st-century Christians. David Tracy in *The Analogical Imagination* argues for preaching as sacrament, the "manifestation" of God. Just as God's ontological reality is in the consecrated elements, the Living Word, Christ, is present in the spoken word. Tracy writes,

If the cosmic and symbolic reality is disallowed, if the paradigmatic power of real manifestation is allowed to slip away quietly under the defamiliarizing blows of the paradigmatic power of the proclaimed word, then the deepest needs of our hearts and imagination are themselves discarded and Christianity eventually retreats into a righteous rigorism of duty and obligation (Tracy 1981, 217).

Gospel preaching is a redemptive event, as Donald G. Miller argues, the "deed of God" in the life of both preacher and congregation. Preaching is more and other than remembering the events of Scripture. It is a reenactment of God's faithfulness to keep His gracious promises. Preaching is not an exercise in rhetoric; it is a participation in Exodus, Resurrection, and Pentecost, all of which point to Christ's triumphant return. The worship of preaching climaxes with *maranatha*, "Even so, come, Lord Jesus" (Rev. 22:20, NKJV).

The ultimate assessment for preaching is what God does in the life of the congregation and in return what the congregation does in the life of the world. God-centered preaching sanctifies the Christian community for supplanting the kingdom of darkness with the Kingdom of Light. Thus, preaching becomes a powerful benediction to enlist and empower Christ's Body: "As the Father has sent me, so I am sending you" (John 20:21, NLT). He is entrusting us with the keys to the Kingdom no less than He did Peter. Preaching breathes on the congregation Christ's words: "Receive the Holy Spirit. If you forgive anyone his sins, they are forgiven; if you do not forgive them, they are not forgiven" (John 20:22-23). Preaching authorizes the Christian to live within Christ's promise, "Lo, I am with you always even unto the end of the world" (Matt. 28:20, KJV).

Preaching as speech differs from preaching as mission. Missional preaching does not simply inform about Christ, it imparts to the congregation the provision that is in Christ. The text of Scripture becomes Christ in us the hope of glory. The purpose of Christ becomes the purpose of the Church to be God's audiovisual. Anointed preaching is the work of the Holy Spirit transcribing the Living Word into the life of the believer. The Spirit without word becomes individualistic subjectivity, and word without Spirit becomes life-killing legalism. The Holy Spirit transforms Scripture into the Church's living reality. Craddock perceptively writes, "The truth is, and by this the church sometimes feels embarrassed, there is no agreement among Christians as to the canon for ascertaining the Spirit's absence or presence at the time of an event. Afterward, of course, the evidence of love, hope, trust, truth, and justice can be read clearly as footprints that say 'yes the Spirit was here'" (Craddock 1985, 29).

Preaching as vision enables the Church to become actors in God's plan, no less than were the apostles. Enactment preaching opens the curtain on the divine drama in such a way that worshipers envision themselves as the actors. Preaching effects the acceptance of a role in God's purpose for the Christian in the surrounding world. Sermonic liturgy conscripts actors for parts as unique and varied as the persons who fulfill them. Prophetical, priestly preaching grants authority to the Christian to become not a bit player but a person of destiny, accepting the divine mandate to determine history. All the feasts of Israel celebrated how God had used people to enact His will on earth: Passover, Booths, Pentecost, and Purim. These feasts were celebrated with the hope that the same God-centered dependence for life's meaning would continue to characterize Israel's distinction as the people of God. Peter who was preaching to the Gentiles transferred vocational election to the Christian Church when he wrote, by borrowing Old Testament language, "But you are a chosen race, a royal priesthood, a holy nation, the people for God's own possession, so that you may proclaim the excellencies of Him who has called you out of darkness into His marvelous light" (1 Pet. 2:9, NASB).

Enactment preaching will at times enlist worshipers to act out the sermon. No one I have observed excels at congregational participation more than Kirby John Caldwell, pastor of Windsor Village United Methodist Church in Houston. In a sermon on the relationship between faith and obedience Caldwell enlisted two persons to chase one another across the front of the church, exemplifying that one always follows on the heels of the other. In challenging believers to not limit God by building a box of unbelief, participants formed a square. The human formation began with many and decreased to few, the space for God's actions becoming almost nonexistent. The point was clear: our "God box" limits what God can do in our lives. Caldwell practices what Pamela Ann Moeller refers to as *A Kinesthetic Homiletic* and Thomas Troeger designates as "logosomantics." Caldwell embodies the gospel by running, leaping, sitting, and any posture appropriate for the particular truth he is asserting. Moeller writes, "When we are embodied by a scriptural passage, when we live it out through group process, we know in our DNA, in the inner workings of our joints, in inhalation/exhalation, that Scripture embodies gospel which is a now interrelationship that depends very much on the persons God addresses participating in that relationship" (Moeller 1993, 83).

preaching as worship

The end of all preaching is worship. Preaching at its best is not persuasion, explanation, or even theological enlightenment. It is the symbolism of words translated by the Holy Spirit into worship of the Triune God. Preaching is an act of worship, the same as every other component of the worship service. Any kind of arrangement that isolates the sermon from the rest of the worship service loses preaching's primary focus, the worship of God. Such isolation is often accented by a practical message directed to the need of the moment rather than the glory of God. The aim of preaching, as David Peterson states, "is to provoke acceptable worship in the form of prayer, praise and obedience, in the church and in the context of everyday life" (Peterson 1992, 153).

The focus of worship in the Book of the Revelation is the Lamb, the Redeemer of humankind. Redemption is the theme of worship in song, creed, Scripture, prayer, preaching, and benediction. Every worship service reenacts the Christological drama of death and resurrection, the acts of Christ that offer salvation to humankind. The sermon announces that Christ is risen, He is alive, and He is presently available to the thirsty, hungry, and empty. Preaching is a liturgical act among other liturgical acts, the certain sound that all are included and can avail themselves of the benefits of the Lamb slain for all who desire freedom from bondage.

The interactive nature of preaching, the dialogue between proclaimer and participant in worship, should preclude preaching as a virtuoso performance complemented by polite parishioners. In "Blood Sacrifice," Dorothy Sayers characterized Garrick Drury, the lead actor in a play, as a man with all the right theatrical gestures even at the door of death. The last words he utters are, "'Brand! Fetch Brand! The curtain must go up!' Garrick Drury's death was very good theater" (Sayers 2002, 743). Preaching preluded by the "curtain going up" undermines, if not completely destroys, its spiritual essence. Preaching honors Christ not as the main event but as part of a seamless flow, thematically placed within the worship service, connected to what has gone before and what will come after. Richard Lischer states, "when it disregards its liturgical matrix, preaching becomes the individualistic, virtuoso performance with which many Protestants are familiar and thereby diminishes both itself and the church" (Lischer 1992, 27). All of us ego-starved preachers need to hear and rehear John Henry Jowett's admonition against self-glorification:

> Yes, men admire, but they do not revere; they appreciate, but they do not repent; they are interested, but they are not exalted. They say, "what a fine sermon!" not, "What a great God!" They say, "What a ready speaker!" and not, "Oh, the depth of the riches both of the wisdom and knowledge of God!" (Jowett 1912, 98).

Can the commonness of an ordinary person, standing in an ordinary pulpit, in an ordinary church, on an ordinary Sunday make a difference in an ordinary person's life? I suspect so if the prayer for each sermon is "God, will you make your presence known?" Once in a while some antiquated, anticipatory soul mistakenly believes that he or she wants to see and hear a preacher. If that is God's perennial means for Him to make himself known, so be it. But even better yet is the preacher who keeps in mind the intention of the Greeks who stated 2,000 years ago, "We would see Jesus" (John 12:21, KJV). The promise is "And I, if I be lifted up . . . , will draw all [people] unto me" (v. 32, KJV). Visual preaching in a day of mass media prays the prayer of the old Irish melody:

> Be Thou my Vision, O Lord of my heart;
> Naught be all else to me, save that Thou art—
> Thou my best thought, by day or by night,
> Waking or sleeping, Thy presence my light.
> > (Sing to the Lord 1993, 460)

the sermon as redemptive matrix

The sermon becomes visible in the Eucharist, the acted Word. Words become the Word, the broken body and the spilled blood of Christ. The sermon invites to the table both those who have repented of their sins and those who desire to enter through the door of salvation. The Eucharist appropriates the spoken word, enabling the hearers to now become doers, partakers in the reality of Christ's presence. These visible symbols of "God with us" fortify and strengthen, providing sustenance for the journey ahead. The table is the sign and reminder that the journey will lead us to the marriage supper of the Lamb, the eternal feast in the presence of God.

The Book of the Revelation celebrates redemption in and through the *Agnus Dei*, the Lamb of God. John the Baptist modeled and prescribed the theme for all preaching when he ushered in the dispensation of Christ by proclaiming, "Behold! The Lamb of God who takes away the sin of the world!" (John 1:29, NKJV). Every sermon, no matter how dark and foreboding the text, becomes an announcement of redemption accomplished by and offered in the sacrifice of Christ. Though more difficult to find in some passages than others, every text sits within a redemptive matrix. Even the most negative text of judgment points toward mercy and grace found in Jesus Christ.

My pastor requested me to preach on the Sunday after Christmas, a day not relished for its homiletical possibilities. The American calendar calls for the preacher to give a rousing challenge for entering into the New Year with more fervent hope and dedicated commitment. The Christian calendar fo-

cuses on an event that would have taken place sometime after the birth of
Christ, even as late as early childhood. The magi, in all likelihood, visited the
Child sometime during that first year. Their visit resulted in the "slaying of the
innocents," that dastardly deed by Herod. Herod slew his two sons, killed his
first wife, and had his mother-in-law executed, prompting Caesar Augustus
to opine, "I would rather be one of Herod's pigs than his son." Yep, Herod
would have thrown his own mother off the train. Which raises the ironical
question: If the star could have led the magi 700 miles across the desert, why
did God have them stop in Jerusalem? Couldn't God have led the wise men
five miles further without them lodging in Jerusalem and asking for directions
at Abraham's Pretty Good Grocery and Chuzak's Chariot Garage? God
would have spared a whole lot of lives and saved mothers a heap of
heartache without looping in Herod. In fact, it was Herod, after consulting
the theological bigwigs, who sent the magi to Bethlehem with the most hypo-
critical request ever concocted: "Go and search carefully for the Child; and
when you have found Him, report to me, so that I too may come and worship Him" (Matt. 2:8, NASB).

The first assumption for all preaching is that no biblical event is a result
of God's oversight. Conjecturing God's motives by working from least plausible to most plausible provides a structural methodology for a sermon on the
magi's visit and the resulting tragedy. Matthew refers to five incidents in the
nativity narrative as being fulfilled by the prophet (Luke none). Concerning
the slaying of the children two years and under he wrote, "A voice was heard
in Ramah, weeping and great mourning, Rachel weeping for her children;
And she refused to be comforted because they were no more" (Matt. 2:18,
NASB). William Barclay dismisses the Matthew connection between Jeremiah's
prophecy (31:15) and the Bethlehem slaughter. Nevertheless, it is clear that
Matthew is attempting to set Herod within God's overall design.

A more convincing reason for God's inclusion of Herod is that the puppet
potentate inadvertently moves the manger on to the world's political stage. A
marginal and peripheral event suddenly becomes the concern of a head of
state? When God is at work, backstage becomes center stage and the side-
lines become the main playing field. God uses the inadvertent choices of people who are caught up in a far bigger game than they realize. Such was the
case for Joseph's brothers when they decided to pawn him off on Ishmaelite
traders. In 1949, an egomaniacal newspaper tycoon, William Randolph
Hearst (Citizen Kane?) memoed his reporters about a young gyrating country
boy evangelist preaching in the big city: "Puff Graham." The rest is history. In

Matthew's nativity narrative, God did not need a memo; He used an already existing rumor mill to get the attention of a paranoid dictator. The word got out that a King had been born.

The more probable reason for risking the Bethlehem atrocity is the acceptance and recognition of an evil world. The anticlimax to Christ's birth erases every sentimental notion of a platonic baby born into a biospheric existence. We recognize in the birth narrative, not the Gerber baby with wings and a halo, but a shriveled-up infant whose scrawny arms and tufts of hair are covered with primordial slime. The birth of Christ not only assaults the senses but is immediately confronted with systemic evil. Christ's birth does not obscure the fact that this is the world, in my lifetime, of Stalin, Pol Pot, Idi Amin, and Saddam Hussein. Henry Wadsworth Longfellow wrote in "I Heard the Bells on Christmas Day,"

> *And in despair I bowed my head.*
> *"There is no peace on earth," I said,*
> *"For hate is strong, and mocks the song*
> *Of peace on earth, goodwill to men."*

All the above serve as tangential reasons why Herod is assigned by God a role in the incarnational drama. But not the real reason. If decisions by the committee of the Trinity are conciliar, the three persons of the Godhead along with a few angels and possibly Moses and Elijah would have had a strategic planning meeting in the celestial boardroom:

"Tell me again why I'm changing zip codes," Jesus asked.

"Well," said the Father.

But before He could go on, one of the less experienced angels said with enthusiastic prediction, "I can tell you right now, things will never be the same. After Jesus assumes an address on the third rock from the sun, Christmas crèches will be built on town squares (He didn't foresee the ACLU). Marshall Fields will have the neatest window displays, KUDL radio station will play nonstop Christmas music from Thanksgiving to Christmas Day, and Dean Martin will sing a gazillion times 'There Is No Place like Home for the Holidays.'"

Everything in the boardroom got quiet, then Jesus spoke, "I'm not sure that's worth putting Joseph and Mary through that much trouble, much less suffering death, even death on a cross."

Then the Father spoke, "Only one reason can suffice for leaving the perfection of heaven for a sin-cursed world. I'm not willing that any should perish but that all should come to repentance."

Again pensive silence, "All?" someone asked. "You don't really mean anybody, no matter what they've done or said, do You?"

"Anybody," said the Father.

"But wouldn't it help to start with respectable, good, pious people to let the religious establishment know we're legit?" somebody asked.

The Holy Spirit chimed in, "Yes, I've already got Elizabeth, Simeon, and Anna lined up. Anybody else?"

"Herod," answered the Father.

"Herod?" responded several committee members with astonishment. "You're not talking about the Herod who paid slave wages to thousands building a temple to secure his own legacy rather than glorify God? Not the Herod who is the hated, half-breed tyrant?"

"Yes, *that* Herod," the Father said with quiet but strong conviction.

And so Herod became the first person by name in the Christmas story to learn that a King had been born. He made the one decision that every single person confronted by Christ's appearance into the world will have to make, "Am I going to be king or is He going to be King?" Far-fetched? Not more far-fetched than the most exaggerated claim in all of history: God became man and died for you and me.

The only way Christ can become Sovereign for my listeners is for Him to be preeminent in my preaching. The proclamation of the pulpit can do no better than the affirmation of the Early Church, "Jesus is Lord." Christ will rule human hearts because He, not the preacher, sits on the throne of the pulpit. Exalting Christ in all of His glory, beauty, holiness, and ultimate triumph will ensure that preaching will continue to be a critical task for God's Church and its servants. Jesus said, "Anyone who has seen me has seen the Father" (John 14:9). May the Holy Spirit enable both you and me to make sure they see Jesus. Preaching is fully realized when knees bow and tongues confess, "Christ, King of Kings, and Lord of Lords."

references

Achtemeier, Elizabeth. 1981. *Creative Preaching: Finding the Words.* Nashville: Abingdon.

———. 1984. *Preaching as Theology and Art.* Nashville: Abingdon.

Adams, Douglas. 1997. *The Prostitute in the Family Tree: Discovering Humor and Irony in the Bible.* Louisville: Westminster/John Knox Press.

Allen, Ronald, Barbara S. Blaisdell, and Scott Black Johnston. 1997. *Theology for Preaching: Authority, Truth, and Knowledge of God in a Postmodern Ethos.* Nashville: Abingdon.

Alter, Robert. 1981. *The Art of Biblical Narrative.* New York: Basic Books, Inc.

Arnheim, Rudolf. 1969. *Visual Thinking.* Berkeley, Calif.: University of California Press.

Babin, Pierre. 1991. *The New Era in Religious Communication.* Minneapolis: Fortress.

Baldwin, James. 1953. *Go Tell It on the Mountain.* New York: Dell Publishing Company.

Barnard, Malcolm. 1995. "Advertising: A Rhetorical Imperative." In *Visual Culture.* Ed. Chris Jenks. New York: Routledge.

Barsotti, Catherine M., and Robert K. Johnston. 2004. *Finding God in the Movies: 33 Films of Reel Faith.* Grand Rapids: Baker Books.

Bartow, Charles L. 1997. *God's Human Speech: A Practical Theology of Proclamation.* Grand Rapids: William B. Eerdmans Publishing Company.

Belton, John. 1994. *American Cinema/American Culture.* New York: McGraw-Hill, Inc.

Bible, Ken, ed. 1993. *Sing to the Lord.* Kansas City: Lillenas Publishing Company.

Boomershine, Thomas E. 1988. *Story Journey: An Invitation to the Gospel as Storytelling.* Nashville: Abingdon.

Boorstin, Jon. 1995. *Making Movies Work: Thinking like a Filmmaker.* Los Angeles: Silman-James Press.

Braaten, Carl. E., and Robert W. Jenson, eds. 2002. *The Strange New Word of the Gospel: Re-Evangelizing in the Postmodern World.* Grand Rapids: William B. Eerdmans Publishing Company.

Bragg, Rick. 1997. *All Over but the Shoutin'.* New York: Vintage Books.

Branigan, Edward. 2006. *Projecting a Camera: Language-Games in Film Theory.* New York: Routledge.

Broadus, John A. 1944. *On the Preparation and Delivery of Sermons.* New York: Harper and Row.

Brooks, David. 2000. *Bobos in Paradise: The New Upper Class and How They Got There.* New York: Simon and Schuster.

Brueggemann, Walter. 1989. *Finally Comes the Poet: Daring Speech for Proclamation.* Minneapolis: Augsburg Fortress.

———. 1995. "Preaching as Reimagination." *Theology Today* 52: No. 3 (October): 313-29.

———. 1988. "The Social Nature of the Biblical Text for Preaching." In *Preaching as a Social Act: Theology and Practice.* Ed. Arthur Van Seters, 127-65. Nashville: Abingdon.

Bryant, David J. 1989. *Faith and the Play of Imagination: On the Role of Imagination in Religion.* Macon, Ga.: Mercer University Press.

Bushman, Richard L. 1977. "Jonathan Edwards as a Great Man: Identity, Conversion, and Leadership in the Great Awakening." In *Encounter with Erikson: Historical Interpretation and Religious Biography,* Eds. Donald Capps, Walter H. Capps, M. Gerald Bradford, 217-52. Missoula, Mont.: Scholars Press.

Buttrick, David. 1987. *Homiletic: Moves and Structures.* Philadelphia: Fortress Press.

———. 1983. "On Preaching a Parable: The Problem of Homiletic Method." *Reformed Liturgy and Music* 17, Winter: 16-21.

Caird, G. B. 1997. *The Language and Imagery of the Bible.* Grand Rapids: William B. Eerdmans Publishing Company.

Camery-Hoggatt, Jerry. 2006. "God in the Plot: Storytelling and the Many-Sided Truth of the Christian Faith." In *Christian Scholar's Review* 35, Summer: 451-70.

———. 1992. *Irony in Mark's Gospel*. New York: Cambridge University Press.

Capote, Truman. 1994. *In Cold Blood*. New York: Vintage Books.

Capps, Donald. 1993. *The Poet's Gift: Toward the Renewal of Pastoral Care*. Louisville: Westminster/John Knox Press.

Chadwick, Samuel. 1972. *The Way to Pentecost*. London: Hadden and Stoughton.

Coppedge, Allan. 2001. *Portraits of God: A Biblical Theology of Holiness*. Downers Grove, Ill.: InterVarsity Press.

Craddock, Fred B. 1981. *As One Without Authority*. Nashville: Abingdon.

———. 1978. *Overhearing the Gospel*. Nashville: Abingdon.

———. 1985. *Preaching*. Nashville: Abingdon.

Crenshaw, James L. 1994. *Trembling at the Threshold of a Biblical Text*. Grand Rapids: William B. Eerdmans Publishing Company.

Cupitt, Don. 1991. *What Is a Story?* London: SCM Press.

Daiches, David. 1984. *God and the Poets*. Oxford, England: Clarendon Press.

Defoe, Daniel. 2003. *Robinson Crusoe*. New York: Barnes and Noble.

Denison, Charles. 2006. *The Artist's Way of Preaching*. Louisville: Westminster/John Knox Press.

Dissanayake, Ellen. 1990. *What Is Art For?* Seattle: University of Washington Press.

Dyrness, William A. 2001. *Visual Faith: Art, Theology, and Worship in Dialogue*. Grand Rapids: Baker Academic.

Eberhart, Elvin T. 1977. *Burnt Offerings: Parables for 20th-Century Christians*. Nashville: Abingdon.

Edie, James. 1976. *Speaking and Meaning: The Phenomenology of Language*. Bloomington, Ind.: Indiana University Press.

Edwards, J. Kent. 2005. *Effective First-Person Biblical Preaching: The Steps from Text to Narrative Sermon*. Grand Rapids: Zondervan.

Egri, Lajos. 2004. *The Art of Dramatic Writing: Its Basis in the Creative Interpretation of Human Motives*. New York: Touchstone.

Ehrenreich, Barbara. 2001. *Nickel and Dimed: On (Not) Getting By in America*. New York: Henry Holt and Company.

Eliot, George. 1999. *Silas Marner*. New York: Signet Classic.

Ewen, Stuart. 1988. *All Consuming Images: The Politics of Style in Contemporary Culture*. New York: Basic Books, Inc.

Fant, Clyde E., and William M. Pinson, eds. 1971. *Twenty Centuries of Great Preaching: An Encyclopedia of Preaching*. Waco, Tex.: Word Books.

Farris, Stephen. 1998. *Preaching That Matters: The Bible and Our Lives*. Louisville: Westminster/John Knox Press.

Faulkner, William. 1965. "A Rose for Emily." In *Idea and Image*. Ed. Hans P. Guth, 168-76. Belmont, Calif.: Wadsworth Publishing Company.

———. 1984. *The Sound and the Fury*. New York: Dell Publishing Company.

Fitzgerald, F. Scott. 2004. *The Great Gatsby*. New York: Scribner.

Fleming, Alice. 1973. *The Moviemakers: A History of American Movies Through the Lives of Ten Great Directors*. New York: St. Martin's Press.

Forde, Gerhard O. 1990. *Theology Is for Proclamation*. Minneapolis: Augsburg Fortress.

Galli, Mark, and Craig B. Larson. 1994. *Preaching That Connects: Using Journalistic Techniques to Add Impact*. Grand Rapids: Zondervan.

Gardner, John. 1999. *On Becoming a Novelist*. New York: W.W. Norton and Company, Inc.

Gayford, Martin and Karen Wright. 2000. *The Grove Book of Art Writing*. New York: Grove Press.

Gerard, Philip. 1996. *Creative Nonfiction: Researching and Crafting Stories of Real Life*. Long Grove, Ill.: Waveland Press, Inc.

Giannetti, Louis. 1999. *Understanding Movies*. Upper Saddle River, N.J.: Prentice Hall.

Glodo, Michael. 2001. "The Bible in Stereo: New Opportunities for Biblical Interpretation in an A-Rational Age." In *The Challenge of Post Modernism*. Ed. David Dockery. Grand Rapids: Baker Academic.

Good, Edwin. 1981. *Irony in the Old Testament*. Sheffield, England: Almond Press.

Green, Joel B., and Michael Pasquarello III. 2003. *Narrative Reading, Narrative Preaching: Reuniting New Testament Interpretation and Proclamation*. Grand Rapids: Baker Academic.

Greenshaw, David M. 1996. "The Formation of Consciousness." In *Preaching as a Theological Task: World, Gospel, Scripture*. Eds. Thomas G. Long and Edward Farley, 1-16. Louisville: Westminister/John Knox Press.

Hart, Darryl. 2004. *Deconstructing Evangelicalism: Conservative Protestantism in the Age of Billy Graham*. Grand Rapids: Baker Academic.

Hayward, Susan. 2000. *Cinema Studies: The Key Concepts*. New York: Routledge.

Hazelton, Roger. 1967. *A Theological Approach to Art*. Nashville: Abingdon.

Heilbroner, Robert L. 1999. *The Worldly Philosophers: The Lives, Times, and Ideas of the Great Economic Thinkers*. New York: Touchstone.

Hendra, Tony. 2004. *Father Joe: The Man Who Saved My Soul*. New York: Random House.

Heschel, Abraham. 1962. *The Prophets*. New York: Harper and Row.

Higgins, Gareth. 2004. *How Movies Helped Save My Soul: Finding Spiritual Fingerprints in Culturally Significant Films*. Lake Mary, Fla.: Relevant Books.

Hildebrandt, Franz. 1963. *Wesley Hymnbook*. Kansas City: Lillenas Publishing Company.

Hipps, Shane. 2005. *The Hidden Power of Electronic Culture: How Media Shapes Faith, the Gospel, and Church*. Grand Rapids: Zondervan.

Holbrook, Clyde. 1984. *The Iconoclastic Deity: Biblical Images of God*. Lewisburg, Pa.: Bucknell University Press.

Hood, Ann. 1998. *Creating Character Emotions*. Cincinnati: Story Press.

Hunsinger, Deborah Van Deusen. 1995. *Theology and Pastoral Counseling: A New Interdisciplinary Approach*. Grand Rapids: William B. Eerdmans Publishing Company.

Jemielity, Thomas. 1992. *Satire and the Hebrew Prophets*. Louisville: Westminster/John Knox Press.

Jenks, Chris. 1995. "The Centrality of the Eye in Western Culture: An Introduction." In *Visual Culture*. Ed. Chris Jenks. New York: Routledge.

Jhally, Sut. 1995. "Image-Based Culture: Advertising and Popular Culture." In *Gender, Race and Class in Media*. Eds. Gail Dines and Jean Humez, 71-81. Oaks, Calif.: Sage Publications.

Johnson, Paul. 1990. *Intellectuals*. New York: HarperPerennial.

Jonsson, Jakob. 1965. *Humour and Irony in the New Testament*. Copenhagen, Denmark: International Booksellers and Publishers.

Jordan, Clarence. 1969. *The Cotton Patch Version of Luke and Acts: Jesus' Doings and the Happenings*. New York: Association Press.

Jowett, J. H. 1912. *The Preacher and His Life and Work*. New York: George H. Doran Company.

Jungel, Eberhard. 1989. *Theological Essays*. Edinburgh, Scotland: T & T Clark Ltd.

Kavanaugh, Aidan J. 1995. "Scriptural Word and Liturgical Worship." In *Reclaiming the Bible for the Church*. Eds. Carl E. Braaten and Robert W. Jenson, 131-37. Grand Rapids: William B. Eerdmans Publishing Company.

Kellner, Douglas. 1995. "Reading Images Critically: Toward a Postmodern Pedagogy." In *Gender, Race and Class in Media*. Eds. Gail Dines and Jean Humez, 126-35. Oaks, Calif.: Sage Publications.

Kierkegaard, Søren. 1967. *Training in Christianity*. Princeton, N.J.: Princeton University Press.

Kilbourne, Jean. 1995. "Beauty and the Beast of Advertising." In *Gender, Race and Class in Media*. Eds. Gail Dines and Jean Humez, 121-25. Oaks, Calif.: Sage Publications.

King, Stephen. 2000. *On Writing: A Memoir of the Craft*. New York: Pocket Books.

Kinlaw, Dennis. *Let's Start with Jesus.* Francis Asbury Society. Audiotape.

Klein, Lillian R. 1988. *The Triumph of Irony in the Book of Judges.* Decatur, Ga.: The Almond Press.

Kress, Nancy. 1998. *Dynamic Characters: How to Create Personalities That Keep Readers Captivated.* Cincinnati: Writer's Digest Books.

Lee, Robert G. 1957. *Pay-Day, Someday.* Grand Rapids: Zondervan Publishing House.

Lewis, C. S., ed. 1966. *Essays Presented to Charles Williams.* Grand Rapids: William B. Eerdmans Publishing Company.

———. 1961. *The Screwtape Letters and Screwtape Proposes a Toast.* New York: MacMillian.

Lischer, Richard. 1992. *A Theology of Preaching: The Dynamics of the Gospel.* Durham, N.C.: The Labyrinth Press.

———. 1995. *The Preacher King: Martin Luther King, Jr. and the Word That Moved America.* New York: Oxford University Press.

Long, Thomas G. 1988a. *The Senses of Preaching.* Atlanta: John Knox Press.

———. 1988b. "Homiletic." *Theology Today* 45 (April): 110-12.

Loughlin, Gerard. 1996. *Telling God's Story: Bible, Church and Narrative Theology.* New York: Cambridge University Press.

Lowry, Eugene L. 1989. *How to Preach a Parable: Designs for Narrative Sermons.* Nashville: Abingdon.

———. 1980. *The Homiletical Plot: The Sermon as Narrative Art Form.* Louisville: John Knox Press.

Lucado, Max. 2006. "Preaching and Story: An Interview with Max Lucado." *Preaching* 21 (March-April): 7-12.

MacDonald, George. 1994. *Diary of an Old Soul.* Minneapolis: Augsburg Fortress.

Macky, Peter W. 1990. *The Centrality of Metaphors to Biblical Thought: A Method for Interpreting the Bible.* Lewiston, N.Y.: The Edwin Mellen Press.

Marsh, Charles. 2001. *The Last Days: A Son's Story of Sin and Segregation at the Dawn of a New South.* New York: Basic Books.

McLuhan, Marshall. 1994. *Understanding Media: The Extensions of Man.* Cambridge: MIT Press.

McClanahan, Rebecca. 1999. *Word Painting: A Guide to Writing More Descriptively.* Cincinnati: Writer's Digest Books.

McCourt, Frank. 1996. *Angela's Ashes: A Memoir.* New York: Scribner.

———. 2005. *Teacher Man: A Memoir.* New York: Scribner.

McFague, Sallie. 1982. *Metaphorical Theology.* Philadelphia: Fortress Press.

———. 2005. *Speaking in Parables.* New York: Fortress Press.

McGinn, Colin. 2005. *The Power of Movies: How Screen and Mind Interact.* New York: Pantheon Books.

Meland, Bernard E. 1976. *Fallible Forms and Symbols: Discourse on Method in a Theology of Culture.* Philadelphia: Fortress Press.

Messaris, Paul. 1994. *Visual "Literacy": Image, Mind, and Reality.* Boulder, Colo.: Westview Press, Inc.

Milbank, John. 1997. *The Word Made Strange: Theology, Language, Culture.* Malden, Mass.: Blackwell Publishers, Inc.

Miller, Arthur. 1998. *Death of a Salesman.* New York: Penguin Group.

Miller, Calvin. 1996. *Spirit, Word, and Story.* Grand Rapids: William B. Eerdmans Publishing Company.

———. 2006. *Preaching: The Art of Narrative Exposition.* Grand Rapids: Baker Books.

Miller, Donald G. 1954. *Fire in Thy Mouth.* Nashville: Pierce and Washabaugh.

Mirzoeff, Nicholas. 1999. *An Introduction to Visual Culture.* New York: Routledge.

Moeller, Pamela. 1993. *A Kinesthetic Homiletic.* Minneapolis: Fortress.

Morley, David. 1995. "Television: Not So Much a Visual Medium, More a Visable Object." In *Visual Culture.* Ed. Chris Jenks, 170-89. New York: Routledge.

Newsweek. December 25, 2006: 106.

Nichols, Aidan. 1980. *The Art of God Incarnate: Theology and Image in Christian Tradition.* New York: Paulist Press.

O'Connor, Flannery. 1988. *Wise Blood*. New York: Library of America.

Oden, Thomas C., ed. 1978. *Parables of Kierkegaard*. Princeton, N.J.: Princeton University Press.

O'Henry. 1988. *Stories*. Bristol, England: Aerie Books, Ltd.

Ortberg, John. 1997. *The Life You've Always Wanted: Spiritual Disciplines for Ordinary People*. Grand Rapids: Zondervan.

Otto, Rudolf. 1958. *The Idea of the Holy: An Inquiry into the Non-Rational Factor in the Idea of the Divine and Its Relation to the Rational*. London, England: Oxford University Press.

Pagitt, Doug. 2005. *Preaching Re-Imagined: The Role of the Sermon in Communities of Faith*. Grand Rapids: Zondervan.

Peterson, David. 1992. *Engaging with God: Biblical Theology of Worship*. Downers Grove, Ill.: InterVarsity Press.

Peterson, Eugene. 2002. *The Message*. Colorado Springs, Colo.: NavPress.

Peyton, Patrick. 1951. *The Ear of God*. Garden City, N.Y.: Doubleday.

Postman, Neil. 1993. *Technopoly: The Surrender of Culture to Technology*. New York: Vintage Books.

Prothero, Stephen. 2003. *American Jesus: How the Son of God Became a National Icon*. New York: Farrar, Straus and Giroux.

Quanstrom, Linda. 1994. *And Some Are Walked Home: Stories of Grace*. Kansas City: Beacon Hill Press of Kansas City.

Ramsey, Ian. 2007. "Talking of God: Models Ancient and Modern." In *Exploring the Philosophy of Religion*. Ed. David Stewart, 285-95. Upper Saddle River, N.J.: Prentice Hall.

Ricoeur, Paul. 1977. *The Rule of Metaphor: Multi-disciplinary Studies of the Creation of Meaning and Language*. Toronto: University of Toronto Press.

Riegert, Eduard. 1990. *Imaginative Shock*. Burlington, Ont.: Trinity Press.

Rose, Lucy A. 1997. *Sharing the Word: Preaching in the Roundtable Church*. Louisville: Westminster/John Knox Press.

Salter, Darius L. 2003. *America's Bishop: The Life of Francis Asbury*. Nappanee, Ind.: Evangel Publishing House.

Sample, Tex. 2005. *Powerful Persuasion: Multimedia Witness in Christian Worship*. Nashville: Abingdon.

Sanders, James A. 1984. *Canon and Community*. Philadelphia: Fortress Press.

Sandmel, Samuel. 1972. *The Enjoyment of Scripture: The Law, the Prophets, and the Writings*. New York: Oxford University Press.

Santayana, George. 1963. *Persons and Places*. New York: Charles Scribner's Sons.

Sayers, Dorothy L. 2002. *The Complete Stories*. New York: HarperCollins Publishers, Inc.

———. 1987. *The Mind of the Maker*. San Francisco: Harper and Row Publishers.

Seamands, Stephen. 2005. *Ministry in the Image of God: The Trinitarian Shape of Christian Service*. Downers Grove, Ill.: InterVarsity Press.

Seters, Arthur V., ed. 1988. *Preaching as a Social Act: Theology and Practice*. Nashville: Abingdon Press.

Shakespeare, William. 1918. *A Midsummer Night's Dream*. New Haven, Conn.: Yale University Press.

Shaw, Mark. 1993. *Doing Theology with Huck and Jim: Parables for Understanding Doctrine*. Downers Grove, Ill.: InterVarsity Press.

Simon, Neil. 1971. *The Collected Plays of Neil Simon*. New York: Touchstone.

Sing to the Lord. 1993. Kansas City: Lillenas Publishing Co.

Steimle, Edmund A., Morris J. Niedenthal, and Charles L. Rice. 1980. *Preaching the Story*. Philadelphia: Fortress Press.

Steinbeck, John. 1939. *The Grapes of Wrath*. New York: Penguin Books.

Stewart, James S. 1946. *Heralds of God*. New York: Charles Scribner's Sons.

Stout, Harry S. 1991. *The Divine Dramatist: George Whitefield and the Rise of Modern Evangelism*. Grand Rapids: William B. Eerdmans Publishing Company.

Stroup, George W. 1981. *The Promise of Narrative Theology: Recovering the Gospel in the Church*. Atlanta: John Knox Press.

Styron, William. 1992. *Darkness Visible.* New York: Vintage.

Tannehill, Robert C. 1975. *The Sword of His Mouth.* Philadelphia: Fortress Press.

Taylor, Mark, and Esa Saarinen. 1994. *Imagologies.* New York: Routledge.

Terrien, Samuel. 1978. *The Elusive Presence: Toward a New Biblical Theology.* New York: Harper and Row.

Thoreau, Henry. 2004. *Walden and Other Writings.* New York: Bantam Dell.

Tracy, David. 1981. *The Analogical Imagination.* New York: The Crossroad Publishing Company.

Traven, B. 1963. *The Treasure of the Sierra Madre.* New York: Hill and Wang.

Troeger, Thomas. 1990. *Imagining a Sermon.* Nashville: Abingdon.

———. 1996. *Ten Strategies for Preaching in a Multimedia Culture.* Nashville: Abingdon.

———. 1988. "The Social Power of Myth as a Key to Preaching on Social Issues." In *Preaching as a Social Act: Theology and Practice.* Ed. Arthur Van Seters, 205-34. Nashville: Abingdon.

Trueblood, Elton. 1964. *The Humor of Christ.* New York: Harper and Row.

Von Rad, Gerhard. 1980. *God at Work in Israel.* Nashville: Abingdon.

Washington, James M., ed. 1986. *A Testament of Hope: The Essential Writings of Martin Luther King, Jr.* San Francisco: Harper and Row.

Webster, John. 2005. "The Visible Attests the Invisible." In *Community of the Word: Toward an Evangelical Ecclesiology.* Eds. Mark Husbands and Daniel J. Treier, 96-113. Downers Grove, Ill.: InterVarsity Press.

Wheelwright, Philip. 1968. *The Burning Fountain: A Study in the Language of Symbolism.* Bloomington, Ind.: Indiana University Press.

———. 1962. *Metaphor and Reality.* Bloomington, Ind.: Indiana University Press.

Wiebe, Donald. 1991. *The Irony of Theology and the Nature of Religious Thought.* Montreal: McGill-Queen's University Press.

Wilder, Amos N. 1964. *Early Christian Rhetoric: The Language of the Gospel.* New York: Harper and Row, Publishers.

Williams, Rowan. 2000. *Lost Icons: Reflections on Cultural Bereavement.* New York: Morehouse Publishing.

Willis, Dennis. 1989. "Noah Was a Good Man." In Eugene L. Lowry, *How to Preach a Parable,* 42-78. Nashville: Abingdon.

Wills, Garry. 1992. *Lincoln at Gettysburg: The Words That Remade America.* New York: Simon and Schuster.

Wilson-Kastner, Patricia. 1989. *Imagery for Preaching.* Minneapolis: Fortress Press.

Wilson, Paul Scott. 2001. *God Sense: Reading the Bible for Preaching.* Nashville: Abingdon.

———. 1992. *A Concise History of Preaching.* Nashville: Abingdon.

———. 1988. *Imagination of the Heart: New Understandings in Preaching.* Nashville: Abingdon.

Winchester, Simon. 2005. *The Professor and the Madman.* New York: Harper Perennial.

Wirt, Sherwood Eliot. 1969. *Passport to Life City: A Modern Pilgrim's Progress.* New York: Harper and Row.

Wolfe, Thomas. 2004. *Look Homeward, Angel: A Story of the Buried Life.* New York: Scribner.

Wright, Ernest. 1958. *God Who Acts.* London: SCM Press.

Zengotita, Thomas De. 2005. *Mediated: How the Media Shapes Your World and the Way You Live in It.* New York: Bloomsbury Publishing.